MW00769983

'Behind God's Back'

Gullah Memories

Cainhoy, Wando, Huger, Daniel Island,
St. Thomas Island, South Carolina

To Mary,
To a lover of books!

By Herb Frazier

With the Art of John W. Jones

Cheer!
Herb
6/7/u

EVENING
POST
PUBLISHING
COMPANY
Charleston
South Carolina

EVENINGPOSTBOOKS
Our Accent is Southern!
www.EveningPostBooks.com

Published by
Evening Post Books
Charleston, South Carolina
www.EveningPostBooks.com

Copyright © 2011 by Herb Frazier
All rights reserved.
First edition

Editors: John M. Burbage, Steve Hoffius
Design: Gill Guerry
Artwork: John W. Jones

First printing 2011
Printed in the United States of America

A CIP catalog record for this book has been applied
for from the Library of Congress.

ISBN: 978-0-9825154-7-1

Contents

Dedication

For my granddaughter

Lauryn Michelle Thomas

Foreword

In 2005 the Coastal Community Foundation of South Carolina wanted to underwrite a history of the Cainhoy-Wando-Huger area with charitable dollars provided by the Daniel Island Community Fund. The plan was to produce the history as a booklet — a modest publication, researched and written in a period of six months and published as a gift to indigenous residents of the area. Our mission was to create a historical sketch that would place an emphasis on the experiences of African Americans who live in the area of the Cainhoy peninsula.

A history professor or a graduate student could have been hired to do the job, but maybe it was the spirits of long-gone residents who whispered Herb Frazier's name to us as the right person for the task. Herb is no stranger to the foundation. He has volunteered to help us award scholarships, and he and others have established a scholarship fund with us to encourage young African-American students to enter the field of journalism.

Two critical elements combined to make this project far more important than we first imagined. As a former daily newspaper reporter, Herb is curious and he seeks out the truth. His curiosity led him to meetings with scores of people and to archival materials in Charleston, Columbia and Washington, D.C.

Love and betrayal, honor and deceit, truth and lies are all part of the human condition, just as they are part of this book that contains stories never before recounted from a single source.

Herb's interviewing and researching didn't take six months. It extended over a period of five years. Out of that effort has emerged a book that tells the true stories of those who lived and died on the Cainhoy peninsula. The Coastal Community Foundation is also grateful to historian and author Steve Hoffius for his masterful editing skills, to Columbia artist John W. Jones for the generous gifts of his artistic talent, to the Daniel Island Company and the Daniel Island Community Fund for moral and financial support, and to the Evening Post Publishing Company of Charleston for transforming what was initially to be a booklet into the real thing.

We are also grateful to the families who have lived here for generations for entrusting to Herb their personal experiences and recollections of love and betrayal, honor and deceit, truth and lies on the Cainhoy peninsula.

Two good things are sure to result from this book. The "bin'yahs" will know that the importance of their lives and those of their forebears is respected. And newcomers to the area — the "cum'yahs" — will have a deeper understanding of those they now call neighbors.

Richard Hendry
Vice President of Programs
Coastal Community Foundation of South Carolina

A Note From the Artist

I am pleased to lend my talents to this project because what is happening in the Cainhoy-Wando-Huger area is similar to changes occurring in other Gullah communities along the South Carolina coast. This is a story that should be told as it unfolds in the Charleston area, on the Sea Islands and elsewhere in the state. This story will encourage readers to support the efforts of Gullah people to preserve their culture.

John W. Jones
www.gallerychuma.com, www.colorsofmoney.com

(Cover art is a marsh view of Cainhoy by John W. Jones.)

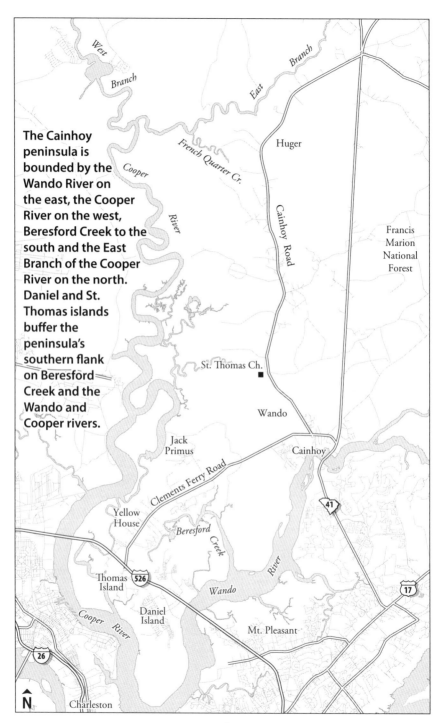

The Cainhoy peninsula is bounded by the Wando River on the east, the Cooper River on the west, Beresford Creek to the south and the East Branch of the Cooper River on the north. Daniel and St. Thomas islands buffer the peninsula's southern flank on Beresford Creek and the Wando and Cooper rivers.

West Branch

East Branch

French Quarter Cr.

Huger

Cooper

River

Cainhoy Road

Francis Marion National Forest

St. Thomas Ch.

Wando

Jack Primus

Cainhoy

Clements Ferry Road

41

Yellow House

Beresford Creek

Thomas Island

526

Daniel Island

Wando

Wando River

17

Cooper River

Mt. Pleasant

26

N

Charleston

14

Introduction

There is no more agreeable mode of passing a day, and thereby breaking in upon the tedium of a long summer's residence in Charleston, than taking advantage occasionally of the opportunity now afforded for a weekly excursion on Cooper River.

— John B. Irving, "A Day on Cooper River" (1842)

The Cooper River flows along the east side of a peninsula that is the cradle of historic Charleston, South Carolina. The port city, founded in 1670 as a British colony, is not a crossroads like the sprawling inland metro areas of Atlanta, Georgia and Charlotte, North Carolina. Rather, Charleston is much smaller by comparison, a place where tourists are charmed by the city's grace, architecture and colonial and antebellum past. Yet only 12 miles up the Cooper River is another large peninsula and nearby islands richly connected to Charleston by a wealth of untold stories.

On this second peninsula are Cainhoy, Wando and Huger, rural communities surrounded by the Francis Marion National Forest. These were among the earliest areas settled in the Carolina colony after European settlers arrived long ago. Although Native Americans were the first people to live on this land, by the mid-1700s their numbers had dropped to near extinction because of disease, exploitation and war.

The broad Cainhoy peninsula is bounded by the Wando River on the east, the Cooper River on the west, Beresford Creek to the south and the

East Branch of the Cooper River on the north. Daniel and St. Thomas islands buffer the peninsula's southern flank on Beresford Creek and the Wando and Cooper rivers.

The village of Cainhoy, tucked in a bend of the Wando, initially served as a river port that linked inland farms and plantations with Charleston. The Cainhoy peninsula was the site of what is believed to be America's first creamware pottery factory and the Carolina colony's earliest brickyards. Along the Wando and Cooper rivers boats and barges transported a variety of commodities to Charleston, making the Cainhoy peninsula and its two island neighbors the colonial equivalent of a modern-day Wal-Mart.

The distinctive place name "Cainhoy" surely is derived from the Native American place name of "Kenha," recorded in 1682 on Joel Gascoyne's "Map of the Country of Carolina." But, unfortunately, the meaning of "Kenha" is lost in time.

Interestingly, "Cainhoy" is also attributed to Cain Walker, a black man who operated a ferry landing on the Wando River after the Civil War. Walker purchased 22 acres along the river in 1880 and began his business. Local lore has it that, when customers arrived at the landing, they'd summon Walker by calling out "Cain, ahoy." However, Cainhoy was recorded as a place name at least a century before Walker was born.

The original Cainhoy was a small community established no later than 1735. Also known today as the "old village," it is situated at the end of Cainhoy Village Road on a bluff overlooking the Wando River. One of the earliest land developers in coastal Carolina was Lewis Fogartie, who established just upriver from the old village a summer retreat where Lowcountry planters enjoyed breezy homes built among the pinelands to escape the heat, humidity and mosquitoes. Between 1788 and 1801, Fogartie sold long narrow lots along the Wando River to develop a planned community sometimes called Lewisville but known as "the new village" today.

The land north and west of Cainhoy is called Wando, which is the name of a Native American tribe that once inhabited the region. The Wando River is also named after the tribe.

Brickyard

Archaeologists recently unearthed a portion of the floor of a brick kiln on the Harper property on the southern edge of the Cainhoy peninsula along Beresford Creek. The brickyard was in operation during the 18th and 19th centuries. Photo courtesy of Brockington and Associates.

In 1673 three land grants totaling 810 acres on Etiwan Island, today's Daniel Island, were granted to William Thomas, who came from North Cumberland County, Virginia, with his wife, daughter, six indentured servants and two enslaved Africans. "Etiwan" is the name of another local tribe, and "Etiwan" is what the indigenous people called the Cooper River. Until the late 1690s, Daniel and St. Thomas islands were known collectively as "Thomas Island."

Daniel Island was named after Englishman Robert Daniell, an influential landowner in the area in the early 1700s. Through the years, the island was known as "Daniell" then "Daniels" and now "Daniel." Before his death in 1718, Daniell served as the colony's deputy proprietor and deputy governor of the Carolinas.

When French King Louis XIV revoked the Edict of Nantes in 1685,

17

French Protestants, or Huguenots, fled France for fear of maltreatment and execution if they did not convert to Catholicism. Among the early Huguenot settlers to arrive in Carolina was Daniel Huger (pronounced "Hu-gee"). His son Daniel Huger II purchased Limerick Plantation in 1713 at the headwaters of the Cooper River's east branch, 12 miles northwest of the Cainhoy villages. Today, the crossroads community of Huger is between Limerick and Wando.

The story of these early settlements mirrors the founding of coastal South Carolina. Relatively few European settlers owned and managed the indigo, rice and cotton plantations while thousands of enslaved Africans actually worked the land, tended the crops, cut the trees for lumber and fuel, dug the clay for bricks and pottery and worked as house servants.

While Daniel Island today is overwhelmingly white in population, the nearby Cainhoy peninsula is inhabited primarily by African Americans, many of them descendants of the enslaved people. Today's residents live in close-knit rural communities throughout the area.

The area around the Cainhoy peninsula today has 22 of these communities, many with wonderfully evocative names. These communities have a combined population of approximately 10,300 people. An exact count is difficult to obtain because no specific Census data is available for these unincorporated areas.

In the Wando area are St. Thomas Island, or "The Ferry"; Pinefield; Yellow House; Jack Primus; Honey Hill; and Cainhoy, or "The Village." Huger-area communities are Brown Hill; Hamlin Corner; Charity Church Road; Baldwin Corner; Richardson Corner; Red Hill; French Quarter Creek; New Hope; Quinby Creek; Smith; Steed Creek; Moore's Corner; Old Joe, or Duffy's Corner; Grant Hill; Kelly; and Greenbay.

These predominantly black communities have preserved an African-based culture called Gullah. As most people know today, Gullah evokes numerous descriptions. It's handmade sweetgrass baskets and cast nets, praise houses, rousing spirituals and syncopated clapping, rice and greens and beans and yams, family land passed down from one generation to

18

the next. Gullah is a distinct and fertile language too that rolls easily off the tongue, a blend of mostly English and African words spoken in rich Caribbean tones.

Gullah crafts, worship, songs and cuisine are rooted with the people who were captured in West Africa and brought to North America in chains more than four centuries ago. Amazingly, their rich and distinctive culture survived primarily along the isolated sea islands of North Carolina, South Carolina, Georgia and northern Florida.

Rivers, creeks and marshes have separated coastal Gullah communities from the mainland, creating isolated pockets where people retained their African ways. Development along the coast, a changing economy and population shifts eventually led many Gullah people to join mainstream America. Changes threaten the continuation of the Gullah way of life. This unique culture and language within the American experience wasn't always so popular. Outsiders once ridiculed Gullah speech as broken English and Gullah folkways as backward. Protection of the culture, however, is now the law of the land.

South Carolina Congressman James Clyburn is the author of H.R. 694: Gullah/Geechee Cultural Heritage Act. Passed by Congress in 2006, the law is designed to enhance the preservation and interpretation of Gullah/Geechee culture. It created the Gullah/Geechee Cultural Heritage Corridor along the coastal lowlands in the four states. (In Georgia and Florida, people of African descent prefer the term Geechee to describe themselves and their culture.) The corridor is the first one in the nation set aside to preserve the heritage and culture of African Americans. The law established a 25-member commission to oversee preservation activities of Gullah/Geechee culture and bring attention to it.

As a result, places such as the Cainhoy peninsula are now at the center of attention. Since Emancipation, Gullah people of the Cainhoy area have scratched out a living through subsistence farming, timbering, fishing and doing domestic work. Some operated moonshine stills deep within the cover of the thick forest.

Until now, the remarkable history of Gullah people on the Cainhoy peninsula and St. Thomas and Daniel islands was passed along orally but seldom compiled and written down. That's because Gullah people had been enslaved, literally and figuratively. Most could not read or write. Few were allowed formal educations. Until Emancipation in the 1860s, most people of African heritage didn't even have surnames. Yet by digging through historical records and newspaper accounts and speaking to longtime residents of the area, the story of the lives of people mortared to this land in a tabby of blood, sweat and tears is now being told in an ordered fashion.

By the early 20th century, millionaires from elsewhere had purchased and consolidated many Southern plantations. They included businessman, publisher, diplomat, horseman and philanthropist Harry Frank Guggenheim of New York. In the early 1930s Guggenheim bought more than 10,000 acres on the Cainhoy peninsula for use as a winter home. He named his plantation "Cain Hoy."

Between 1946 and 1955, Guggenheim made two purchases to acquire the 4,000-acre Daniel Island, where his herd of Hereford cattle grazed. At that time, the Cainhoy peninsula and nearby islands were out-of-the-way places that required long drives or river travel. In more recent times, two paved roads provided circuitous routes to this area at the southern end of Berkeley County. A drive to Daniel Island from Charleston, just 3.5 miles upriver, could take 40 minutes.

This began to change dramatically after the June 1992 opening of the Mark Clark Expressway (Interstate Highway 526), which cuts across St. Thomas and Daniel islands.[1] Two months later, an interchange opened, allowing traffic to flow north on Clements Ferry Road to Wando, Cainhoy and Huger and south to St. Thomas and Daniel islands. In 1999 a second exit opened on Daniel Island.

Prior to the expressway, Clements Ferry was a lonely road that stopped

---

1 The expressway is named for World War II and Korean War Gen. Mark W. Clark, who was president of The Citadel, the Military College of South Carolina, from 1954 to 1966. He is buried on The Citadel's campus in Charleston.

at the southern tip of St. Thomas Island. Now a seven-mile stretch of it from the expressway to Cainhoy is lined with new businesses, gas stations, entrances to subdivisions and four traffic lights. The names of some new developments pay homage to Richard Beresford, one of the area's wealthiest landowners in the 1700s.

Jack Primus, Yellow House, Wando, Cainhoy and St. Thomas Island are the communities closest to the development. But Daniel Island has been altered the most. In 1991 the city of Charleston annexed Daniel Island, although it remains in Berkeley County. Farms and hunting grounds quickly disappeared to make room for upscale communities and commercial enterprises, the relocated Bishop England high school, soccer and tennis stadiums and more traffic lights. A series of subsequent annexations also brought Guggenheim's Cain Hoy Plantation into the city.

The threads of this quilt tie together memories of black resistance during Reconstruction, a pioneering nurse midwife from Charleston, a community that banded together to build a school, black entrepreneurs whose boats and buses carried workers to Charleston and the midnight movement of men making moonshine to feed their families. This story has recollections of murders and a court fight over land that ripped a family apart.

This story of a place once isolated and described by the locals as "Behind God's Back" begins with the voices of two men: One who grew up in the Jack Primus community and stayed to raise his family, farm and chauffeur Guggenheim; the other who, as a boy, boarded the ferry at Daniel Island and moved to Charleston where he worked hard for the rest of his long life and became a world-class blacksmith.

Voices: Harold Lincoln

The rivers provide direct links from Charleston to the Cainhoy peninsula and Daniel and St. Thomas islands. Ferries once carried people, farm animals and commodities back and forth. When older residents reminisce, their stories flow to the rivers.

Harold Lincoln is one of them.

A roaring fire in the hearth warms Lincoln's living room. His wife, Gladys Vanderhorst Lincoln, sits in a kitchen equipped with two stoves, one fueled by gas and another by wood. In the living room, Lincoln wraps sweet potatoes in aluminum foil and puts them in the embers as he talks about his life in the Jack Primus community, his home since the day he was born on October 12, 1913.

The Lincolns were married in 1940. They had known each other all of their lives. They have 11 children, 30 grandchildren, 48 great-grandchildren and one great-great-grandchild. Before Gladys Lincoln died on February 5, 2008, at age 86, the Lincolns were the oldest couple in Jack Primus.

Four generations of Lincolns have lived in or near the family compound close to the Cooper River. Lincoln built his home in 1954 not far from the house where he was born. It is across the yard from a cluster of five other residences. His daughter Ethel McKnight lives in a dwelling on the spot where Lincoln's boyhood house stood before it burned in the early 1940s. In this compound, the Lincolns raised 11 children: Verna, Harold, Fred, Ethel, Barbara, Henry, Jeanette, Deloris, Kenneth, Sharon and Steven. Lincoln doesn't know how the community came to be called Jack Primus.

Harold Lincoln's birthday celebration

In Jack Primus, a few hundred people gathered on October 10, 2009, to celebrate Harold Lincoln's 96th birthday at the family's compound. The birthday party for Lincoln has been arranged every year on the second Saturday in October for more than a decade. Photo by Herb Frazier.

"I met that name here," a spry 92-year-old Lincoln said in early 2005.

About 300 people live in Jack Primus, a horseshoe-shaped community wrapped around the former Venning Plantation. Before Emancipation, William L. Venning was the plantation owner. "He was the old slave master. After the slaves got free, he sold this land to the ex-slaves, including the Broughtons, the Greens, the Vanderhorsts, the Wigfalls, the Bryants, the Lawrences, the McNeals, the Vennings, the Walkers and the Lincolns."

Lincoln's grandfather, Peter Lincoln, was one of the former slaves who

Greater St. John AME Church

In 1877 William L. Venning Jr. sold an acre for $1 to the trustees of St. John Chapel, which later became Greater St. John AME Church. Harold Lincoln is a deacon at the church, which was once part of the Hartford Plantation. Painting by John W. Jones.

bought land. Lincoln didn't know his grandfather. "You could buy as much land as you wanted. The average was 20 acres. I never heard how much it cost. I know when I bought my property in here it was twenty-and-a-half acres, and I paid $175 in 1948."

No one knows when Peter Lincoln died. He is buried in an unmarked grave in the cemetery on the old Venning place, which became part of Harry Frank Guggenheim's Cain Hoy Plantation. Peter Lincoln was laid to rest long before undertakers got involved. The community handled the arrangements. Ashes from the hearth were mixed with water and used to stain the yellow pine coffins black, Harold Lincoln said as he poked a stick at the sweet potatoes roasting in the glowing embers. "I saw people do that. It ain't been like it is now."

Most people grew what they needed. They planted corn, rice, potatoes and cotton. Until the late 1950s, Lincoln grew cotton, which he hauled to a gin in Moncks Corner. "You couldn't do nothing else but sell the cotton. You couldn't eat the cotton. The corn was fed to the cows and hogs."

When Harold Lincoln was a boy, his father hoisted him on his shoulders as he walked a log bridge across a rice field. "They used to make bricks here, too, and cut crossties for the railroad and logs for timber. Peter Lincoln did all of that. My father, Mike Lincoln, also did that kind of work."

Mike Lincoln worked on the river mostly while his wife, Sarah Lincoln, kept the house and cared for their 10 children. Harold Lincoln's father captained *The Brothers*, a sailboat owned by Thomas Sinkler, a white man who lived in Charleston. Mike Lincoln sailed between landings along the Cooper River. He stopped at the Redding, Venning, Red Bluff, Bushy Point and Simmons landings — important jumping off points to the city.

Sinkler owned another boat that hauled firewood from the Huger area to Charleston. James Baldwin was its captain. The vessels left on different days and at different times on schedules dictated by the tides. Mike Lincoln brought goods that were sold in the city and returned with items needed in the country. As a boy, Harold Lincoln accompanied his father on numerous trips across the Cooper River that took up to two hours, depending on the conditions. At the dock in Charleston, the Lincolns unloaded firewood and vegetables and returned with food, kerosene and other necessities that were sold in Cainhoy stores. In later years, they also brought back caskets.

Cainhoy was accessible by land back then, but a trip by a horse-drawn wagon could take all day. It was slow going over dusty roads scarred with ruts cut deep by wagon wheels and erosion. "Anybody who come ya almost had to come by boat," Lincoln said. Mules and horses bought as farm animals experienced a kind of baptism on the way to Cainhoy. "Farmers bought them from stables in the city. They took the animals to Mount Pleasant by ferry, walked to the Wando River and swam over at low tide."

Another boat carried mail and people to and from Charleston. It left Cainhoy at 8 a.m. with passengers and brought them back later in the day. Robbie Lucas captained the mail boat.

Boats didn't haul trees cut on the Cainhoy peninsula and sent to the mill. Logs were lashed together and floated across the river to the Tuxbury sawmill just below the old Charleston Navy Yard on the Charleston Neck.

Marie Fordham was the principal of a school in the community. Classes were initially held in her home before moving to Greater St. John African

Methodist Episcopal Church. Sessions ran only from January through March to allow students to work in the fields most of the year. Lincoln did not attend. "I had to get out and work. Everything I learned, I learned from scratch. In the winter, I'd go and catch raccoon and get the fur and sell them for 50 cents. That is what I used to do. I used to catch mullet and row from here to North Charleston and sell them." Lincoln also hunted "kuta," a Gullah term for turtle.

Lincoln's father worked on the river until the late-1920s, when the advent of electricity and natural gas reduced the demand for firewood in Charleston. So he took up farm work to earn a living, digging potatoes and cutting cucumbers and cabbages for American Fruit Growers Company on Daniel Island.

Harold Lincoln eventually obtained a small boat of his own and rowed across the river to work in fertilizer mills and cotton presses in the Charleston Neck area. He moved to the North in the late-1940s in search of a better paying job. He lived briefly in Baltimore with his aunt and her husband. "I worked in Baltimore. I was 35 or 36 years old. I'd catch part-time work, and I didn't like it. So I come back. When I was young, I worked all the time."

Twenty-two years before Harold Lincoln retired in 1974, he worked on the land where his grandfather was enslaved. As he stood near the marsh along his property, he pointed to a huge white mansion at modern-day Cain Hoy Plantation, primarily a hunting retreat just upriver. "You see that white thing yonder? That's the Guggenheim house. When he built that house way back yonder in the early part of the 1930s, it was $250,000 then." Lincoln was a driver on Cain Hoy Plantation when Guggenheim's visitors came to hunt.

"It was a plantation to raise turkey and quail. Senator (Harry) Byrd and all them used to be there. General Patrick, he headed the Air Force at Myrtle Beach. They were Guggenheim's guests. I was their chauffeur. They had a wagon with four seats, a water kit and medicine kit, a rack for the gun and a man who handled the guns. When the dog pointed, I drove them to a point, they'd get off and shoot."

Lincoln bent easily at the waist to duck through an open' leading to his pasture where grazing cows keep the green gra' ground. Ant hills and cow dung dot the ground near the Coo, marsh. Lincoln offered a simple formula for staying young. "The only secret I can tell you is, do the right thing, love your neighbor as you love yourself and trust in God. He will never tell you no."

Lincoln became a born-again Christian in 1931 at Greater St. John Church. "It was Hoover times," Lincoln said, referring to President Herbert Hoover and the Great Depression. Mike Lincoln was too ill to work. Harold Lincoln found employment with the Works Progress Administration in his father's place. He joined a crew that filled in a section on Clements Ferry Road that flooded at high tide. It was then that he learned to write his name by watching a white man scribble "Harold Lincoln" on his paycheck.

Harold Lincoln's father died in 1934. "Back in those days, people didn't have the education like they do nowadays to read and write to record important events like deaths, births and marriages. I could be a millionaire," he added as he walked his property along the river. "I have all of this for the children. Because at my age all I need is a good place to stay, food to eat … and one old truck will suit me. I've never been a person who needed much. I just want to enjoy my days and sit by my fire. I don't owe a man a dime. I've always had that old-timey way about me. I grew up around old people, and I am glad I did, too, because if I didn't I might have been an old drunk. Being with old people made it better for me today."

Voices: Philip Simmons

Harold Lincoln's cousin, the late Philip Simmons is a national treasure. The Cooper River took Simmons from his birthplace on Daniel Island to Charleston, where he became a nationally known blacksmith and artisan.

"We used to call this Dan's Island," Simmons, 93, said in his usual slow, instructive tone of voice in late fall of 2005. "That name hold fast until the Northerners start calling it by its right name. Everybody on this island made a living either hunting, fishing or farming. Everything we had on the table came from that island. On the farm we cured our meats such as pork, beef, chicken and wild game. Everything in the air, we eat that. Everything in the water, we eat that."

Until his death in 2009, two weeks shy of his 97th birthday, Simmons fashioned more than 500 pieces of ornamental wrought-iron gates, fences, balconies and window grills that adorn many of Charleston's homes; some historic and others not so well known. He is best known for his gates.

The Smithsonian Institution has his "Star and Fish" gate on display in Washington, D.C. Others are displayed at the South Carolina State Museum in Columbia and the Charleston Visitor Center on Meeting Street. His gates include images of birds, fish, trees and stars — all elements of his boyhood surroundings. The works are accented with whimsical touches and graceful scrolls. Simmons also hammered hot metal into the shape of a gazebo that stands in the lobby at the Charleston International Airport.

The wall of his tiny office in his Blake Street home on Charleston's east

Philip Simmons made this hand rail and installed it in the mansion at Cain Hoy Plantation. Photo by Herb Frazier.

Philip Simmons. Courtesy of the Philip Simmons Foundation.

side was crammed with mementos and accolades, including South Carolina's highest civilian honor, the Order of the Palmetto; a South Carolina Folk Heritage Award; and a certificate noting his induction into the South Carolina Hall of Fame. His office was a mini-museum that included a photo of him with President Ronald Reagan at the White House and another with Peter Simmons (no relation), the man who taught him the blacksmith trade.[2]

---

2 Peter Simmons' son Lonnie Simmons at age 10 played in the Jenkins Orphanage Band. He later became a Chicago-based musician.

That fall in 2005, Philip Simmons reminisced about his early life as he toured Daniel Island by car. The area had changed drastically since he left at age 8 to attend school in Charleston and begin his apprenticeship.

Philip Simmons was born June 9, 1912, in his grandfather's house, surrounded by a field of nutgrass on the Wando River side of Daniel Island in an area called the Furman Tract. His grandparents, William and Sarah Buncombe Simmons, raised him. His grandmother was Cherokee. "I heard that my great-granddaddy was a slave," he said.

"I worked on the farm as an eight-year-old boy. I picked up white potatoes. We worked on the American Fruit Growers' farm. There were more blacks than whites on Daniel Island. Black people were making $1 a day. Everything you picked we shipped it north. Back in those days whites and blacks got along because they lived closer together."

About 100 families lived on Daniel and St. Thomas islands at that time, he said. "A lot of local people worked for American Fruit Growers Company and a lot of people came from elsewhere to work on the farm. They came from St. Stephen, Bonneau and Moncks Corner to get that dollar-a-day job."

Simmons said he could pick about three bags of potatoes a day, but because he was a boy, he was paid only 50 cents a day plus an additional 10 cents per bag. A horse-drawn plow turned the soil followed by workers who collected the potatoes. Simmons worked in the field for a year.

"It was hard work, bending your back all day. We started about 9 a.m., stopped at noon, back at 1 and worked until 5 p.m. I worked during the potato, cabbage and bean seasons. I came (to Charleston) when I was eight years old to go to school. I first went to school on Daniels Island in St. Luke Church and St. James Church. Our parents would go to the school early and start a fire so it would be warm by the time the children got there. I worked more than I went to school.

"I first went to Charleston on the ferry. The 8 a.m. boat from Cainhoy would stop and pick up passengers from Daniel Island. I paid 15 cents to come on the boat. My mother paid 25 cents."

Philip Simmons said children attended school at St. James AME Church when the church was located on Daniel Island. Painting by John W. Jones.

Simmons left Daniel Island with his friend Reuben Mitchell, who was five years older. "I can't remember what I had for dinner yesterday, but I can remember all of my friends. I was following him. He was like a big brother to me. Our parents decided to send us to Charleston for a better education. I left Daniel Island during Hoover time and moved to 9 Vernon Street in the city. I lived with my mother, Rosa Simmons."

Simmons was glad to leave Daniel Island in 1920 because he wanted to live "in the big city." Rosa Simmons enrolled her son in Buist Elementary School at the east end of Calhoun Street, not far from the Cooper River. Philip was one of about 700 students on the first day of classes at the new three-story brick school. After graduating from Buist after the sixth grade, he went to the Burke school on the west side of Charleston's peninsula.

Charleston had about 15 blacksmith shops when Simmons arrived in the city from Daniel Island. Not only was he excited to see the city but the blacksmith shop sparked his interest even more. "The horses and wagons! The horses were kicking up! There was Peter (Simmons) and another man, Jim Davis. They were partners."

Peter Simmons opened his Calhoun Street business in 1890 on Charles-

Charleston blacksmith Peter Simmons. Courtesy of the Philip Simmons Foundation.

ton's east side. He was one of nine black men employed in the trade and one of four in a five-block area along the waterfront. Peter Simmons was part Cherokee, too. "He was like a father to me. His blacksmith shop was near Vernon Street. He wouldn't hire me at eight years old ... Peter was careful. He said, 'Boy, I can't hire you until you get to 13, when you can take care of yourself.' "

So, Philip Simmons went to school, sold the Charleston Evening Post newspaper and shined shoes until he was old enough to learn blacksmithing. "The paper cost a nickel, the same price for a shoeshine."

When he reached 13, Philip returned to Peter's shop, which had been moved closer to the river. "I had it made then. I used to come out of school and go into the blacksmith shop. The first thing I made was an ice pick." Years later, Simmons fashioned hand-held hooks that dock workers used to load bales of cotton on cargo ships.

Peter turned the business over to Philip in the early 1930s and moved across the Cooper River where he set up another shop in Mount Pleasant near Shem Creek. After working in his Calhoun Street shop, Philip would take the ferry over to help Peter in Mount Pleasant. Peter died in 1953, two days shy of his 98th birthday.

Philip Simmons was on his own when the country went to war. "I didn't go into World War II. I think one of the reasons is that I was in the blacksmith shop and they needed all of the tradesmen here. I think that's why I didn't go. I registered; I wasn't drafted."

When people became more dependent on automobiles than horse-drawn transportation, it had a direct affect on his business. He was 16 years old when the John P. Grace Bridge across the Cooper River opened in 1929, linking Charleston with Mount Pleasant and beyond.[3] "I thought that was the best thing that could have happened," although most blacksmith shops closed as cars increased in popularity. "People asked me, 'What are you going to do now?'" Simmons began to make iron gates. "The first gate I made was for (Charleston clothier) Jack Krawcheck in 1944."

Do you have a gate in Cainhoy?

"Let me see. In 'Cain Hi' I have a step railing up there," he said, referring to those at Guggenheim's mansion at Cain Hoy Plantation. After Harold Lincoln introduced Simmons to Guggenheim, the millionaire commissioned the blacksmith to make the railing. Upon completion in July 1963, Guggenheim paid Simmons $18.

Do you have a gate on Daniel Island?

"I have an entire park!" Simmons boasted.

Philip Simmons Park is at Seven Farms Road and River Landing Drive and features a large iron gate.

"I designed the gate, but I didn't build it," Simmons explained as he walked around the park with his hands clasped behind his back. He said he was honored that the Smithsonian purchased one of his gates and even more so to have a park named after him on Daniel Island. "This is home."

What is the significance of the fish design in the Daniel Island gate?

"I don't know... I am a lover of fish," he said with a laugh. "I am a lover of birds. I am a lover of wild game."

Simmons turned and looked beyond the island's towering tennis stadium in the direction of where his grandfather's house once stood, surrounded by nutgrass.

He was silent.

---

3 A second span over the Cooper River, the Silas N. Pearman Bridge, was built in 1966. It paralleled the Grace bridge. Both bridges were demolished and replaced with the Arthur Ravenel Jr. Bridge in 2005.

Raymond Varner insisted that his children be identified as Indian and he encouraged other Native American families to do the same. Photo courtesy of Heidi Varner.

Chapter 1: Native Americans

Before Europeans and Africans settled the Cainhoy peninsula, Native Americans lived there for millennia. Their departure marked the area's first great transformation. But without the present rush to develop the peninsula and adjacent islands, evidence that Native American people lived on this land would have remained hidden just below the surface of the soil and along marshy riverbanks.

State and federal laws now require builders in South Carolina's coastal zone to conduct studies before construction begins to ensure that historically significant sites are documented and preserved to some degree. Archaeologists have found the remains of cultures that existed on this land thousands of years before Europeans and Africans arrived.

Scholars estimate that people lived on this land as many as 10,000 years ago. Stone tools, arrowheads and pieces of pottery discovered throughout the nearby Francis Marion National Forest tell of their existence. Archaeologists have determined that some of the pottery is about 4,000 years old. The stories of the people who made and used these objects are partially told by studying vessels they used to carry water, store food and cook.

A large concentration of broken pottery was found buried near the Jack Primus community on the site where the Charleston Regional Business Center now stands. Archaeologists retrieved thousands of shards of what is known as Thom's Creek pottery, made between 2500 and 1000 B.C. This distinctive style of pottery features depressions made in the wet clay for either decorative or functional purposes. The pottery came from thick clay deposits along Lowcountry waterways and lagoons.

Four tribes – Wando, Etiwan, Sewee and Sampa – inhabited the lands on and around present-day Charleston and the Cainhoy peninsula when settlers from England and the British colony of Barbados arrived in April 1670 at Albemarle Point on the Ashley River.

The Etiwan lived primarily on the upper Cooper River, but claimed land as far down as Charleston and Daniel Island. Etiwan and Wando are the names the indigenous people gave to the Cooper and Wando rivers, respectively. The Ashley River, on the west side of the Charleston peninsula, was called Kiawah, after another tribe.

Spanish explorers encountered the Etiwan and the Kiawah in 1605 and 1609. Shortly after the English arrived, they made contact with the Wando and Sampa, who had settled north of the Kiawah. The northernmost tribe, the Sewee, lived near the mouth of the Santee River. In the early years of English settlements, the Native Americans supplied the colonists with fish, venison and other wildlife. They also traded the skins of deer and other animals.

In appearance, the Indians were strikingly different from the Europeans — not just in the shade of their chestnut-colored skin and texture of their hair but also the manner in which they carried their "straight bodies." The Europeans described them as having excellent posture, with straight, strong backs. They were also admired for other physical attributes.

Artist and explorer Mark Catesby wrote: "I have never seen a crooked Indian in my life. Both men and women could run miles without tiring. Most were robust and athletic, capable of lifting great burdens and enduring hard labor."

The Etiwan altered their looks to meet what they considered a physical ideal. The process started early in an individual's life. A colonist in 1711 reported seeing a small bag of sand pressed hard to a baby boy's forehead to make it flatter. This made his eyes stand out, supposedly improving vision and allowing his hair to fall over his forehead like an over-hanging roof. This not only improved a hunter's ability of spotting prey but also increased his chances of being selected for the prettiest girl.

Before the settlers arrived, the Indians' clothing was scant. Women wore moss skirts. In referring to the Etiwan, Richard Ludlam wrote: "They will not themselves nor let their children learn to wear a decent apparel." When they did wear clothing, he wrote, it was usually made from the skins of bear and deer.

The men had little or no hair on their chins. But the long, straight black locks of men and women were smeared with bear oil to keep it clean and to foster growth. The oil had no strong odor, but it did repel mosquitoes.

Autumn was a time for celebration. Throughout the Southeast, the most important one was the celebration of green corn rites. In preparation, men and women adorned themselves with paint, feathers and beads. At other times, they paid homage to the sun, moon, planets and ministers of the Great Spirit who provided for them.

The Rev. Dr. Francis LeJau, a French Protestant and early settler, was an ordained Anglican minister who lived near the Native Americans. In 1707 he became the first rector of St. James Church at Goose Creek where the nomadic Etiwan built temporary shelters. LeJau, who observed their burial practices, wrote that, after an Etiwan died, the women of the tribe anointed the body with the oil of either "the bear or Ikkerry (hickory) nuts."

Each year, the Etiwans assembled for a great dance, the minister wrote. Men danced by themselves for three days. Then the women arrived, and they danced by themselves at night. LeJau asked an Etiwan man the reason for the separation: "To remember a time where a Man was made alone and there was no woman; but after, God took somewhat out of Men and made the Woman." When LeJau asked the man what it was that God took, the man placed his hand upon his breast. LeJau's wife, Elizabeth Harrison LeJau, called it a bone. The Etiwan man smiled and said yes. The practice may have reflected the influence of earlier Spanish missionaries who were in the area.

Most Indian couples had only one or two children. The number was controlled through herb-induced abortion, a practice reported throughout North America. It made them sterile, although occasionally it was fatal. In either case, it reduced the population. But the use of herbs for medicinal purposes probably helped some native people live to see their fifth-generation descendants.

Settling along the Cooper and Wando rivers before the Europeans and Africans arrived, the Native Americans were well placed for fresh water, fish and shellfish. They used hand lines and hooks made from fish bones and made fish traps and nets.

When living near the coast during the summer, they shared the work of planting corn and, for the Etiwan, pumpkins. Corn and shellfish were roasted. They did not plant more than they needed. In the fall and winter, tribes moved inland, possibly to be closer to seasonal food sources. During the fall migration, families lived on game, roots and nuts, including acorns and hickory.

The area was crisscrossed with their trails. They also traveled the rivers and streams in canoes made of pine and tulip trees. Before they obtained European tools, the Indians split hardwood trees and burned the centers and scraped them hollow with oyster shells and stone hatchets.

Because they migrated, coastal Indians were acquainted with customs far beyond their territory. They traveled as far south as St. Augustine, Florida, and as far north as Cape Fear, North Carolina. They also went hundreds of miles inland. Although they traveled widely, few native people were multi-lingual. The Etiwan and Sampa probably spoke Eastern Siouan, an ancient dialect distantly related to the Dakota Siouan.

The Sewee traded with tribes that came down the Santee in canoes. The Sewee primarily offered salt and fish from the coast for copper from the mountains. Eventually, the tribe also traded with the colonists, but they weren't content with such a limited access. They wanted to trade directly with England, but an attempt to do so ended in tragedy.

The Sewee had observed that the European ships always came from the direction of the rising sun. Because so many ships arrived, they assumed that England could not be far away. So, the Sewee decided to sail east.

The tribe assembled a fleet of gigantic canoes filled with skins and other wares. According to an English explorer, "The affair was carried out with a great deal of Secrecy and Expedition, so as in a small time they had gotten a Navy, Loading, Provisions and hands ready to set sail, leaving only the old, impotent and Minors at Home, 'till their successful return. The Wind presenting, they set up their Mat-Sails, and were scarce out of Sight when there rose a tempest." The Indians' vessels sank; survivors were captured and sold. None was heard from again.

After Charles Town was settled, more and more colonists moved inland and many settled along the Cooper River. Before 1700 small settlements, farms and plantations lined both banks along the river. The settlers traded with the Indians. Some made fortunes exchanging a variety of goods for cured furs, which were shipped back to England. The settlers provided rum, guns, gunpowder and shot along with an assortment of trinkets.

Before European settlements, the coastal tribes had generally established land boundaries and conflict was not a cause for major wars. This peace ended when Europeans began displacing tribes and various colonies persuaded native warriors to align with them militarily. Often, prisoners of war were sold off as slaves. LeJau wrote: "I suspect there is no other necessity for those Nations to war against their neighbors but that of making slaves to pay for the goods the traders sell them, for the skins trade do's not flourish as formerly." Early laws prohibited the enslavement of Native Americans but were seldom enforced.

The upper Wando River may have the distinction of being one of the first Indian reservations in the American colonies. In 1680 colonist Maurice Mathews wrote that all the land on the Wando beyond three miles of its mouth had been reserved for the Indian tribes displaced by the settlement of Charles Town at Oyster Point, the present-day White Point Garden. These included the Etiwan, Wando and Sampa, who previously lived closer to the harbor.

By 1699 smallpox had probably wiped out the Wando, and tribal lands between Charles Town and the Santee River were declared by the British available for white settlement. The Sampa were pushed beyond the Santee delta. The Kiawah lost all of Kiawah Island and were forced north to Wappaoola Creek on the Cooper River.

Within 50 years after the establishment of Charles Town, the native population had decreased greatly. Scattered groups remained throughout the Lowcountry but most moved inland. Settlers took their land while European diseases decimated their populations. Smallpox was especially deadly. Provincial Governor John Archdale believed it "pleased Almighty God to send unusual sicknesses amongst them, as the Smallpox, etc., to lessen their numbers … the Hand of God was eminently seen in thinning the Indians, to make room for the English."

At the time of European contact, the coastal region's Indian population was estimated at 2,300. By 1715 the number had dwindled to 533. From 1562 to 1751, 19 tribes lived in the coastal area. After 1751 they had been pushed out by the settlers or killed by war and disease. The Sampa eventually moved northward. The Sampit River near Georgetown was named for them. The remaining Wandos also may have moved north. The Etiwan are mentioned in colonial records in 1743 and again in 1751. After 1751 no coastal tribe is again listed as a separate group.

Native Americans, however, didn't vanish. A community still exists.

The Wassamassaw tribe, centered in today's Varner Town community, is largely descendant from the Edisto and Etiwan, who were members of the Cusabo, the first people to inhabit James Island south of Charleston. The Cusabo included the Ashepoo, Cumbahee, Coosa, Edisto, Escamacu, Etiwan, Kiawah, Stono, Wando and Wimbee.

Varner Town residents also are related to Catawba and Cherokee and other tribal groups. Native American families of Catawba and Cherokee heritage from the interior of South Carolina settled in the area in the late 19th century and became part of the community.

The Varner Town Indians live in Berkeley County near the intersection of Highways 17-A and 176 — known locally as Carnes Crossroads — between Moncks Corner and Summerville. Between 150 to 200 tribal members live on 52 acres in Varner Town while as many as 800 others reside in the surrounding area.

Heidi Varner, a former member of the Wassamassaw Council, said, "By carrying on this community, it is our way of honoring our ancestors to make sure we survive and our children are educated about their culture. The Edisto and the Etiwan and other area tribes banded together for survival."

It is also possible the community includes descendants of the Sewee and Sampa. After the Sewee's failed attempt to sail to England, she said, "they left some of their women and children here, who mixed with the other Indian groups.

"After the Yemassee War around 1724, the Etiwan and other neighboring tribes asked for their own land to settle their people," she said. The colonial government granted the request and land was secured for them on the west side of the Wassamassaw Swamp. Varner Town is west of the Wassamassaw Swamp. (Wassamassaw is a Catawba word that probably means connecting waters.) "The agreement to officially grant this land was never carried out, and that is why Lowcountry Indians today do not have official reservations," she said. "It is very probable that the area where Varner Town is located was either inhabited by the Etiwan before the land was secured, or this area was the designated land that was secured for them and they were told to settle in this area. Even though the land was not officially granted, people remained in the same area. This area was considered to be the frontier of the old districts of St. James Goose Creek and St. John Berkeley at that time.

"Families of the Varner Town community have formed a distinct Native American community. Like other Native American communities in the Southeast, Indian ancestry was the identity and motivating factor that kept these communities together and caused them to live separately from other ethnic groups."

Varner Town is holding on to its remaining customs. The men play the drums and clean the graveyard, said Edmund Varner, Heidi Varner's brother and leader of the community's five drummers and a member of the Tribal Council. "Playing the drum is honoring the ancestors and the creator." Women don't play drums. They stand behind the drummers and sing tones, not words.

A large drum sits in a rear corner of the community center on U.S. Highway 17-A. Its head is made of buffalo hide. Its wide body was carved from the trunk of a large pine tree. It is one of three drums made from the tree. The United Methodist Church paid to have them made. The other drums are owned by the Keeper of the Wild, a shelter for sick, injured, orphaned or displaced wildlife in St. George and the Methodist Church Native American Ministry.

Although residents don't speak the languages of their ancestors, they've protected their identity. Seventy years ago, when Indians filed birth records and other official documents, state and county officials gave them the option of identifying themselves as black or white. Many people chose white. Heidi Varner's paternal grandfather Raymond Varner insisted that his children be identified as Indian.

"It's a miracle that we still exist today as a Native American community after all the struggles and pain my family had to endure over the past hundreds of years," she said. "I am proud of my ancestors who fought and stood their ground for their heritage and their history."

Heidi Varner has spent years researching her family's connection to the community. Even though she knew that she descended from the Etiwan, she never had a desire or need to visit Daniel Island until she was hired as a customer-service representative for a cell phone company there. The daily trips bring her close to a moss-draped tree in the marsh near the Long Point Road exit off the Mark Clark Expressway in Mount Pleasant.

"When I drive past that tree, I get a feeling that my ancestors walked here hundreds of years ago. This should be our land."

Main house at Middleburg Plantation, built between 1697 and 1699, is believed to be the oldest wooden structure in South Carolina. Painting by John W. Jones.

Chapter 2: Africans and Europeans

Carolina was settled in the late 1600s as a private venture. Eight Lords Proprietors received huge land grants from King Charles II for helping him regain the British throne. They encouraged colonists to come to America for profit. But the enterprise was short-lived. By 1729, less than 60 years after the founding of Charles Town, the British government took control of Carolina. The colonists rebelled against the Proprietors for proposing restrictive laws and failing to protect them from the Spaniards and their Native American allies.

In addition to the prospect of owning land and making a living, Carolina, although officially Anglican, offered white God-fearing settlers a rare guarantee in the 17th century: freedom of religion. The Fundamental Constitutions of Carolina guaranteed that, "No person whatsoever shall disturb, molest or persecute another for his speculative opinion in religion or his way of worship." This was an open invitation to Quakers, Jews and Protestants, although Roman Catholics were not welcome initially.

The Cainhoy peninsula was located in the Parish of St. Thomas and St. Denis as defined by the Church Act in 1706, which divided the province of South Carolina into 10 parishes. St. Thomas was the English-speaking area of the parish. The French-speaking Protestants in St. Denis arrived in Carolina in 1680 on the *Richmond*. Some of them settled in the Orange or French Quarter on the Cainhoy peninsula. The 1699 census listed 101 French settlers in Orange Quarter or about 25 families of between four to five persons in each family. By 1725 the population had dwindled to

16 French families.

Land grants were based on the "headright" system. Land was guaranteed to each head-of-household in the colony in exchange for working his assigned acreage. Heads of household were always men. Their families included relatives, indentured servants and enslaved Africans. The development of labor-intensive rice plantations soon increased the need for enslaved Africans who quickly became the majority in Carolina. Of course, they had virtually no rights.

In 1703 the colony's population was estimated at 9,580 people, of whom 42.6 percent were white, 42.8 percent were black and 14.6 percent were Native Americans. However, the black-white ratio in rice- and indigo-growing coastal areas was as high as 15 blacks to every one white. By the 1790s the population in St. Thomas and St. Denis Parish was 431 whites and 3,404 Africans.

Simon Lewis, co-director of the Carolina Lowcountry and Atlantic World Program at the College of Charleston, said as many as 200,000 enslaved men, women and children from Africa's west coast arrived in Charleston before the United States government outlawed the importation of slaves in 1808. That number represents approximately 40 percent of all Africans who were brought to continental North America. "After that date, slave-trading was still legal within the slave-holding states and some illegal slave trading from overseas continued," Lewis said. The slave population continued to grow because the children of slaves became slaves themselves.

The physical isolation of plantations allowed Africans to preserve many aspects of their traditional way of life. The Africans not only brought their ability to grow rice, they also continuously adapted and modified the old ways with the new. Gradually their language, religion, music, customs and culture were incorporated into everyday life. Today, the people, their culture and language are called Gullah.

The origin of the word Gullah is unclear. It might be a shortened form of the African nation of "Angola" or a variation of "Gola," an ethnic group in Sierra Leone. People of African descent in Georgia prefer to be called

"Geechee," which may also have roots in Sierra Leone from a tribe there known as the Kissi (pronounced Gee-zee). However, a river south of Savannah, Georgia, called the Ogeechee, appears to be a Native American name.[4]

Gullah is a beautiful language that is more easily understood by listening to it than trying to read its words, which have various spellings. For instance, some Gullah people pronounce "Cainhoy" as "Cain Hi," which evokes an eloquent description by the late Virginia Geraty, a Gullah scholar who wrote that Gullah is spoken softly, with a rolling rhythm. "As the Gullah speaks, you can almost hear the wind ruffling the marsh grasses. Their words sway like the long banners of moss that hang from oak trees that grace their homeland."

Remote and almost entirely self-sufficient, Lowcountry plantations were like small towns inhabited by people who seldom left the place. The planter's "big house" typically stood at the highest point on the overwhelmingly flat and low property. The main house was usually surrounded by gardens — formal as well as vegetable — along with barns and other buildings, all of which overlooked well-kept rice fields, hand-dug trunk lines and gates that were used to control the water levels during the planting season. Most of the fields were fed by brackish water from adjacent rivers and creeks. Others used water from inland swamp reservoirs.

Not far from the master's main house was the slave community. Their small cabins, typically lining a dirt "street," were primitive in comparison. They were usually one room and used primarily for sleeping. Some may have had a fireplace and chimney to provide warmth at night. Cooking was done outside in the yard or in the "kitchen house," which was adjacent to the master's living quarters. Fresh water was extracted from primitive wells and springs.

African workers typically tended their own vegetable gardens near their cabins and some raised a few chickens and some livestock for food. Most

---

4 Some life-long white residents of Charleston are also called Geechees because of their distinctive brogue, which sounds like a mixture of Scots-Irish and Gullah.

of their bare necessities were provided by their owners.

Plantation boundaries changed as owners bought and sold the land, but many of the original names of the places live on. Middleburg Plantation is one example and nearby Limerick Plantation is another. Twenty miles from Charleston, the Cooper River divides sharply at a place known as the "T." Middleburg is on the East Branch of the Cooper River in an area Native Americans called "Pimlica Maptica."

In 1693 French-born Benjamin Simons received a Proprietor's warrant to farm a 100-acre tract of high land and swamp there. At age 15 Simons, a Huguenot, escaped from France following the execution of his parents. He got to the Dutch town of Middelburg. From there he traveled to London where he joined his aunt and uncle. They immigrated to Carolina. Simons eventually married his first cousin Mary Esther DuPre. They named their two-story, clapboard plantation house Middleburg.

The house, constructed between 1697 and 1699, is believed to be the oldest wooden building in South Carolina. No doubt, black hands erected the beams and nailed the siding onto the dwelling. Simons later acquired more land from another grant in 1704, seven years after his original warrant, increasing Middleburg Plantation to 350 acres.

In 1772 Middleburg had 59 enslaved workers living on the place. By 1790, nine years before Jonathan Lucas II married Simons' great-grand-daughter, Sarah Lydia Simons, the African population at Middleburg was 90. Middleburg's main house was near a cluster of houses built for African workers. A 1786 map of Middleburg shows tiny squares identified as "12 cabins for the Negroes."

On this site, archaeologists found pottery made by enslaved workers, imported English ceramics from the 18th century, a slew of nails, glass shards, buttons and broken clay tobacco pipes and pipe stems.

Lucas became concerned about his family's safety in 1822 following a failed slave revolt in Charleston organized by freedman Denmark Vesey. After one of Lucas' slaves was charged and hanged as one of the "primary leaders" in the revolt, Lucas moved his wife and 10 youngest children to his London estate, according to Max "Macky" Hill III, whose parents Jane and Max Hill own Middleburg. If the revolt had succeeded, or so the story goes, a conspirator would have received one of Lucas' daughters as a prize.

The story, however, isn't consistent with an account published after Vesey and 34 of his alleged co-conspirators were tried, convicted and hanged. Three prisoners – Brand, Richard and John – the property of a certain "Jon. Lucas," presumably Jonathan Lucas, were acquitted by a court of two magistrates and five freeholders (landowners) and released.

According to the Lucas family history, "A Lucas Memorandum," written by William Dollard Lucas, Jonathan Lucas II moved to London after the English government invited him to build rice mills in England. Lucas erected large rice-cleaning plants in London and Liverpool, other European cities and in Egypt.

"A Lucas Memorandum" does not indicate that Jonathan Lucas II was a full-time resident at Middleburg. The account says he lived in Charleston and all but one of his children was born on the Charleston peninsula. His third child, Benjamin Simons Lucas, was baptized in May 1806 at Middleburg.

Instead of attempting a Vesey-inspired insurrection, many enslaved people on the Cainhoy peninsula took steps to emancipate themselves. They simply ran away. Newspaper advertisements for runaways provide valuable details about their personalities and styles of dress. Because teaching enslaved people to read and write was illegal, few of them left written accounts of their lives. They are not generally documented as individuals in legal records either. Therefore, advertisements for runaways are among the few descriptions available.

In March 1786 a three-guinea reward was offered for the return of Molly Dean, a "very smart, good looking woman" who spoke English well. She was formerly owned by a butcher named Bealer and well known about Cainhoy. Her husband lived on "Mr. Daniels'" plantation and there was reason to believe she was "harboured thereabouts." Unlike most enslaved people, Molly Dean had a first and last name.

Another was a woman whose name was Manemia. Before she ran away in January 1809, she had been known by two other names, Amelia and Peggy. Manemia spoke in a soft, low voice. One of her ears had been cut from the "boring" for her earrings. The cut portion of her ear "resembles an old-fashioned ear drop of the largest kind." She used a kerchief to cover the ear.

Manemia was raised on Andrew Deveaux's plantation on the Cooper River in the St. Thomas area of the parish. She had been sold to Necca DeCoster in Charleston before she disappeared. "She has numerous acquaintances in … Cainhoy and to the southward as well as in this city (Charleston). She was seen about two weeks since in King near Queen streets, and last week at the upper end of King Street, but from the many friends she has in various parts of the city it is impossible to point out the most likely place to find her."

A missing slave named Sam was advertised as having pit marks on his skin from smallpox. Sam, a house carpenter, left his owner, John Fogartie of Cainhoy, in the fall of 1787. Sam was wearing a shirt and trousers made from a coarse cotton cloth called osnaburg. The heavy cloth was used primarily to make sacks for grain, upholstery and draperies.

When Sarah, a woman from Angola on the southern end of Africa's west coast, ran away from her owner in Cainhoy, she was not alone. In April 1787 she was captured and taken to the Work House in Charleston for punishment. Sarah belonged to Mrs. Bushett of Cainhoy. She fled with two of her children, one three years old and the other 18 months. Sarah knew what it was like to be free because she had been captured in Angola and survived the Middle Passage to bear children in America.

A "mustee lad" named Primus, who was 17 or 18 years old in December 1786, ran away on Christmas Day without waiting to see if his owner would follow the tradition of giving him a present. "Mustee" was a term used to describe a person who is descendant from a white person and a person with one-fourth black ancestry. At least six weeks later, Primus still hadn't been found. He was well known in Charleston and St. Thomas "where it is supposed he is harbored at a plantation called Free David's on Cainhoy." Sometimes slave owners described a runaway's style of dress. In May 1798 after Moses fled, he was said to have been wearing a "blue Negro coat" made with coarse cloth that had a red cape and cuffs. He also wore overalls. In addition to his dark complexion, Moses had other distinguishing features. "He has some marks of a whip about him," the advertisement said.

Ads announcing runaways usually listed the person's height. At six feet, Moses, a 19-year-old mulatto was exceptionally tall for the times. He was a housepainter who ran away in October 1795. His skin was pocked by smallpox scars. He had long, bushy hair and wore an osnaburg jacket and overalls.

According to the ad seeking his return, Moses didn't spend much time in the streets during the day. On Sundays, he went fishing or headed to Sullivan's Island. His owner said if he wasn't hiding out on Sullivan's Island he most likely "will conceal himself amongst Negroes, and go fishing for some time, until he gets employment on board some coasting vessel, or those which bring wood to town, as he formerly went in such vessels." Moses' mother was a free mulatto woman who had lived at Cainhoy but moved to Johns Island, south of Charleston, where her son rambled often.

A case of homesickness in early 1821 caused 30-year-old Massa to run away from her owner near Columbia. Massa was born on Daniel Island and enslaved in Charleston before she was bought and moved to Columbia. Her new owner placed an ad in the City Gazette and Daily Advertiser in Charleston offering a reward for her return.

Sometimes an advertisement ended with the promise that if the runaways turned themselves in they would be forgiven. Rewards were generally higher for white informants than for blacks.

Not all slaveholders were white. Nathaniel Williams was a free black slaveholder on Daniel Island and was known as "Black Nat." Williams was a carpenter and is said to have owned 500 acres and at least one boy named Joseph. In his will, dated November 16, 1729, Williams granted Joseph his freedom, 25 acres and half of his clothing.

The Charleston district also had a significant number of "brown aristocrats," skilled free tradesmen of African descent who were tailors, carpenters, millwrights and others with special skills. Many owned slaves, usually employed as servants in their homes or laborers in their workshops. In 1830, 11 black men and women owned 236 slaves in St. Thomas and St. Denis Parish. The black slave owners were: Thomas Bonneau, William G. Grown, Henry Cannady, Catherine Edwards, the estate of George Elfe, John Glenn, John L. Geyer, George A. Hazelhurst, John Johnson, Mary Lord and Thomas Mitchell. Catherine Edwards was the largest slaveholder, owning 73 people.

After the Civil War, some who had been enslaved left the country for the city in search of work. Those who didn't find employment often found a home in jail. When the war ended, Charleston opened the House of Corrections on the upper west side to confine vagrants and people who violated city ordinances. From the opening year of the House of Corrections in 1868 and until 1884, at least six prisoners, evenly divided between men and women, came from St. Thomas. By 1886 the facility was closed. Records list the inmates' ages, but not the reasons for their confinement. Some prisoners were as young as nine years old. The building once stood in the area of today's Johnson Hagood Stadium near The Citadel.

July Pinckney, 65, a "colored" field hand from St. Thomas, was among the oldest prisoners. He was locked up twice, first in May 1868 for 15 days and again the following month for four days.

On May 21, 1868, Scipio Green, an 18-year-old "colored" fish hawker from St. Thomas was arrested and held for four days. On the same day, another "colored" fish hawker from Beaufort County, Joseph Pinckney, age 20, was arrested, placed in the House of Corrections and released after five days. The arrest of two fish hawkers on the same day could have been a coincidence, or it may have been the result of a city crackdown on salesmen suspected of violating city ordinances. Or perhaps the men got into a dispute that led to their arrests.

The other St. Thomas residents who served time between 1871 and

1884 were Godfrey Bryant and Rose Alston, each 20 years old. In different years, two 17-year-old girls from Cainhoy who could have been related were jailed. In August 1882 Rose Hardgraves was held for one month; a year later, Anna C. Hardgraves spent 15 days in confinement. The record does not list the race of these detainees.

Two weeks before Christmas in 1889, an enterprising boy from Cainhoy was mentioned in an article in The News and Courier. To tell this story, the newspaper did not hesitate to use a term African Americans would find offensive today. The newspaper specifically called the boy a "little coon" and mentioned that "coon" was used to describe a black youth from Cainhoy. The newspaper story also offers an interesting glimpse into what Lowcountry families were willing to put on their dinner tables.

"A little 'coon' … made his appearance in the market … with a bunch of 13 squirrels, another of 12 rabbits and a single 'coon' (raccoon). He said that the game had been shot in the vicinity of Cainhoy, and had been given (to) him to sell. He asked 10 cents each for the squirrels, 12 cents each for the rabbits, and wanted a whole half a dollar for the coon, which was singed and dressed. And he got the money. There has been more four-footed game in the market this year than has been seen for many years. The rabbit market has been simply over-stocked, and prices have been consequently very low. One can purchase a pair of fat hares for from 20 to 25 cents, a half a dozen squirrels for 30 cents, or a fat coon for 25 to 30 cents."

Emancipation changed the way some black people on the Cainhoy peninsula handled their money. Instead of burying it, they now had the option of opening bank accounts. On March 3, 1865, Congress created the Freedmen's Savings and Trust Company, commonly called The Freedmen's Bank. Along with the Freedmen's Bureau, the bank was designed to aid freedmen in the transition from slavery to freedom.

The bank operated 37 branches in 17 states and the District of Columbia, where it was headquartered. The bank was one of the first multi-state financial institutions in the nation. By 1870 nearly all the local branches were run by black employees.

Massive fraud among upper management and among the board of directors by 1874 took its toll. The bank fell into even deeper trouble due to rapid growth and economic instability during the economic panic the previous year. On June 29, 1874, the bank closed.

Some of the Freedmen's Bank records survived and provide information to document black families for the period immediately following the Civil War. At least four people from the Cainhoy peninsula had money in the bank's Charleston branch.

Sixty-year-old Ann Horlbeck opened an account on September 17, 1869. She was born on John Ball's place on the Cooper River and was a daughter of Dinah and Hector Ball. After Emancipation, she remained on the plantation. She listed her occupation as "planting." Horlbeck and her husband, Jacob, had 10 children: Jacob, Michael, Lewis, Syke, Dinah, Stepny, Ben, Ellen, Lemiel and Hector. Her brothers were September, Areulies and Gabriel Ball.

A year after Horlbeck opened her account, John Dixon (mother Juliette, father John), who was born in Cainhoy, placed money in the bank. Like Horlbeck, farming was Dixon's occupation. He reported that he worked for "J.S. O'Hair." Dixon, 25, was married to Chloe, and they were childless.

In the summer of 1871, three years before the bank failed, Frank Robinson and George H. Allen, both from Cainhoy, entrusted their money to the bank.

Robinson (mother Rial, father, Robbin), age 18, opened an account when he was living at 17 Market Street in Charleston. He drove a wood cart and worked for a man named "Simmons." He was single and had no children. His siblings were Sambo, Robert, Amaria and Lucas.

Allen (mother Rebecca, father Jack) was a 53-year-old self-employed carpenter married to Susan Ann. They had seven children: William Henry, Mary, Hannah Rebecca, Elizabeth Ann, Isaac H., Catharine L. and Martha. One of Allen's daughters married James Smalls. The couple lived at the intersection of Calhoun and East Bay streets in Charleston. George Allen's only sibling, a brother named Isaac, had left St. Thomas and moved to Texas.

Although emancipation gave the plantation workers the option to leave the area, some felt such a bond with the land and had so few options they chose to work for their former owners as sharecroppers. The areas they settled just beyond the plantation gates gave rise to communities that exist today in the Cainhoy-Huger area.

The former slaves continued to labor under difficult times, conditions made even harsher when Union soldiers, assigned to serve as Freedmen's Bureau agents, forced sharecroppers to sign contracts with their former owners. Captain F.M. Montell, who had a desire to "get a place on Cooper River," bargained with four East Branch planters in July 1865 to collect 10 percent of any contract he obtained on their behalf. Montell used his rifle to encourage them to sign.

Tober, a former slave, described Montell's mode of persuasion. Montell had him "cornered up against a brick chimney with the muzzle of a musket against his breast and ordered him to sign the contract."

The year after the war ended, Edward F. O'Brien, a Union officer stationed at Mount Pleasant, reported on conditions in the parishes to A. Mc.L. Crawford, of the Freedmen's Bureau office in Charleston. In his September 1866 report, O'Brien wrote: "I found a great amount of destitution existing and more particularly in St. Thomas Parish. There the people were living on green corn, pond lily beans and in some instances have used alligator meat to prevent actual starvation. I consider the corn crop a failure and I fear that during the forthcoming winter the suffering amongst the aged and infirm will be appalling."

The poor economy in St. Thomas also may have led one resident to get more rations than he deserved by exaggerating the size of his family. In his report, O'Brien also wrote: "I have one more case to call your attention to, and that is the case of Mr. McDowell of Cain Hoy. He is the reputed father of some six children and has been drawing rations for them from the Government under the plea that they were orphans and as such entitled to be fed."

O'Brien recommended that McDowell be punished for fraud and required to repay the government the value of rations he received.

While some former slaves left the plantations, others chose to work and live on the land of their former owners. Susan and Scipio Green didn't leave Middleburg. They worked for the John Coming Ball family when Ball acquired the plantation. During and after slavery, Susan Green was a cook and Scipio Green was a horseman.

When Scipio was a boy, the Balls entertained Northern guests who sometimes denounced slavery. For those who criticized it, the Balls would summon Scipio. Ball told his guests: "No, we treat them well, and even educate them." Then he told Scipio to recite verbatim what he had learned. Scipio's performance surprised the guests. The Balls quietly reveled in the deception, believing that Scipio didn't have a clue as to what he was saying. Some black workers, however, knew that little Scipio could read, a skill kept hidden from the Balls.

After Emancipation and before the turn of the 20th century, when it was no longer against the law to teach black people how to read and write, the Greens' granddaughter, Mary Ida Boney, received an education at Middleburg. Ida lived with her grandparents there and played with two of the white children, Annie and Marie Ball.

Ida wanted so badly to identify with her white playmates she desired straight hair as long as theirs even though her own hair extended past her shoulders. To satisfy her, Ida's grandmother cut a horse's mane to weave into her granddaughter's hair.

Aside from getting what may have been the first hair extension, Ida's association with the Ball girls benefited her in another way. The Ball girls had an English teacher who was brought from the North to teach them to read. Ida also learned from the teacher. Her reading skills rose to the third-grade level.

Ida's parents, William and Dianna Boney, had five other children: Annie, Daniel, Susan, Hannah and Laurie Mae. It isn't known why Ida was selected to live with her grandparents at Middleburg. Ida's family believes her early exposure to education predestined her daughter, Lela Haynes Session, to become supervisor of Berkeley County's schools for black students.

Bricks and Creamware

Because of the Wando River's high salinity, the nearby Cooper River was better suited for rice cultivation. By the mid-19th century, rice cultivation along the Wando was largely replaced by more profitable endeavors such as brick making, cotton growing and livestock. In the 1850s the value of beef more than doubled. This along with growing corn for feed provided plantation owners with a significant supplemental income.

Although brick making was common on many plantations, it had not been done on a large scale until a series of fires in Charles Town in the mid-18th century destroyed large sections of the city. In 1715 the Colonial Assembly passed an act requiring all new buildings within fortified Charles Town to be of brick or stone construction. But this act was not enforced until a fire on Tuesday, November 18, 1740. Approximately 300 buildings from Broad and Church streets to Meeting and Tradd streets were consumed. With almost one-third of the city destroyed, bricks were suddenly in great demand.

To be economically viable, a brickyard needed proximity to navigable water, clay and sand for temper and wood to fuel the kilns. Lands along the Wando and Cooper rivers fulfilled those requirements. Eventually, 23 brickyards were located along the Wando and its tributaries and the Cooper River.

In many cases, the brick maker was the property owner, who typically had a primary residence in Charles Town and ran other enterprises. James and Deborah Fisher, for instance, were Charles Town merchants who owned a brick plantation near Cainhoy in the 1740s. Indentured servants and enslaved people developed the skills needed to make bricks and did the actual work.

Brick making on the Wando River lasted until the onset of the Civil War. The 1850 census lists Daniel Island-Cainhoy brick makers as John

This chimney at Middleburg Plantation was once part of a steam-powered rice mill Jonathan Lucas II built in the 1800s. Painting by John W. Jones.

Sanders, John L. O'Hear, John Marshall, J.B. Gordon, J. Venning and G. Thompson. Their total output topped more than four million bricks a year. Unlike the huge labor force needed for growing rice, brick making required fewer workers. Sanders' plantation made 700,000 bricks a year with 33 workers and John L. O'Hear made 580,000 bricks annually with 22 hands.

Daniel Island's subsoil provided another remarkable yield, a fine white clay called kaolin, which could be transformed into ceramics. In the 1760s Englishman John Bartlam established the first American creamware factory on a site near Cainhoy at present-day St. Thomas Point. Bartlam's pottery factory was particularly important because, up to that point, all fine ceramics and porcelain were imported. Englishman Sir Josiah Wedgwood was so worried about competition from the American factory that he visited Charleston to investigate.

"The simple fact that Bartlam was making pottery to rival that made in England ... and that Wedgwood was concerned about the effect Bartlam's factory would have on his export of ceramics to America, is evidence for the importance of this pottery," University of South Carolina archaeologist Stanley South notes.

Although Bartlam's endeavors eventually failed and the factory was abandoned, his work at Cainhoy is of special significance in the history of American ceramics. Few examples of this rare American-made creamware remain.

Slave Jail: Myth or Fact?

John Coming Ball, who was among the few successful rice planters following the Civil War, bought Middleburg in 1872. Ball was the first owner of the plantation who was not descended from the Simons family. Soon afterward, Ball married the great-great-granddaughter of Benjamin Simons III.

In April 1926, The News and Courier published a story by Emma S. Gilchrist that heralded Middleburg as a great rice plantation with a house still in perfect condition. The story also mentions Middleburg's "plantation jail," described as an imposing building with cypress shingles on a high brick foundation. The upper story was used as a "corn house" and the ground level was a place to confine delinquent slaves. Depending on the offense, an enslaved worker got time in the jail following a trial by the plantation owner.

A son of a later owner, Macky Hill, maintains that the building was never used as a jail. He believes it was the plantation commissary and a barn to store seed rice that would ensure Middleburg's ability to replant and thrive.

"In 1981 John Gibbs, John Coming Ball's grandson, who sold Middleburg to my parents, told me that the name 'slave jail' was kind of a jokey

It is rumored that the Middleburg Plantation seed house was used to incarcerate unruly workers. Painting by John W. Jones.

name used for two small, cell-like rooms on the east end to get him and his three little brothers excited and scared," Hill said. That was around 1910, when the commissary served as a neighborhood store.

"The small, high, barred windows of the brick first story are serious-looking, but were to keep people out, not in," Hill said. "They protected one of the most precious commodities on the plantation — the seed rice, carefully grown and harvested each year specifically for seed and preserved with extreme caution between seasons."

The term "slave jail" apparently stuck as a memorable name for the entire building. It was picked up and used in newspaper and magazine articles and became part of the plantation's lore, he said.

Hill cited a 1998 archaeology study done by graduate student Kerri Barile, who was under the direction of University of South Carolina professor Leland Ferguson. Barile based her master's thesis on research and archaeological excavations inside and outside of Middleburg's commissary. She determined the so-called jail addition dated from the mid-1870s to the 1880s, decades after the slaves were freed, Hill said.

Barile's conclusion does not preclude that the building was used for incarceration, Professor Ferguson said.

"We know for a fact that from time to time slaves were locked in various plantation buildings in the South. While John Gibbs may be correct in his story, he also may be wrong. Descendants of the people enslaved (at Middleburg) called the whole building a slave jail, and they may have had reason."

Colonial-era Philanthropist, Richard Beresford

Colonist Richard Beresford and 20th century northern industrialist Harry Frank Guggenheim have had the most lasting influence on the Cainhoy peninsula.

With his enormous wealth, Beresford created the "Beresford Bounty" in 1721 for the support of schools in St. Thomas Parish. The fund was nearly destroyed during the Civil War, but it survived and today is managed by the Episcopal Diocese of South Carolina, which owns the St. Thomas Church. The fund provides a small amount of money that offsets a portion of the cost to maintain and insure the property.

By 1711 Beresford had acquired nine land grants in St. Thomas and Christ Church parishes for a total of 4,350 acres. Three years later, he acquired another 450 acres. On January 4, 1712, he married Sarah Cooke by whom he had one son, John. She died less than a year later, perhaps from complications arising from childbirth.

Beresford's public career in South Carolina was impressive. He served on the Grand Council from 1690 to 1708 and in the Assembly beginning in 1702 and ending in 1717. He was appointed a commissioner of

The estate of Richard Beresford provided the fund in the mid-1800s to build this 17-room house that was a school for poor white children and parish rectory in the old village of Cainhoy. Photo courtesy of Beverly Avinger Lahmeyer.

the Indian Trade in 1707 and, in that year, was named public treasurer, a position he held throughout the proprietary period. By 1708 he was a Lords Proprietor's deputy. He was a commissioner of the Free School at Charles Town for two years, beginning in 1710. With Joseph Boone, he was named the colony's agent in 1715. He also was a commissioner of the High Roads for St. Thomas and St. Denis Parish. While serving in England as South Carolina's agent, he met and married Dorothy Mellish. They had two children.

Beresford's life was cut short. On March 17, 1721, a falling tree limb killed him. Though his untimely death no doubt caused great difficulties for his family, it benefited the parish's poor children. Beresford's will provided money for the expansion of a school that had been active in St. Thomas Parish since 1718. It was called the Beresford Free Grammar School. On December 4, 1765, the school caught fire and was consumed.

The following January a notice in the South-Carolina Gazette called for subscriptions for its rebuilding.

Beresford's estate provided the funds for a new school. An act was passed on December 10, 1856, giving the vestry and wardens of St. Thomas Parish the power to purchase land "situate in the Parish of St. Thomas and Dennis, on Wando River, near the village of Louisville, containing two hundred and twenty five and one-half acres." The land became the site of a new schoolhouse and parish rectory called Beresford House.

It was a three-story building fronted by a large porch with tall columns. Its 17 rooms served the multiple purposes of home for the rector and his family, a chapel on the bottom floor, including stained-glass windows, school rooms and rooms for boarding students.

The parish suffered from the effects of the Civil War and Reconstruction. Without parishioners, St. Thomas Church as an active entity was eventually discontinued. The parish house and former school were used at various times as a private residence. In 1937 Harry Frank Guggenheim paid $3,000 for the Beresford Bounty property.

Huguenot Cross

On March 25, 1922, the heirs of Altis Dickson, a "worthy colored man of the neighborhood" who owned property in the Orange Quarter, gave the Huguenot Society of South Carolina a one-acre plot on which stands a granite cross that marks the former location of a Huguenot church.

The original church for the French congregation of Orange Quarter on the Cainhoy peninsula was built before 1700. A second church was built in 1708 after the 1706 Church Act. The church was in a small wooden building, which may have been built on or near land formerly belonging to Caesar Mauzé. After about 1715 the Orange Quarter was called the French Quarter.

Although the French in the area were served by a succession of itinerant ministers before 1700, the Rev. Jean LaPierre was the first permanent minister in the parish, serving from November 1706 until his death in

Huguenot Cross at French Quarter Creek. Photo by Herb Frazier.

1728. He was followed by the Rev. John James Tissot. Though he was Anglican, Tissot officiated in the French language. He served from 1730 until he died in 1763.

By the mid-1750s most residents in the Parish of St. Denis spoke English. In 1768 the Parish of St. Denis was dissolved into the Parish of St. Thomas and the church building was sold. The money went to benefit poor residents of St. Thomas and St. Denis Parish.

The granite cross erected on the site has inscriptions etched on two sides of the stout monument that fronts French Quarter Creek Road. On one side, the inscription reads: "Erected A.D. 1922 by the Huguenot Society of South Carolina on this God's Acre." On the other side: "Site of the old and extinct Protestant or Huguenot Church of Orange Quarter St. Denis with its surrounding graveyard constructed about 1687 A.D." French Quarter Creek, formerly known as Lynch's and originally Wisboo Creek, is barely visible through the underbrush.

Early roads

Trading with Indians to supply England required moving large amounts of goods. The Cooper River served as a "superhighway" to get commodities to Charles Town. But roads also were necessary to make this connection from the farm and plantations to the seaport. In the settlement's early days land travel was difficult. There were few roads and many of those were mere footpaths, often the "broad paths" formerly used by Native Americans. Some of the broad paths evolved into roads.

One of the earliest roads was on St. Thomas Island. By 1698 the island had developed to such an extent that a 16-foot-wide road was built. An act required all males living on the island to keep it clear. The act was amended in 1701 and again in 1707; the second amendment provided not only for a road in Christ Church Parish but referred to the first bridge across the Wando River.

In 1712 an act was passed "for Raising Sum of One Hundred and Nineteen Pounds on those persons ... especially appointed to make a Highway or Common Road upon Thomas Island on the NW Side of Wando River." The act required residents to maintain the bridge over the creek on the northwest side of Thomas Island, commonly called the Wading Place. It also reimbursed Robert Daniel Jr. for his expense to build the bridge.

Fogartie's Landing at Cainhoy was widely used, particularly by inland plantation owners who did not have direct water access. When the trade in naval stores and with the Indians declined, the river did not lose its importance. Gov. James Glen reported in 1751 to the Lords Commissioners for Trade and Plantation in England that the "Cooper River appears sometime a kind of floating market, and we have numbers of canoes boats and pettyaguas that ply incessantly, bringing down the country produce to town, and returning with such necessaries as are wanted by the planters."

In 1731 a law was passed establishing a ferry from the lower bluff on Long Point on the Charleston Neck to Richard Codner's plantation on Daniel Island. This ferry was invested to Joseph Scott in 1765, then to John Clement in the 1790s.

Clement's ferry had many names during its existence, but it was popularly referred to as the "Dover and Calais" ferry. Because many people who lived in St. Thomas and St. Denis were of French descent and the people who lived on Charleston Neck were of English background, the name was a joking comparison to the English Channel ferry between Dover, England, and Calais, France.

The ferry ran between Calais Ferry House on Daniel Island and Dover Ferry House just outside the City of Charleston. Clement established it in 1793. The road leading to the ferry on the Cainhoy peninsula was named Clements Ferry Road. Milestones were positioned along the road to mark the distance to the Calais and Dover Ferry. Vandals have since stolen many of the milestones. A few of them remain. According to the S.C. Department of Archives and History, the location of the highway appears to have changed to its present location in 1825. It is assumed that the milestones could have been placed in their present location at that time. The unadorned stones are inscribed near the top with "__ to Calais."

The names and path of Clements Ferry and Cainhoy roads over time have been switched. The highway that is called Clements Ferry today once passed in front of the St. Thomas Church. Maps of Harry Frank Guggenheim's Cain Hoy Plantation show how the path of the roads changed over time.

A 1937 map of Cain Hoy Plantation shows Clements Ferry Road passing in front of the church. It also went through an area marked "Negro," which is likely today's Jack Primus community. Another road south of Clements Ferry is marked Cainhoy Road. It took travelers to the village of Cainhoy.

By 1952 Clements Ferry Road had been erased from a map of the Cain Hoy Plantation, and today's Cainhoy Road at that time was called Clements Ferry Road. The changes didn't end there. A 1958 map identifies the road between Cainhoy and St. Thomas Island as Cainhoy Road, but today it is called Clements Ferry Road.

Six mile marker to the Calais to Dover Ferry. The marker is along the original route of Clements Ferry Road and located on the Cain Hoy Plantation. Photo by Herb Frazier.

— MAP OF —
CAINHOY PLANTATION
SITUATE IN ST. THOMAS PARISH, BERKELEY CO. S.C.
OWNED BY HARRY F. GUGGENHIEM OF
PORT WASHINGTON, LONG ISLAND

This 1937 map of Cainhoy Plantation shows three major roads of that period. Clements Ferry Road no longer exists in its 1937 location. The road labeled Public Road is now known as Cainhoy Road and the road labeled as Cainhoy Road is now known as Clements Ferry Road.

St. Thomas Church, site of 1876 Cainhoy Riot. Painting by John W. Jones.

Chapter 3: The Cainhoy Riot

On January 1, 1863, President Abraham Lincoln signed the Emancipation Proclamation, ending slavery in those states that had seceded. But freedom did not spread to the entire South until the Civil War was over in 1865. The end of the fighting ushered in a 12-year period in South Carolina called Reconstruction, during which people of African descent made huge political gains. But it also was a time of dramatic racial hostilities and violence. That violence reached Cainhoy on October 16, 1876.

After four years of war, South Carolina's social needs were enormous, while financial resources were scarce. Industry was crippled. Fields went unplanted. Tax revenue sagged. Whites, alleging corruption, refused to cooperate with the state government, which included black legislators and white "carpetbaggers" from other regions of the country. Eventually, white and some black South Carolinians banded together to regain control of state government. In 1876 whites started a campaign of violence to support a "straight out" slate of white Democrats, rejecting the notion of "fusion" with black Republicans. They traveled the state on horseback wearing uniforms with red flannel shirts. They were called "Redshirts" and their goal was to intimidate black voters.

As the election neared, one tactic was to call for "joint discussions" at Republican rallies. Sometimes the black gatherings were broken up; sometimes black voters gave the Democrats a fair listening. Either result was a victory for the Democrats. Before an October 16 rally near Cainhoy, county Democratic Party Chairman Charles H. Simonton asked Republican Chairman and Charleston County Sheriff Christopher Columbus Bowen, a white man, to allow his party to share the speaking time at the St. Thomas Church — also known as Brick Church — near Cainhoy. Bowen went along with the plan but requested that both sides come unarmed. Simonton agreed.

In those days, a Southerner considered bearing arms to mean carrying a rifle or shotgun. There was an assumption that every man carried a pistol. Most of the whites in attendance did not bring their heavier guns. Black people, however, had reason to be more than a little cautious about arriving totally unarmed at a meeting with whites. Already that year, whites had killed black people in riots at Hamburg and Ellenton, South Carolina. Many black people in the audience brought shotguns and muskets, which they hid in the nearby woods and in a dilapidated shed to the left of the speaker's platform.

That Monday morning at 9:30, about 150 white Democrats, musicians and two dozen Republicans left Charleston on the steamer *Pocosin* for Cainhoy. The boat ride up the Cooper River was pleasant. To amuse themselves, both sides fired their pistols at objects in the water. When the boat docked, carts and wagons carried passengers to St. Thomas Church about 2.5 miles outside Cainhoy. An hour later, a crowd of about 500 people, the majority of whom were black, assembled on the church grounds.

A prominent speaker at the rally was Dr. Martin R. Delany, a dynamic black leader. A native of Pennsylvania, he was the most famous of the five black physicians in Charleston. He studied medicine at Harvard, but a protest by white students forced him out. He intermittently worked as a medical doctor in Charleston and Pittsburgh. During his career, he was known for his activities as an abolitionist, an African ethnographer and a black nationalist. He also was the first black man to serve as a field officer in the Union Army, holding the rank of major.

Delany surprised many by publicly backing former Confederate Gen. Wade Hampton, the Democratic Party candidate for governor. Delany had grown frustrated with the Army's and Republican Party's failed attempts to help newly emancipated black people start small farms and achieve economic independence. Hampton pledged that he'd be a father to the state's family, black and white. He promised equal protection under the law, an end to violence, better public schools and fair political campaigns.

Delany took Hampton's promise seriously even though the former general was supported by whites who advocated violence against blacks. Critics said Delany had betrayed his race, and it certainly didn't endear him to black Republicans. Throughout the Lowcountry, Hampton spoke to large crowds, both black and white. But black people who defected from the Republican Party were shunned and sometimes victimized for supporting Democrats.

At the Cainhoy rally, a News and Courier reporter described the black audience as "the most uncouth, savage and uncivilized that I have ever seen. ... When it was understood that Col. M.R. Delany, who is probably the most intelligent man of his race in the State, was to be one of the speakers on the Democratic side, your correspondent asked Mr. Bowen if they would hear him speak. 'Yes,' replied Mr. Bowen, 'I reckon I can keep them still but it will be just about as hard as to hold a wild elephant or a lion without tying him.'"

What happened next is confusing. As soon as Delany mounted the wagon to speak, black Republicans started beating drums, and many of them walked away. They refused to listen to "de damned nigger Democrat." They ignored requests to return. As they marched off, women crowded around the wagon with bludgeons, shouting threats at Delany. Bowen was not able to restore order until he leaped from the wagon and ordered the crowd to calm down.

Delany was invited to continue, but declined. Instead, he complained that he had been to Europe and Africa and in the presence of nobility of many countries, and he had never been insulted as he was that day by people of his own race. But the interruptions continued.

The next speaker was Republican W.J. McKinlay, described as a gentle, inoffensive Charleston teacher. He was a member of a prominent and wealthy free black family. He had served in the Constitutional Convention of 1868 and was Charleston's recorder of deeds. Moments after McKinlay began to speak, a shot was fired, reportedly by someone who had mistaken McKinlay for Delany.

Pandemonium ensued. The white Democrats, many of them unarmed, had no choice but to run as other shots rang out. Some fell wounded during the onslaught. The rest made it to the village of Cainhoy where they gathered at Beresford House, the parish rectory and old schoolhouse. In all, six white men and one black man were killed. Sixteen people were wounded, some seriously. Only three blacks were injured, all of them Democrats.

Reconstruction Governor Daniel Chamberlain ordered an investigation and Federal troops were sent to restore order. Statements were taken from all those present.

Two days after the Cainhoy riot, R.M. Wallace, the U.S. marshal in South Carolina, submitted an incident report to U.S. Attorney General Alphonzo Taft and acknowledged that white Democrats went for their guns first.

Wallace emphasized the Democrats were following an "intimidation policy" of demanding to speak at Republican gatherings, backing up their demands with "Winchester repeating rifles in the hands of men who knew how to use them." Because of those previous experiences, the Republicans came armed, but were told by party leaders to store their weapons away from the rally.

Wallace wrote, "Soon after McKinlay commenced speaking a commotion was observed in the crowd and the side next to the dilapidated building, and McKinlay jumped off the stand and said, 'Those white men in that house have guns and are going to shoot.'

"The colored men raised a shout that the Democrats had seized their guns and made a rush for the other guns. The white men, who had secretly slipped into the house and seized the guns, then fired; and the first shot killed an old colored man about 70 years of age who was leaning on a stick. … The colored men returned with their guns very soon, attacked the party at the old house and then commenced a general fire on the Democrats, who were generally armed with pistols, but forced to retire rapidly toward the boat under a heavy fire. The colored men became furious when their arms were seized and their old man was dead.

"Sheriff Bowen, whom they recognized as their personal and political friend, rushed among them and tried to stop the firing, but they did not cease until all the white men were driven away from the church. ... As soon as the fight ceased the steamboat returned to the city for arms and reinforcements, and over 100 men went back on her on two hours' notice, with arms for themselves and their 100 men already there." Fearing a second attack after the gunfight, white women and children gathered at the residence of the Rev. E.C. Logan.

The News and Courier denounced Wallace's report for what it claimed was "suppression of truth and downright misstatements." However, Jim Alston, a Civil War veteran who had once been enslaved at Hampton Plantation, witnessed the shooting and agreed that whites fired first. Alston was standing next to John Lachicotte, the old black man killed at the start of the gunfight.

Speaking in thick Gullah tones, Alston gave this account in 1926: "The riot started this way. Solicitor Jervey was the first speaker, then as soon as he got through, then this colored man Mr. (Mc)Kinlay, as he got up, all he could say was, 'Fellow Citizens, hear what I got to say,' and right from then the drum keep beating. And the first news we know after the drum beating, four or five of these little boys from the city, white boys, one tall white gentleman was with them, and he made them take the guns from a little vestry house that (is) broke down now, and (they) form a line."

Alston said he and Lachicotte approached the boys who held the guns. Lachicotte announced to one of them, "Gimme mi gun." Alston explained further, "As he walk up, de boy hole de gun in his hand and de ole man walk up to him and de boy fire de gun off and hit him right in bress — whole charge. An I was rite there next to him when it happened. ... Dat started de shooting.

"Five got shot around de church an fall on de groan cripple so they couldn't move. The fuss (victim) I brought to de schoolhouse was a little boy — good size chile. I tink he mother don't know where he is. I bring he to the school house; died there."

After the shooting, Alston said he also rendered aid to the whites who had been shot. Alston said whites appreciated his help, but black people didn't see his reasoning for aiding the white victims. "De nigger all said dey would kill me – no more than for fun," Alston said.

The white victims were Thomas Whitaker, William E. Simmons, Alexander McNeil, William Daly, J. King and Walter Gradick. John Lachicotte was the only black man to die at the church. Blacks in Cainhoy were perceived to have won. The gunfight soon became legendary. To some, it was a matter of black resistance to white attacks; to others it was an example of unjustified black violence.

Within a week after the Cainhoy riot, there were tense moments in Mount Pleasant and on James Island. About 400 black militiamen marched through Mount Pleasant and threatened to kill white residents and burn the village. They shouted, "Remember Cainhoy!" Witnesses said some of the militia there had also been involved in the gunfight at Cainhoy. About 40 white residents and 50 black Democrats gathered their guns and huddled together in a house. They were prepared to defend themselves, but no violence ensued.

On James Island, about 150 armed local black militiamen and an equal number of armed Republicans held a political rally. This time, the Republicans refused to allow any black Democrats to speak. The stage was set for a bloody clash as at Cainhoy, but most of the Democrats left the scene. Nonetheless, the meeting broke up in a row with Republicans firing their weapons. Maria Knights, a black woman and wife of a Democrat, was shot in the jaw by Sergeant Green, a James Island militiaman. He was jailed.

Controversies continued beyond the election when both Democrats and Republicans claimed to have won the South Carolina governor's seat. Finally, the federal government decided that General Hampton had won.

Jim Alston, a witness
to the Cainhoy Riot.
Source: S.C. Historical
Society.

As a result, black legislators were thrown out of office and soon almost all
black elected officials lost their seats.

In the following years, a series of political injustices and violent attacks
against black people occurred in South Carolina. The new order eliminated
the political gains that black citizens had enjoyed during Reconstruction.
The cry of "Cainhoy," however, remained powerful.

In August 1888 white political candidate Benjamin "Pitchfork" Tillman
invoked the village's name during a speech in Charleston. Standing at the
railing around the steps of City Hall under rain-threatening skies, Tillman
berated white Charlestonians for not seeking revenge after the Cainhoy
gunfight. "You sent a score of men over to your Cainhoy over there, and let
them be shot down, and you never even killed a nigger for it," he screamed.

Tillman boasted that he had taken part in another 1876 riot, in the town of Hamburg. In that incident, influential white men in Edgefield County, including Tillman, decided to "seize the first opportunity that the Negroes might offer them to provoke a riot and teach the Negroes a lesson."

Tillman held up the Cainhoy riot as an example of what would never happen if he and his supporters held office. Eventually, Tillman was elected South Carolina governor and later a U.S. senator. His rise to power opened the way for enactment of the hated Jim Crow laws designed to intimidate and disenfranchise blacks.

For decades the riot remained a topic of discussion around the dinner tables of black families on the Cainhoy peninsula. In the early 1900s, Jake Howard who lived in the Huger area, told his children about the "Cainhoy war." He said whites had for too long taken advantage of black people. White people, he said, came to the political rally to kill black people, but the blacks stood their ground.

Fred Lincoln, Harold Lincoln's son, said his maternal grandmother, Sadie Vanderhorst, warned him the area around the Brick Church was haunted by a headless man who roamed the church grounds. Even as a teenager in the 1960s, Lincoln said, he was afraid to drive by the church at night.

When the Cainhoy Historic District was listed on the National Register of Historic Places in 1982, the gunfight of 1876 was cited as "unusual in the history of racial confrontations in South Carolina during Reconstruction because blacks were the victors."

The confrontation was most certainly on the minds of local people years later when the village came to the brink of another bloody racial dispute. This time, however, the confrontation was not over politics. This disagreement began when the black mother of two boys confronted a white storeowner after her sons said he had cheated them out of 15 cents.

On September 12, 1911, W.W. Jordan hired Jane Johnson's sons to haul some freight from the steamer landing to his place, a few miles from Cainhoy. After the boys hauled a "good-sized load" to Jordan's place, the boys asked to be paid. Jordan offered them a dime. He said he'd pay them the rest when they delivered the remainder of the freight. But the boys insisted they had agreed to haul one load for 25 cents. The boys said they would send their mother to see Jordan to get the rest of their money.

That night when Jane Johnson went to see Jordan, he pistol-whipped her. Even though Jordan thought he had killed her, he went to Magistrate P.R. Donnelly to take out a warrant for her arrest. Unbeknownst to Jordan, Johnson also went to the magistrate and demanded that Jordan be arrested.

Black residents were told inaccurately that the magistrate had issued a warrant for Johnson's arrest. The false report spread quickly through the community. Within a short time a crowd of about 150 people gathered at the magistrate's office and declared they would not allow Johnson to be arrested.

The crowd also was out to get Jordan. Things grew so hot for him that he was forced to take his wife and child from Cainhoy to Conifer, a logging camp where he owned another store. Black Cainhoy residents warned that, if Jordan returned, they would lynch him. A week later, Berkeley County Sheriff R.G. Causey came to Cainhoy. He organized a large posse and arrested suspects that onlookers said led the demonstration to protest the warrant against Johnson. Witnesses estimated that the size of the posse varied from 40 to 80 men.

Even though the protesters were arrested, many people were quick to acknowledge that the hostility in Cainhoy did not represent normal racial relations in the village. Before the Jordan-Johnson case erupted, white residents had circulated a petition calling for Magistrate Donnelly to be replaced. Those who wanted him removed believed he was wrong when he refused to issue a warrant for Jordan's arrest.

The News and Courier reported on September 28, 1911, that "the Negroes did not, or do not, harbor any unfriendly feelings toward the white people of Cainhoy in general but only to those directly concerned in the case, and to Jordan in particular, who, they say, started all of the trouble."

An older black man — who was described in the newspaper as a person "of the antebellum type" — said the black people were merely asking what would have happened if the races had been reversed; that is, if Jordan

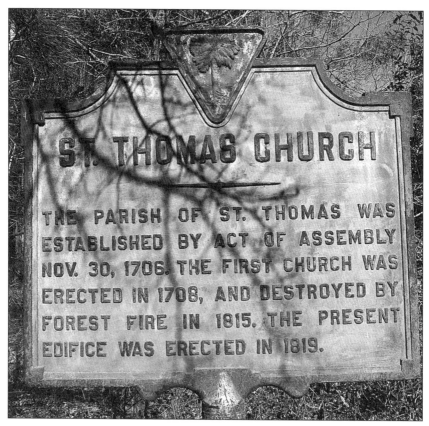

Historical marker at the St. Thomas Church on Cainhoy Road, just west of Cainhoy. The marker does not mention the Cainhoy Riot. Photo by Herb Frazier.

had been black and Johnson were white. He answered his own question: "Dey would a chopped him to leetle pieces." The old man said white men would have lynched Jordan if he had beaten a white woman the way he beat Johnson.

The ringleaders were arrested and jailed in Moncks Corner. James Gray, Mack McGinnis, Fred Lawrence, Sam Brown, Kit Mitchell, Mace Bennett and Marsha Caison were charged with rioting. Lawrence and Brown were acquitted. The others were convicted and each fined $50. It is unclear whether Jordan was arrested and charged for beating Johnson.

Following the arrests of the rioters, white residents breathed a collective sigh of relief. While there had been several disturbances among the black people in Cainhoy since the 1876 gunfight at the church, whites in the village said that, in practically every case, an outsider had caused the trouble.

* * *

Jim Alston, who stood next to the only black casualty during the Cainhoy riot, later applied for a pension that was due to him because he served in the Confederate Army during the Civil War.

The majority of the South Carolina agricultural workforce in 1860 was black, many of whom were pressed into service in support of Confederate troops. Calls went out to plantation owners to provide enslaved workers for construction crews, camp aides and cooks. Some planters procrastinated or ignored the requests. Before the war began, Alston was enslaved at Hampton Plantation on Wambaw Creek near McClellanville. Years later Alston moved to St. Thomas Parish.

In an interview in 1926, Alston said he had "bin tru de war." From 1861 until the end of the fighting, he served as a camp attendant under Confederate Colonel Henry Middleton Rutledge of the 25th North Carolina Regiment. Rutledge owned Hampton Plantation. Whether Alston served voluntarily is not known, but it is likely he and thousands of other enslaved black men were "impressed" into working for the Rebels.

In February 1928, five years after applying for a war pension from the South Carolina government and identifying himself as a resident of Cain Hoy, Alston began to receive his money. His application was endorsed by Thomas P. Rutledge, son of Col. Rutledge, Alston's commanding officer. The pensions could not exceed $25 annually.

Jim Alston is listed in the 1920 Census as being 77 years old and his wife, Jane, 69. Other members of Alston's household were Christopher Alston, 34; Richard Norton, 12; and Arnal Robinson, 9.

Guardian of St. Thomas Church

While attention today is focused on the housing and business development that has brought rapid changes on the Cainhoy peninsula, Tammy Wilson Giannelli is on a solo campaign to protect a small piece of the area's history. She is the caretaker at St. Thomas Church, site of the 1876 Cainhoy gunfight.

The Episcopal Diocese of South Carolina owns the sanctuary that once received support from a trust established by Harry F. Guggenheim. Peter Lawson-Johnston II, Guggenheim's cousin and the managing member of Cain Hoy Land and Timber Co., said that after Guggenheim died, the assets of the trust in 1999 were transferred to the Episcopal Diocese. The title to the St. Thomas Church land and cemetery is held by the Episcopal Diocese.

Giannelli said she is in regular contact with the diocese asking for repairs to the sanctuary, which is no longer used for regular services. She keeps an eye on the church to prevent vandalism and to note wear and tear on the building. She's also the church's unofficial tour guide for anyone who stops by.

The church has been a part of Giannelli's life since she was a child living on Cain Hoy Plantation. Jake Wilson, her father, looked after the church grounds as the assistant caretaker of the Guggenheim property. "My dad worked there for 41 years," she said. "He started out working cattle on Daniel Island where he was like a cowboy."

When the church's caretaker, John Murray, died her father took over. Giannelli herself became the caretaker after another caretaker John Slayton and his wife moved to Michigan.

When she was a student at Wando High School, the "high-class kids" called her a country bumpkin because of her passion for horses, fishing and raccoon hunting. After graduation in 1988, she lived briefly in Miami and Summerville before returning to Cainhoy. "There was a time when I knew every single person in Cainhoy. But today that has changed because of development. Daniel Island will never be the same."

A view of the cemetery at the St. Thomas Church through a semi-circular window in the sanctuary. Photo by Tammy Wilson Giannelli.

The Cainhoy-Wando area is too crowded; Cainhoy Road too busy, she said. Tammy and her husband, Michael, own 28 acres on three tracts near Huger. She said they would like to pack up their three children and move away from the advancing development.

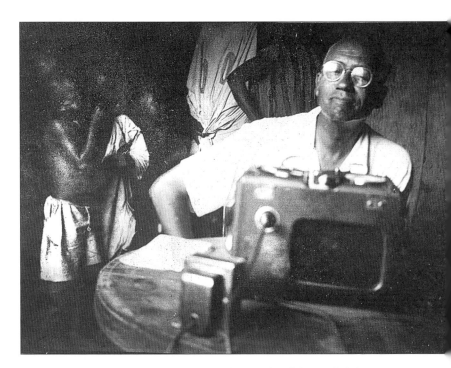

Lorenzo Dow Turner was a pioneer in the study of the Gullah language. Turner is pictured here taping informants in Africa. Turner set up his recording machine wherever he could. Coutesy of The Anacostia Community Museum, Smithsonian Institution.

Chapter 4: Turn of the Century

The number of people who experienced slavery, the Civil War and its aftermath dwindled through the early part of the 20th century. Through this closing window on the past streamed poignant and sometimes romanticized memories.

One recollection comes from the daughter of a former slave owner who owned Limerick Plantation at the headwaters of the East Branch of the Cooper River. Another is told by a woman with many talents who was enslaved on a plantation along the Cooper River. Two men from Cordesville also shared their memories with a Fisk University professor, who later became known as the father of Gullah studies.

Limerick Plantation

Lydia Child Ball was born in 1873 at Limerick. Four generations of her family, beginning with Elias Ball Sr., owned the plantation from the mid-18th century until the late-19th century. The E.P. Burton Lumber Co. acquired a portion of the land in the early 20th century. Former South Carolina Governor James B. Edwards is its current owner.

According to Ball's description of antebellum Limerick that was published in The News and Courier on August 8, 1929, black workers were considered to be family dependents. They were included in family prayers and given religious instruction. The Balls also provided care to the sick and aged.

Domestic servants were given titles. Women were called "Maum," followed by their first name. Men were called "Daddy," followed by their first name. Maum and Daddy were courtesy titles to personalize the slave-owner relationship without being overly respectful of the person in servitude.

"Maum Hetty" was among many of the trusted servants at Limerick. During the Civil War she confronted a Union solider who tried to steal a shoulder of meat from her. "Gimme my meat; how you say you come yah for mek me free, and you try for tek me meat from me."

Other servants were Daddy Handy, formerly the coachman and later gardener and cook; Daddy Edward; Maum Eve; Maum Betty and Maum Flora. But Robert Nelson, or "Robty," was most beloved.

Nelson was the butler who also served as nurse, caretaker and all-around handy man. He made traps and cedar boat paddles, and he dazzled the children with stories of Br'er Rabbit and Br'er Wolf. He was never too tired to hunt 'possum and 'coon with his owner's boys. His soothing presence made their world seem better. At mealtime, he stood as though carved from ebony with his aristocratic head cocked high, a veritable "black prince" with eyes that never missed a need.

According to Lydia Child Ball, a ghost haunted the main house at Limerick, leaving footprints on the wall, ceiling and stairway. The prints appeared as though the foot had stepped in cream-colored paint. Black people on the plantation called the ghost the "Weegee (Huger) Sperrit" or "Weegee ghost."

Another "sperrit" haunted the road between Limerick and Kensington Plantation. It was called the Kensington Path. This ghost sometimes appeared as a pig, sometimes as a calf. One night a "faithful servant" from Limerick claims to have heard it but didn't see it. She heard a loud crashing noise, like something was breaking down a fence along the road. When she saw the fence still intact, she yelled and ran and didn't stop until she got back to "Limbrick."

After the Revolutionary War, the widow of Gen. Francis Marion was said to have spent time at Limerick during the winter. She was a timid soul who requested that Maum Marsha sleep in her bedroom "to keep off the ghosts."

The Gullah Language

Dr. Lorenzo Dow Turner, the late chairman of the English Department at Fisk University in Nashville, Tennessee, collected the memories of Gullah people who lived during slavery times. Turner wasn't attempting to document the oral histories of former slaves during visits to coastal South Carolina in 1932, 1933 and subsequent summers. Instead, he took a voice-recorder with him to the Sea Islands of South Carolina and Georgia and captured the speech of Gullah people.

Turner understood that Gullah people spoke a "creolized" language. Their speech in the 1930s was influenced by the approximately 30 related African languages of their ancestors and had mingled with English during the centuries of enslavement. Their speech remained intact in the relative isolation of Gullah communities.

Turner asked his Gullah informants questions about themselves and their communities. He also studied West African languages and was able to catalogue thousands of African words in Gullah speech.

Among them are: *guba* (peanut), now called "goober;" *gumbo* (okra), that now refers to a stew containing okra; and *bohboh* (boy), used now as "bubba." He also showed that Gullah is a language with its own rules. In 1949 he published his findings in the book "Africanisms in the Gullah Dialect." It was the first and remains the only full-length study of the Gullah language.

Lorenzo Dow Turner was a pioneer in the study of the Gullah language. Coutesy of The Anacostia Community Museum, Smithsonian Institution.

Turner was so accepted by Gullah people that they shared with him closely held secrets about their identities. He found that most Gullah people had two names, a public name like "Bill Jones" or "Sally White" for the outside world and a "basket name" of African origin for use within the community. Turner cataloged hundreds of African names used as basket names among Gullah people, including, Isatu, Fatu, Sanie, Salifu, Sesay, Kanu and Kabbah.

Most older residents of the Cainhoy peninsula today aren't familiar with the term "basket names," but they do use nicknames such as Boogie, Doc, Banks, Bootsie, Comesee, String, Stinky, Twocent, Dribble, Jooham and Boochie.

Florence Jessie Dickerson of Huger recalls that one man in the community got an unusual nickname after his family thought he was dead. Before undertakers came to the Cainhoy peninsula, bodies weren't embalmed. As a result, at least one man in Huger came close to being buried alive. As the casket was about to be lowered into the grave, he banged on the casket from the inside and the burial was stopped. The lid was removed, and the man sat up. For the rest of his long life, Dickerson said, the man was known as Cheat Death.

Turner focused his research on the barrier islands of South Carolina and Georgia. He traveled to them by boat before bridges connected many of the islands to the mainland after World War II. On other occasions, his informants met him on the mainland.

Twice in 1932, Turner went inland to Cordesville, near Huger, where he interviewed Frank Roper and Hope Lloyd. The recordings of Turner's interviews include the haunting voices of each man. It is difficult to understand all of what they said because of their dialects.

Moncks Corner resident Richard Roper was 16 when Frank Roper, his grandfather, met Turner. Bertha Roper Davis, a retired Riverside, California, teacher who returned to her native Moncks Corner in 1997, never met Roper, her paternal great-grandfather, or Hope Lloyd, her maternal great-granduncle. Along with Richard Roper's wife, Cleola Reid Roper, they sat in a meeting room at the Berkeley County Library in Moncks Corner in 2009 and listened to Turner's recorded interviews with Lloyd and Roper.

" 'Cordesville, South Carolina. Life as a slave.' Oh, my word," Davis said as she read from a list of Turner's recordings in South Carolina and Georgia. The originals are in the Indiana University Archives of Traditional Music in Bloomington, Indiana. "I think Hope Lloyd was older than my great-grandfather. That's probably why he can remember slavery," she said.

Cordesville resident Frank Roper was interviewed by linguist Lorenzo Dow Turner in May 1932. Photo courtesy of Bertha Roper Davis.

"Great to see his (Hope Lloyd's) name in print," Richard Roper said. "I remember him because he had a beard. He was the only man in the Cordesville area who wore a beard. It was white."

Davis invited her uncle and aunt to listen to the recordings with her. They sat erect and attentive as Lloyd described his experiences as an enslaved man. Because of his thick Gullah accent, each of the listeners strained to recognize words and phrases.

"I'll tell you what I used to know in the olden time. I had a boss who was very good news in a sense, and he was bad in a sense," Lloyd explained.

He also mentioned the feared patrol groups of whites who regularly rode the trails between plantations looking for runaway slaves and checking the identities of others who traveled from one to the next.

Lloyd said he often walked the roads without the fear of being detained. "Many of the servants were saved by that boss man of mine. But, Lord, after he dead and gone, I catch the dickens."

Lloyd said he once was stopped, tied up and lifted off the ground with a rope. "I thought I was going to die. That same party dat done dat I had to get 'em bread. I am glad to find out that somebody take an interest in what we came through in dem days. I remember when we had to go into the woods at night to have (church) class meetings. I could go in the woods at night and make fire."

Lloyd also described the method of getting a pair of shoes that fit properly. "If you want to buy a pair of shoes, I mean if you are going to get a pair of shoes, you got to measure your foot with a stick, you know," he said with a soft chuckle. "You take dat stick and that your shoe."

Lloyd mentioned the war's end and the uncertainty among whites that Union officers would prosecute former slaveholders for the way they treated their slaves. "When peace was declared, master come to the house and beg us not to put him in trouble even though he was very good master."

Frank Roper is buried at Emanuel AME Church in Cordesville. Photo by Herb Frazier.

During Christmas enslaved workers traditionally got a day off. "Oh Lord, come Christmas time if you dance, you get two days. If you don't dance, you get but one," Lloyd said.

Lloyd did not mention the name of the plantation where he lived and worked. It probably was one of the following: Winter Grove, Brick House, Pawley, Glebe, Rice Hope or Mepkin plantations near Cordesville. Lloyd is buried in the Cordesville United Methodist Church cemetery on Dr. Evans Road, previously called River Road. The church was known as St. Luke Methodist Church originally. No one knows exactly when he passed away.

Frank Roper's interview is easier to understand.

"I'm no great talker. Why? 'Cause what little I do know of God, I take from the Bible. And that is all I depend on." He said his parents would not let him leave his house without first kneeling and praying. "Anybody who knew my father never heard him use a bad word or cuss. I trained that way. What little I know about Christ, I take the Bible, take the Bible for my guide."

Then Roper, in his rich Gullah accent, prayed: "Oh Heavenly Father, I am asking you once more. I'm asking you for forgiveness. Oh Lord, hear me. This is my true word what I am supposed to say.

"Lord, have mercy. … Oh Lord, thy are so merciful to be with me … and today I have a glorious opportunity to say blessed thanks be to God.

"I am not confined in the bed, wrapped up. I can say thanks be to God I am able to walk, and I am able to talk.

"Through the mercy of Christ, Jesus blessed me to see this day and, oh God, I ask you most merciful God to keep me in the middle of the road. Don't let me go astray. Don't let Satan have the dominion over me."

He asked God to help him remember that he has a throne waiting for him in heaven after he dies and for the Lord to have mercy on him.

"Lord you know thou have been good to me, and I say thanks be to God. I am asking thee night after night, day after day, to don't let me go astray until I can get home to Jesus.

"Oh Father, you know my desire. You know what I want. I am asking you, Master, to don't let me be no stumbling block; no difficulty in nobody way. That is my desire, Master."

Frank Roper was 85 when he died April 4, 1936, a year after his grandson Richard Roper joined the Army and left home. Richard Roper was stationed at Fort Benning, Georgia. He could not return to Cordesville for his grandfather's funeral and burial at Emanuel AME Church, where he serves as a trustee today. He's also a retired Army sergeant.

The epitaph on Frank Roper's headstone reads: "Though thou art gone, fond memory clings to thee." He never told his grandson that Turner had interviewed him four years prior to his death.

"People back in that time didn't tell us much about sex, who is this child or that child or what not," Richard Roper said. "They use to say, you teach a boy, he becomes too mannish. He has been gone since 72 years ago. He was a positive man and independent. He owned land and often said, 'If you make a dollar, try to save part of it.' "

As Roper listened to his grandfather's voice, he flinched each time his ancestor said "Jesus." "If I hear Jesus called, it runs through me," Richard Roper said. "I pray sometimes, and I jump. I don't know why. The spirit. Even on the television, I hear 'Jesus' and I jump."

Cleola Roper said her husband's voice sounds more like his grandfather's than his father's — Richard Roper Sr. His father and mother, Eva Gillins Roper, had four children: Dan Porcher Roper, Julia Roper Chisolm, Tony Roper and Richard Roper, the youngest.

By today's standard of travel, Cordesville is not that far from Huger. But it was a long way to go when Richard Roper was a boy on the farm. "We had only a few modes of transportation; mule, horse or by foot. Going to Huger was out of the way. I was born and raised in that community, and I stayed in that community until I went into the service."

No one knows why Turner chose to conduct interviews at Cordesville, which is not a Sea Island community. The best possible explanation could be that Dr. Walter Evans, Berkeley County's first black physician, suggested it. When Turner was concluding his master's degree studies at Harvard University in 1917, he may have met Evans, who was studying medicine at Boston University. Evans may have told Turner about the Gullah people in Cordesville and arranged for him to interview Lloyd and Roper.

Dr. Margaret Wade-Lewis, a linguist at the State University of New York at New Paltz, is the author of Turner's biography, "Lorenzo Dow Turner: Father of Gullah Studies." In an interview before she died in December 2009, Dr. Wade-Lewis suggested that Turner went to Cordesville to compare inland and coastal Gullah speech.

Frank Roper left his family with more than the memories captured by Turner's voice-recording machine. He showed them how to feed themselves, a skill that was useful during the Depression. When the commercial production of rice ended in the early 20th century, black families did not suddenly lose their rice-growing skills or their taste for it. Richard Roper was reared in the Buckhall section of Cordesville, ten miles northwest of Huger. He remembers how his family grew rice when he was 12 years old in 1928. The rice-growing knowledge was passed down from Roper's grandfather Frank

Roper. He instructed his children and grandchildren, who provided the muscle to plant, harvest and clean the rice.

The Ropers farmed 22 acres on River Road, which is now called Dr. Evans Road. When it was time to plant, rice seeds from the previous harvests were retrieved from the barn where they had been stored during the winter. An ox-drawn plow cut trenches in a low-lying half-acre too moist for other crops. Rice seeds were sprinkled along the trenches and covered. The plants emerged about a week later.

During warm weather, rice plants grew a foot and a half in

Mortar and pestle on display in the Berkeley County Museum in Moncks Corner. Photo by Herb Frazier

about three months. They were cut while still green with a reap hook — a hand tool with a sharp, curved blade and long handle. The stalks were bundled and laid out in the sun on the high ground for two weeks. When they turned brown, the Ropers placed them in a sheet of crocus sacks that were sewn together and then beat the grain on the ground. They scooped up rice, which was still in the husks and poured it into a wooden mortar. Richard's job was to pound the rice in the mortar with the pestle to remove the husk.

Roper's family didn't make the heavy mortar and long pestle that were set up in a shed next to the barn. A local craftsman carved out the trunk of a pine tree to make the mortar and fashioned a tree branch into the pestle. To make the mortar's tapered bowl, the craftsman began with an auger to bore a hole in the center of the trunk, which was 12 to 18 inches in diam-

A fanner basket on display in the Berkeley County Museum in Moncks Corner. Photo by Herb Frazier.

eter. He poured kerosene in the hole and set it on fire. Repeated burnings enlarged the hole, Roper explained. Wet clay smeared inside the hole guided the burning wood to form a deep bowl, narrow at the bottom and wide at the top.

A straight section of a branch, at least five feet in length, was selected for the pestle. With a drawknife, the craftsman shaved the limb's midsection to a circumference small enough to grasp. One end was made blunt to pound the husk; the other was pointed to polish the rice.

After Roper beat the grain, the rice and loosened husks were placed in flat fanner baskets and gently tossed in the air on a windy day. The breeze blew the husks away and the heavy rice remained. "That was our way of life at that time."[5]

The Ropers grew and processed about 100 pounds of rice this way until Richard Roper joined the Army. They, like many other black families in those days, ate rice only on Sundays. "Rice was special at that time," Roper said. "We ate more grits than we did rice."

---

5 The mortar and pestle is an African invention. Fanner baskets were made from bulrush, a long, course grass-like plant that grows in the marsh. The fanner basket was an antecedent to the popular sweetgrass baskets made today by Lowcountry African Americans. As the commercial production of rice declined so did the need for bulrush fanner baskets, according to College of Charleston historian Dale Rosengarten.

Richard Roper is flanked by his wife, Cleola Reid Roper (right) and his niece, Bertha Roper Davis in the parking of Emanuel AME Church in Cordesville. Photo by Herb Frazier.

Tena White

In 1936 during the Depression and three years after Dr. Turner conducted his ground-breaking Gullah research, the Works Progress Administration launched the two-year Federal Writer's Project to put unemployed people to work documenting American life and history. One of those efforts turned into a collection of oral histories of Africans who had been enslaved on Southern plantations. Thanks to the Federal Writer's Project, writers and journalists interviewed more than 2,300 people who knew the old stories.

None of the WPA oral histories for the Charleston area include people from the Cainhoy peninsula. However, Tena White told Charleston writer Martha E. Pinckney she was enslaved on the Venning Plantation at Remley's Point in Christ Church Parish, adjacent to St. Thomas Parish. Her experiences surely were similar to those of enslaved people in St. Thomas.

By the time Pinckney had interviewed White in the mid-1930s, White's memory of life as an enslaved person had faded to the point that she couldn't remember "ma pa's name," but she had retained vivid recollections of "when de war come through." White was about 90 years old when Pinckney came calling at her home in Mount Pleasant. As Pinckney walked up the stairs to the porch, a friendly cur (dog) wagged itself toward her but White shooed it away. On the piazza, a baby lay asleep on a folded cloth with a pillow under its head. Pinckney quickly established a rapport with White. She reminded White of her owner at Remley's Point.

"As soon as my eye set on you, I see you favor the people I know," White said. "My people belong to Mr. William Venning." His plantation was in Christ Church Parish at Remley's Point just down the Cooper River from Daniel Island. It is possible that William Venning, who owned Tena White, was related to or could have been the William L. Venning who sold the land that became the Jack Primus community on the Cainhoy peninsula.

White reflected on the Civil War, first recalling the drumming as federal troops marched through. "Oh de drum; I nebber hear such a drum in my life. De people like music; dey didn't care nothing bout de Yankees, but dem bands of music. My mother name Molly Williams. My pa dead long before that.

"When de Yankee come through, we been at Remley Point. My Ma took care ob me. She shut me up and she grab me. De Yankee been go in de colored people house, an dey mix all up, and dey do jus what dey want. Dey been brutish.

"All de beautiful ting smash up, an all de meat an ham in de smoke house e stribute um all out to de people, an de dairy broke up, an de horse and de cow kill. Nothin' leave. Scatter ebberyting. Nothin' leave."

White said she was known as "Tena White, the washer; Tena, the cook; Maum Tena; or Da Tena, the nurse." She was accomplished in each task but best as a nurse.

White gave thanks to God for a long life. "I know I got for die some day ... but when I look an see my flesh, I tenk de Lord for ebbery year what pass on my head. Taint my goodness, tis His goodness. Nothing but the pureness of heart will see Him."

Sue Coaxum was a domestic worker at Middleburg Plantation after the Civil War. Painting by John W. Jones.

Chapter 5: Domestic Workforce

The profession of domestic worker is a legacy of enslavement that ties numerous white families with black women who cook for them, raise their children and do house work. Black women stroll along Charleston's blue stone sidewalks with white children in tow. Black men often work as chauffeurs and handy men.

Domestic jobs were plentiful in the early 1900s and people from rural areas were eager to fill them. John Sanders and Margaret Wilder were among hundreds who left the Cainhoy-Wando-Huger area to join Charleston's domestic workforce. Ernestine Singleton Taylor, however, continued to live in Huger but commuted to the Isle of Palms, Sullivan's Island and Mount Pleasant to work.

John Sanders

John Sanders was born in 1897 at Cainhoy. His parents, Sergeant and Miley Horlbeck, were farmers. At 20 years old, Sanders joined the U.S. Army during World War I. Assigned to a transportation unit, he was one of about 27,000 black men from South Carolina who served during the war. Sanders enlisted on November 4, 1918, at Newport News, Virginia. He reached the rank of sergeant. On March 20, 1919, he was honorably discharged three months before the war ended. The roster of black servicemen from South Carolina does not indicate whether he saw combat.

After the war, Sanders went to work for Langdon Cheves (1848-1939), a Charleston attorney and a descendant of wealthy Lowcountry planters. Cheves lived in a mansion in downtown Charleston. Sanders, who also lived on the property, was Cheves' chauffeur and handyman. Cheves had a vacation home in Flat Rock, North Carolina, a mountain retreat where many Charlestonians spent their summers. Sanders would go up to Flat Rock alone to prepare the house for Cheves' wife, Sophie. He stayed with her until Cheves joined them later in the season. On one occasion in the spring of 1920, Sophie Cheves sent letters to her husband to tell him how well Sanders had cared for her and the house.

On the morning of May 19, 1929, Charleston physician Edward Rutledge was called to Cheves' house at 61 South Battery to examine John Sanders, who had a tetanus infection. The doctor asked Sanders if he had cut his hand. Sanders said he had stepped on a nail that pierced his shoe and left foot. Within a week, Sanders was gravely ill. The doctor admitted him to Roper Hospital in Charleston. Before 8 p.m. the next night, Sanders rose up in the bed, cried out, fell back and died. He was only 32 years old. Two days later, Cheves sent a letter to Sanders' wife Evelyn Sanders, who lived in New York City.

"Evelyn," he wrote, "I have sad news to send. John died on last Monday evening 20th May. Dr. Rutledge came at once as he was taken to the hospital. Serum injections made and every care taken of him. But it was too late!"

Cheves received letters of condolence from his friends who praised Sanders for his exceptional service to his employer as well as his integrity. Henry Comer of Charleston wrote: "I sympathize with you so entirely in the loss of John. Not only (was he a) satisfactory chauffeur but so satisfactory all round – a nice character. You find about one like that in a lifetime. John was always so polite and nice to me. I will miss him myself. His smile as I passed him on the street or in the car. You liked him and he liked you, and it's pretty hard to have him go."

Another letter came from O.M. Drake of Hendersonville, North Carolina, not far from Flat Rock: "I was very sorry to hear of the death of John, your faithful servant. We all liked and respected John for the many better qualities found in him. I know you will miss him very much."

Later that year, Sanders' widow began inquiring about death benefits or an "adjusted service certificate" for his military service.

In August 1929, she wrote to Cheves: "Mr. Cheves, this is my second letter I have written to you. ... You must please tell me some thing about John's war money. If not I will seek it up hear (sic)." Cheves wrote back saying he had contacted the Veterans Administration, but because Sanders died without a will, the matter had to be settled by the probate judge before she could get the death benefits, which amounted to $425. It is not clear whether she got the money from the VA or got a share of Sanders' estate, valued at $500.

Edwin G. Harleston at Harleston Funeral Home handled Sanders' arrangements. The mortician's bill, presumably including the casket and other burial expenses, came to $105. Four days after Sanders died, his body was taken by boat to Cainhoy where he was buried. A marble slab that cost $235 was placed over his grave. Because Cainhoy was so remote, it was customary for an undertaker to spend the night there and return to Charleston on the next day's ferry. Cheves paid the expenses for Sanders' funeral and marker as an expression of his appreciation for his friend's longtime service.

Margaret Green Wilder

Margaret Green Wilder left her family in Huger and worked for the next 40 years in Charleston for Virginia and Wade Hampton Logan, a prominent Charleston couple who lived on Church Street. The Logans had three children, Julia, Wade Hampton III and Harry.

"I have no memory of life without Margaret, just like I have no memory of life without my parents or without my brothers. I thought of her as family," Julia Logan said. Wilder raised Julia and her brothers as if they were her own children. When she tucked Julia in at night, she told thinly veiled morality tales and sang "Kum Ba Yah" and "Climbing Jacob's Ladder" to her. Julia was 6 years old when she realized that Margaret was not a blood relative.

Wilder was perhaps closest to Julia, whom she called Jule. As Julia grew in the 1960s into a rebellious flower child, her views on life occasionally crossed with her parents' conservative outlook on the social order of Charleston society. Julia wondered why she seemed more like Wilder and less like her mother. Then she realized she had two mothers.

"Margaret wasn't black or white. She was Margaret. Her love was non-judgmental and respectful, but demanding of respect back," Julia explained. While her parents criticized her at times for not living up to their expectations, Julia got a different message from Wilder. "She rarely said, 'I am disappointed in you.' She would say, 'You know better because I have taught you better.'"

As Julia approached her teen years, her mother placed on her bed a pamphlet titled "All About You," a sex education primer. In a trembling voice, she told her to check back with her if she had questions. But Julia went to Wilder instead. "She talked to me about how to protect myself," Julia remembered. "She talked about the emotional relationship between men and women. I never had that kind of discussion with my mother."

Wilder was Julia's refuge. "When somebody teased me and I needed comfort, Margaret was there," she said. "She represented comfort, unconditional love. I knew my mother loved me, but it wasn't this all-encompassing, take-care-of-me love. That was Margaret's love."

Ernestine Singleton Taylor

If Ernestine Singleton Taylor wasn't working in the dry-cleaning business or picking cotton, peas and beans on farms in the Huger area, she was cooking and cleaning for white families who lived east of the Cooper River. Being a domestic servant was humiliating, according to her daughter Dorothy Scott, who later became a civil rights advocate and president of the Charleston Branch of the National Association for the Advancement of Colored People.

"The domestic worker/white family relationship was one of ownership," she said. "Even though they told my mother 'we love you,' it didn't matter what was going on with her own children or family. She had to get there to take care of their children first."

This sort of attitude was hard on many black women who did domestic work, she said. Many were told they could not enter a white family's house through the front door or that they were not allowed to ride in the front seat of a white person's car. Yet they were entrusted with the responsibility to care for their white employers' children.

Such demoralization was designed to keep domestic workers in their place, she said. "For the most part they were treated with little or no respect and spoken to as children rather than adults," Scott said. "I didn't see anything positive that Mom brought to us (from her domestic job) that made us feel empowered. However, what Mom did instill in us was the importance of a good education and the rewards of hard work and perseverance."

Scott remembers the afternoon the sheriff and her mother's white employer stormed into their house on Cainhoy Road. The white woman accused Scott's mother of stealing from her. "While it was quickly determined that there had been no theft as alleged by what appeared to be a very intoxicated white woman and a very disrespectful law enforcement officer, the humiliation and lack of fairness leveled at my mother and our family served as a reminder that black people had no rights that white people had to respect," Scott said. "It made me determined that I didn't want to be in a position that I couldn't speak out against what I believe is wrong."

After Scott graduated from Cainhoy High School, she went to work as a short-order cook in a North Charleston restaurant. When she was told she was expected to do janitorial work, she refused, saying it wasn't part of the original agreement. She later had conflicts with the white manager at the Army/Navy Surplus Store on King Street. Although he was cordial to Dorothy, he was less than respectful to her sister, Evelyn, who also worked at the store. Dorothy let him know that she wouldn't tolerate him verbally abusing her sister. When she worked as a cashier at the all-black Lincoln Theater on upper King Street, she clashed with the white manager because of the lack of cleanliness of the place.

She applied for a clerical job with the local telephone company. She was told that blacks could only work as switchboard operators and janitors and that graduates from city schools were preferred over those from rural schools. When she married, she moved to New York City where her husband worked for the Postal Service and she first got a job as a credit investigator at Macy's Department Store, then landed a clerical position with the New York Telephone Company. She returned to Charleston in 1971 and applied again for a clerical job with the local phone company but was offered a job as an operator. Eventually, she was hired in a clerical position. "That's when I began to cut my teeth on true civil-rights advocacy," she said.

She was elected to the NAACP presidency in 2001. "Every time I stand up for what I feel is a just cause, I think about my mom. She paid a high price for her children to be treated fairly. How dare she not get the return on her investment!"

Jack Primus resident
Joseph Broughton
(above) was convicted
in 1939 of killing Yel-
low House storekeeper
James Elias DuTart.
Photo courtesy of the
S.C. Department of
Corrections.

James Elias DuTart
served in the U.S.
Navy during World
War I. Photo courtesy
of Mary Ann DuTart
Silver.

Chapter Six: Family Tragedies

A few weeks after Mary Ann DuTart was born at Cainhoy on July 13, 1938, her family moved to Bennett Street in Mount Pleasant. When America entered World War II, her father, Philip Pepper DuTart, went to work as a civilian employee at Fort Moultrie on Sullivan's Island. Her mother, Frances Johnson DuTart, stayed at home to care for Mary Ann, the eldest of six DuTart children. When Mary Ann began grammar school in the early 1940s her mother gave her a chilly warning one summer day after a boy walked past their house and waved hello.

"Don't talk to that boy," Frances DuTart said. "His grandfather killed your grandfather."

Though startled, Mary Ann never asked her mother for the details. It wasn't until years after her mother had died in 1963 and Mary Ann was married to Alton Silver that she read a newspaper story about a fatal shooting that happened three decades before she was born.

On August 11, 1908, The News and Courier reported: "L.A. DuTart Killed at Cainhoy. C.E. DuTart wounded and will probably die."

At the time of the DuTart family's first heartbreak, Mary Ann's grandfather Charles Edward DuTart was 49. Her granduncle Lawrence Archibald "Archie" DuTart was 20. The DuTarts operated the *Erna H. Lucas*, a launch that carried freight and passengers between Cainhoy and Charleston. Charles was also a farmer and lumberman and former Cainhoy magistrate. His son Archie and some of his other children worked on the boat.

DuTart's competitor was Julius B. Hyer, who ran another boat called

North Star. The men's relationship went beyond competition for business on the river. It was a personal feud. Their animosity toward one another reached a boiling point on August 10, 1908, when Charles and Archie were mortally wounded and Hyer was charged with murder.

On November 9, 1908, Hyer went on trial at Moncks Corner for killing the DuTarts, but after two days of testimony, he was acquitted. The jury believed Hyer shot the men in self-defense. Hyer later found "peace and seclusion" on Dewees Island north of Charleston after marrying Charlotte Deleisseline, whose family owned the small barrier island just north of the Isle of Palms.

In 2004 Mary Ann Silver first read the newspaper accounts of the shooting. "It made me sad for my father," she said. "He was 18 years old, and had to take care of the business, and my grandmother lost a son and husband on the same day. She was so young when this occurred."

It wouldn't be the last time the DuTart family suffered from such a tragedy. Silver remembers stories about James Elias DuTart, her father's brother and her godfather. He was murdered July 31, 1938.

"He was very outgoing, and he could dance his feet off," she said. James DuTart operated a store in the Yellow House community near Wando. Downstairs he sold clothing from one side of the building and food and dry goods in the other. He lived over the business with his wife, Inez Adams DuTart.

Around 2 a.m. on a Sunday, DuTart, 44, was awakened by a noise downstairs. He carried a flashlight and pistol as he descended the stairs. At the bottom of the steps DuTart yelled out: "Who's down there?"

He held out the flashlight and scanned the dark store when someone fired a shotgun at him. Birdshot struck him in the left hand, in which he held the light. Pellets also pierced his heart. "Lord have mercy," DuTart exclaimed as he struggled back upstairs to the bedroom where he fell on the floor and died. His wife got out of bed and stumbled over her husband's body.

Later that morning lawmen searched the homes of black people in Yellow House, Wando, Cainhoy and Jack Primus for a suspect. Everyone knew somebody was going to jail. The only question was who?

Jack Primus resident Gussie Bryant was arrested and held a few days before he was released. He was questioned because he had recently purchased shotgun shells. The next day police also arrested Joseph Broughton, who also lived in Jack Primus. Barefoot and frightened, Broughton was stopped as he walked along the King Street Extension in the Ten Mile community north of Charleston.

After repeated grilling by police, Broughton confessed to killing DuTart. In an 800-word statement, Broughton said that Saturday he walked about three miles from his mother's house to "Cap'n Tart's store." He arrived at the store around 9 p.m. He removed his shoes and sat in the bushes where he could see the store. He watched DuTart lock the building. But DuTart didn't close one shutter over a window. Hours later, Broughton said he tore the screen and entered the store. He had a pipe wrench and a single-barreled shotgun. He used the wrench to pry open the money drawer. The noise woke DuTart, and he came downstairs to investigate. From behind the counter, Broughton fired at DuTart's flashlight. "I sh-shot him, but I ain't m-mean to shoot him," Broughton told police as he stuttered from a speech impediment. He tried to shoot the flashlight from DuTart's hand.

Broughton told police he returned to his mother's house about 3 a.m. but he could not sleep. He went into the woods near the Cooper River and paced back and forth. He returned to his mother's house, ate and went to bed. Later that day, he returned to the river, where he met Ben Wigfall. Broughton asked Wigfall to row him across the river to the Oakdene cotton press. Once on the other side, he walked up the King Street Extension toward Moncks Corner.

Broughton's twin brother, Jacob, was arrested along with another man the day after DuTart was shot. Jacob told police he overheard Joseph talking to another man earlier in the week about plans to rob a store or steal a cow.

Indeed, before DuTart was killed, Joseph Broughton and Francis Odom stole an ox from Benjamin Venning, a black man who lived in Jack Primus and sold it for $20. They got an initial payment of $5. Police detained them briefly and forced them to refund the money and return the ox to its owner.

Jack Primus resident Harold Lincoln remembers the murder and Joseph Broughton, who was considered "slow" because he could not read or write and he stuttered. Lincoln and Broughton played together as children, but later in life Broughton became an outcast in Jack Primus. Fred Lincoln, Harold Lincoln's son, recalls that his father told him that older people in the community didn't trust Broughton because he occasionally molested seniors he encountered alone in the woods, and he stole lunches from workers in the forest.

On May 11, 1939, less than 10 months after the killing, Broughton sat at the defense table in the county courthouse in Moncks Corner where he was on trial for murder. The "death gun" was found in the marsh near Broughton's grandmother's home.

Clerk of Court P.E. Myers, the only defense witness, identified a letter from Dr. C.F. Williams of the State Hospital in Columbia in which Broughton was described as being "mentally deficient."

It took 13 minutes for an all-white jury to find Broughton guilty of murder. Judge William H. Grimball sentenced him to die in the electric chair the following month.

At 6 a.m. on Friday, June 23, 1939, Broughton was escorted from a cell at the state penitentiary in Columbia to the death room. Before guards strapped him in the electric chair, Broughton told witnesses: "I want to say that I am sorry that I killed that man, but I wanted to pay with my life for the life I took."

At 6:02 a.m. the current flowed into his body and three minutes later, he was declared dead. Prison records list Broughton's age as 40, although he was actually in his late-20s.

In a note to his mother Celia and his sister Bell, Broughton said: "Meet me in Heaven. I am ready to go. I am sorry I killed that man but I am ready to pay my debt. Jesus has saved my soul."

Thirty people witnessed the execution. They included Rembert C. Dennis, who was then a member of the State House of Representatives; and

Mary Ann Silver's father, Philip DuTart.

Broughton's body was returned in a pine coffin to the Jack Primus community and left on the steps of Greater St. John Church. His funeral was held inside the church the following Sunday and the burial was in nearby Venning Cemetery on Cain Hoy Plantation.

Questions then and now remain about the role Broughton played in the murder. Some people doubt that Broughton killed DuTart and question whether he was mentally fit to stand trial.

Ernest Christopher Avinger Sr. of Cainhoy had been picked for the jury, but he asked to be excused because he already had an opinion. Cainhoy resident Beverly Avinger Lahmeyer said, "My grandfather knew that (Broughton) was not guilty because he was retarded."

Effie Chaney of Wando was born after her uncle Joseph Broughton was electrocuted. When she was a teenager in the 1960s, her mother, Lavenia Broughton Porcher, said her uncle was innocent. "He didn't do what they said he did. A white killed that man," she said.

Two men who remember the murder and Broughton's execution also believe he was innocent. "Joseph didn't kill that man," said the Rev. Benjamin Dennis, an associate pastor of Intercession Reformed Episcopal Church on St. Thomas Island. DuTart was well liked among black people in the Yellow House community because he "would bend over backwards to help you. If you needed something and didn't have the money, you'd still get it."

DuTart's generosity toward black people didn't sit well with some whites, said Johnnie Rivers, who lived in the Pinefield community at the time. He and Dennis said DuTart was killed by a white man who often bragged about framing Broughton. After the white man shot DuTart, he gave Broughton the murder weapon to hide, Rivers and Dennis said. Broughton hid it in the marsh near his grandmother's house.

Eugenia Broughton stands in the doorway of a mobile clinic that she towed with a car from the early 1950s to the late 1960s to bring health-care services to residents on the Cainhoy peninsula. Source: National Library of Medicine.

Chapter 7: Birthing a Community

Geneva Alethia Broughton and her younger cousin Anita Eugenia "Genie" Broughton sat on the steps at 16 Dewey Street during the 1920s wondering about their future as black girls in Charleston. They knew the only way they'd avoid working in the "white man's kitchen" was to get good educations.

Geneva's father, Julius Broughton, was a brick mason who sent his daughter to Burke Industrial School. After graduation, Geneva married Thomas Dansby and began her career as a teacher after graduating from Allen University in Columbia. In 1928 she was hired at Buist Elementary School where she taught arts and crafts.[6]

Genie's father, the Rev. Ralph Sanders Broughton, an Episcopal minister, would've been disappointed if his only daughter didn't enter a profession befitting their status as an upper-class family. After elementary school at Burke, Genie was enrolled at Avery Normal Institute on Bull Street in Charleston.

In her final year at Avery, Genie displayed acting, singing and musical talents that her friends say she inherited from her mother, Jessie Williams Broughton. Genie enjoyed taking the stage to play the piano, sing and act. Her final school performance was a piano solo of "A Spirit Flower" during Avery's June 1933 graduation ceremony at Morris Street Baptist Church.

John Wilson courted Genie while she was at Avery. After graduation

---

6 Mrs. Dansby retired in 1971 after 42 years in the classroom. She celebrated her 102nd birthday August 20, 2010.

she expected that he would become her husband. But he married another girl. It broke Genie's heart. Genie Broughton remained single for the rest of her life.

Yet Genie fulfilled her lifelong dream of becoming a nurse and midwife. Along with Maude Callen, they pioneered in the training of lay midwives in Berkeley County. In South Carolina, nearly 5,000 lay midwives in the early 1900s delivered most of the babies in the state's rural communities, including those on the Cainhoy peninsula.

Genie earned a nursing diploma in February 1937 from Charity Hospital in Savannah and the following winter she became a special community nurse in Berkeley County. She went to work initially at a starting monthly salary of $25 for the first three months. The health-care service was supported by the Reformed Episcopal Church, based in Summerville. She was assigned to the Cainhoy peninsula. She lived with a local family and went home to Charleston on the weekends on the line boat that traveled between Cainhoy and Charleston.

During the week she walked the dusty roads of the Cainhoy peninsula until a church member in Philadelphia who owned a car dealership gave her a used Buick. Nurse Broughton traveled the county in the donated car to see her patients. When it was necessary she even drove them to see doctors in Charleston.

She also sang and preached to her patients, most of them expectant mothers, many single and immature. She tried to explain the facts of life to them in no uncertain terms.

With so little money to provide medical service for low-income people, Broughton turned to Harry Frank Guggenheim for help. In an April 19, 1939, letter, she told Guggenheim that Dr. William Kershaw Fishburne, director of the Berkeley County Health Department, treated patients at the weekly clinics, "but we don't have an adequately equipped place in which to do thorough examinations."

She asked Guggenheim for money to build a small examining room at the rear of Trinity Church, which probably was at the intersection of

Cainhoy and Clements Ferry roads. A 1950 highway map shows the location of a "colored" Episcopal Church at that location. The letter was the first of many that Guggenheim and Broughton would exchange over the next three decades.

Not all of Nurse Broughton's patients in the early 1940s were expectant mothers. One was Beverly Avinger (now Lahmeyer), a 7-year-old white girl who lived with her family in the old Beresford School House and Episcopal Church rectory at Cainhoy. She was very sick with sores that covered her body.

"She saved my life," Beverly said years later. Broughton came to the house and told Beverly's mother how to make the hot baths for her daughter. "Eugenia was a Godsend. There was something very special about her."

Johnnie Rivers, who was 10 years old at the time, also remembers Nurse Broughton, who usually wore a dark-blue uniform and white apron. Sometimes she'd stop by the Rivers' house at Pinefield at the end of her workday. "When she came to my mama house, she'd eat and lay cross the bed and relax until she was ready to jump in her car and go back to Charleston," he said.

His mother, Eva Rivers, would always prepare a package of fresh vegetables for her to take home. The vegetables included yellow squash, okra and Broughton's favorite, green peas. In exchange for the hospitality and food, she treated the Rivers children for minor medical problems and administered their vaccinations. "I still have the mark on my arm today," Johnnie Rivers said, pointing to his left shoulder.

By 1940 Broughton had traded in the Buick for a newer car, which she bought on credit. She later wrote to Guggenheim saying she needed money to cover her car payments.

"I am sorry that you're in a temporarily difficult situation," Guggenheim wrote in an April 1940 letter. "I take pleasure in enclosing my check for $32.26, which you request in order to make the payment that is coming due."

When her car needed new tires, she again asked Guggenheim for help.

"Nurses are able to get priority for tires so that is one consolation," she explained to him in a letter postmarked in February 1942 when war was raging and rubber was rationed. "The car is in fair condition now and with new tires it will last me for quite some time, I hope." She added a postscript: "I learned that the tires are $10 apiece."

The State Board of Health, through the Berkeley County Health Department, took over supervision of the rural medical program in 1947 from the Reformed Episcopal Church. Broughton then began two years of additional training at hospitals in Virginia, New York City and Washington, D.C. and became a registered nurse and midwife. She also taught midwifery classes at Penn Center on St. Helena Island near Beaufort, S.C.

In 1951 Broughton and Callen were among 49 registered midwives in Berkeley County.[7] They conducted one-day training courses at Cross, Jamestown, Moncks Corner, Pineville, Black Creek, Ridgeville and St. Stephen as well as at Broughton's clinic at Wando.

The clinic was six miles from Vernelle Dickerson's house on Cainhoy Road in Huger. In the 1950s Dickerson went there to receive her shots before school began. If she couldn't get a ride on cousin Britton Lockwood's flatbed truck or on the family's mule and wagon, she, her siblings and mother, Florence Dickerson, walked to the clinic. It was a slow journey on a sandy road.

Beatrice Smalls McGirth and her siblings also got their shots from Broughton. They walked 10 miles round trip from their home in Huger on what was called at that time Smith Road to Henry Lee Johnson's store, where Broughton had set up a temporary clinic to administer the vaccinations.

McGirth praises Broughton as a "Trojan" for the work she did to train nurse midwives, including her grandmother, Carrie Ladson. But McGirth also remembers the sting of the nurse's needle as well as her tongue. If she saw dirt on the cotton swab after she wiped a child's arm before giving a shot, Nurse Broughton would launch into a long and loud lecture. She

---

7 See Appendix I: Berkeley County licensed midwives in 1951.

didn't hesitate to publicly embarrass the mother of an unwashed child.

By the late summer of 1952, she began visiting Guggenheim's cattle ranch on Daniel Island to check on his employees and their living conditions. They included five black families on Daniel Island — the Browns, Washingtons, McNeils, Foys and Jenkinses.

"The homes were found to be remarkably clean and well kept," she wrote to Guggenheim. "Because of the availability of electricity, each home is equipped with a radio, which enhances the little pleasures they receive."

She suggested that electric refrigerators would greatly improve living conditions. "Those of us in the low-income group with the high cost of foodstuff cannot afford to 'waste' anything."

She noted that the Brown and Foy households were growing and each of their dwellings needed an additional bedroom to relieve cramped sleeping quarters. "If this could materialize in the very near future, it would be a blessing since both are expecting new babies in the early autumn."

The following month Guggenheim asked Nurse Broughton to continue urging the employees on Daniel Island to improve their living conditions. "If they could be encouraged in every way in cleanliness and hygiene and to plant both flower and vegetable gardens, it would be beneficial."

To bring routine medical services closer to people, the church bought a trailer in 1953 that was used as a mobile clinic for residents of Wando, Huger and Jamestown. During a service at Grace Reformed Episcopal Church in Moncks Corner to dedicate the trailer, the congregation asked God to "watch over thy servant Nurse Broughton and others who may use this unit and that their going out and their coming may always be in safety."

Broughton, with the help of the Berkeley County board of health, established regular stops and a schedule, providing a general medical clinic for residents of the rural communities. Expectant mothers, new mothers and children comprised most of the clients.

Broughton also continued the monthly visits to Daniel Island to inspect workers' living conditions. She praised Guggenheim for improvements in their lives. "It is due to your making their homes more livable and comfortable and the personal interest you have in the welfare of each tenant," she wrote in an April 29, 1954 letter. "Their egos have been boosted and they hold you in such esteem that they try to do everything that will please Mr. Guggenheim, or 'the boss,' as well as help themselves."

Guggenheim had set aside land for a baseball field for the children. "I do hope that the Negro youths will use it to all advantage," Broughton wrote. She expressed a hope for additional recreational facilities, especially for girls who've prematurely become mothers. "Of course, I realize that it all takes time and education."

In the 1920s Guggenheim had become fascinated with horse racing. Initially, he raced his horses under the colors of the Falaise Stables, named for his Long Island estate. But after acquiring the Cainhoy property, he changed the designation to Cain Hoy Stables. His horse, Dark Star, won the Kentucky Derby in 1953, defeating previously unbeaten Native Dancer. Broughton acknowledged the victory in a letter to him the following year.

"Although belated, I think that congratulations are still in order to you for having won the Derby," she wrote. "I was quite proud to say that I know you. I only wish I could have said the same about the horse."

In mid-January 1956 fire destroyed the home of Marie Fordham, principal of the Keith School in the Wando community. Broughton wrote to Guggenheim saying Fordham had "given 25 years of untiring service as a teacher and servant in the Cainhoy community. Her congenital deformity did not retard her activities whatsoever and she has done more to enhance the programs of the area. Two weeks ago, her home burned to the ground. All of her earthly possessions went up in flames. What took a lifetime to accumulate was whisked away in a matter of seconds … but despite this catastrophe, she said, 'God helped me to build this house, and He will help me again.' "

Guggenheim sent money to Fordham as requested. A new brick cottage was constructed for her on Cainhoy Road near Clements Ferry Road. The cottage still stands today.

In a February 7, 1956, letter to Guggenheim, Marie Fordham thanked him for his generosity. "I wish to express my appreciation for the kindness that you have showed me in the time of my distress. When I was told about the wonderful offer you had given me, my heart was overjoyed with gladness. The Lord will always open up a way, if you try to do the right thing. Today I was given the check, and words cannot express my feeling. The house is beautiful. I trust that God will ever keep you for the goodness that you have contributed to me and the community."

In the spring of that year, Broughton again wrote to Guggenheim saying she hoped that someday she could shake his hand and thank him in person for all he had done for the people of the Cainhoy area through the years.

"I've always been somewhat afraid to say other than a casual greeting to one in your category, but somehow I feel that you are different from the majority, and I don't think I am wrong," she wrote.

That summer Broughton again wrote to say she was two months behind on her car payment. "A most unfortunate predicament to be in, and although it greatly hurts my pride to ask assistance from you, I really have no other alternative since I have exhausted other resources."

She reminded Guggenheim that 15 years earlier he had helped her pay her car note, adding, "I am quite sure, however, that this will not happen again." Two weeks later, Broughton received a check for $75.

It appears that they did not exchange any more letters until March 1965.

"You may not remember me, but I am the nurse (at) Cainhoy," Broughton wrote. "Years ago you helped to attain a room behind Trinity Church for clinical purposes, and you gave me personal assistance just when I needed it most to make a car payment. Today, I am again faced with this emergency and there is nowhere to turn because of other commitments and problems. One would think that, after 25 years of service in a community, life should be beautiful, but it is quite the contrary. Instead of getting better, things seem to get worse."

She had purchased another car. The payments were $89.56 a month for 26 months. She was three months behind. That wasn't her only problem. Pulling the mobile clinic with the car had taken its toll on the vehicle.

In addition to that the small wooden building that housed the clinic at Cainhoy was razed after it became a fire hazard. Her life personally and professionally seemed to be as bad as it was in the 1940s. To repay him Broughton said she'd work off the debt. She offered to do any health-related work. She even humbled herself, offering to do "domestic" work at Guggenheim's Cain Hoy Plantation. Before the month was over, Guggenheim sent her a check for $85.

Broughton most likely sat in the "colored" section on the line boat to and from Cainhoy early in her career. But when treating patients, everyone knew that she was in charge. In 1963 she reported to the Episcopal Church that she was pleased that white residents were also coming to her clinic.

"The generalized program under which I work covering 26 or more services has gone on as usual. The remarkable exception is that more white people in the Huger-Wando area are soliciting and accepting these services. It is truly gratifying that confidence has been built up to that extent. An all-white well-child clinic is conducted every fourth Friday at the Protestant Episcopal Mission in Huger with 25 or more usually in attendance. Can you imagine a Reformed Episcopal clinic at a Protestant Episcopal church building?"

As a young black nurse, Broughton was better educated than most people in the community, which surely made for tense moments early in her service at a time when African Americans, only two generations from slavery, were expected to show respect and deference to whites no matter what. It's difficult to imagine that Nurse Broughton would have deferred to anyone, even in Cainhoy where only four months earlier Joseph Broughton, a black man but no relation to her, was charged with killing white storekeeper James Elias DuTart.

Nurse Broughton's mobile clinic continued to operate throughout the area until 1969. That year the South Carolina Board of Health received federal money to build a clinic at Clements Ferry and Cainhoy roads. The Wando Health Center was dedicated December 14, 1969, on the site of the black Episcopal church.

People admired the clinic's large waiting room, office and two examination rooms at the end of the hall. With dreamy eyes, a smiling Nurse Broughton removed her glasses to peer out at the audience as she spoke during the dedication.

Five years after the clinic opened Broughton received a certificate from South Carolina in recognition of more than 30 years of service.

The following year, Nurses Eugenia Broughton and Maude Callen were special guests at a ceremony in Columbia during which South Carolina honored the state's lay midwives for their service throughout the state. A portrait of the state's oldest midwife at the time, Josephine Matthews of Wagener, was unveiled and hangs today in the board room of the S.C. Department of Health and Environmental Control in Columbia. The inscription on the painting reads: "Portrait in recognition of the 'granny midwives' at their retirement in May 1975. Josephine Matthews delivered approximately 1,800 babies prior to her retirement at the age of 77."

After 1969 no new lay midwives were licensed by the state. As the older practitioners retired their duties were assumed by physicians and nurse-midwives trained at the Medical University of South Carolina in Charleston. By 1975 hospital services and physician care had been expanded while retirements reduced the number of lay midwives in the state to 121.

Beginning in the 1970s people arrived at clinics around Berkeley County to enroll in the Special Supplemental Nutrition Program for Women, Infants and Children, commonly called the WIC Program. Vouchers to buy milk, eggs and cheese were given to pregnant women, breast-feeding mothers and women with children under five.

Carolyn Britt, a young clerk in the county's WIC Program, first met Broughton in the winter of 1975 at the busy Wando Health Center, one of seven clinics in the county where mothers enrolled in the WIC program. The other sites were at Cross, Pineville, St. Stephen, Jamestown, Goose Creek and Moncks Corner.

The waiting room was filled when Britt and another WIC clerk arrived at the Wando clinic. Those who couldn't find a seat inside stood in the yard. Although the scene appeared overwhelming, Broughton, as usual, was in control.

Broughton truly cared for people, Britt said. "She wanted to make sure they got the health care they needed. If people didn't show up or missed an appointment for some reason, she'd chastise them and tell them when they needed to be there."

The young Broughton cousins, who many years before sat on the porch of Genie Broughton's home to ponder their futures, never strayed far from one another. By the 1980s Geneva Dansby regularly stopped by her younger cousin's house each workday en route to teaching at Buist school. One morning, however, Dansby's "sweet cousin" didn't answer the door.

Genie Broughton had suffered a stroke and collapsed on the floor. For the next three years a home-care nurse came to Dewey Street to care for her, and Geneva Dansby cooked her meals.

Nurse Broughton died on February 18, 1983, at the age of 68. A week after Broughton's death, Callen gave a tribute from the Berkeley County midwives during the funeral at Holy Trinity Reformed Episcopal Church on Bull Street in Charleston. She was among the mourners who gathered that day for a "service of triumph" for the beloved nurse. A poem in the program captured the sentiment:

> "Noteworthy service to duty's call;
> "Unselfish and faithful, you gave to all;
> "Resourceful and talented in doing His work.
> "Sincerely dedicated, no duty you shirked.
> "Eternally grateful we'll always be.
> "Because you cared and shared your gift,
> "Relying on the Almighty to help you lift,
> "Others were eased of burden and pain,
> "Understanding that you worked in His name.
> "God will reward you; of this we are sure;
> "He does inflict, but with patience endure.

"To Him who keeps you in His care,
"Our voices rise in fervent prayer,
"Never ceasing to ask that He hold you near."

Harry Frank Guggenheim

Harry Frank Guggenheim's grandfather, Simon Meyer Guggenheim, began building the family fortune in mining after he immigrated to the United States in 1848 from Switzerland.

Born in August 1890 at West End, N.J., Harry Frank served an apprenticeship in mining and metallurgy with the American Smelting and Refining Company from 1907 until 1910 at its plants in Mexico. He later became the senior partner in the mining and metallurgical firm of Guggenheim Brothers, the head of several foundations, ambassador to Cuba, an author and a Navy aviator during World Wars I and II.

He was married three times. His last wife, Alicia Patterson of Port Washington, N.Y., was the daughter of Joseph Medill Patterson, founder and publisher of the New York Daily News, and great-granddaughter of Joseph Medill, founder of the Chicago Tribune. In 1940 Harry Frank and Alicia Guggenheim established Newsday, based on Long Island, N.Y. He was the president, and she was editor and publisher until her death in July 1963. Two years later, Guggenheim became the newspaper's publisher and editor. He sold the newspaper in 1970 to the Los Angeles Times.

Guggenheim's uncle, Solomon Guggenheim, who spent his winters at 9 East Battery in Charleston, introduced Harry Frank to the city. During the early years of the Depression, Guggenheim purchased several parcels in the Cainhoy area, consolidating the property into a retreat of more than 10,000 acres that he called the Cain Hoy Plantation. In 1937 he built a cream-colored mansion topped with a tile roof.

After realizing the land on his Cain Hoy Plantation could not be kept as permanent pasture, Guggenheim bought 2,900 acres on Daniel Island in 1946 where the soil was more fertile. The island had been covered with Sea Island cotton until the early 1900s, and later it was planted in fruits

Harry Frank Guggenheim.

Jockey Henry Moreno rode Guggenheim's Dark Star to a win in the Kentucky Derby in 1953. Photos courtesy of Peter Lawson-Johnston II.

and vegetables. Guggenheim bought the island from John F. Maybank Jr. for $75,000. In 1946 Guggenheim purchased the lower portion of the island and nine years later he bought the Furman Tract on the northern end of the island. With that purchase he had the entire 4,000-acre island. Guggenheim used the island to breed cattle, one of the largest herds in the country. He planted winter and summer grasses for his Hereford cattle. In 1970 he sold the herd for more than $1 million.

On the 35th floor in the Equitable Building, a New York City skyscraper, Guggenheim's office overlooked Wall Street, the financial heart of America. The opulent setting seemed far removed from the sprawling marshes and Lowcountry pinelands where he spent winters.

"If it hadn't been for that man," he said, pointing to a portrait of his bearded grandfather, "I might have been tending dairy cows on an Alpine slope today instead of raising beef cattle in South Carolina."

Guggenheim died in January 1971 at his Falaise Estate on Long Island. He was 80.

A timber worker in 1929 in Berkeley County.
Source: Forest History Society.

Chapter 8: Timber

Trees covered the landscape when European colonists first settled on the Cainhoy peninsula. The forest was more than a source of timber for homes, shops and ships. Trees provided naval stores — tar, pitch and turpentine — drawn from the abundant Southern longleaf pine, the most prolific resin tree in North America. Naval stores were the first goods exported to England as those items were in short supply there.

As the 19th century was ending, timber companies in the Great Lakes states and Northeast turned to the South for new sources of trees. The early 20th century signaled the beginning of large-scale industrial timber harvesting in the coastal pine belt of South Carolina. In the area around the Cainhoy peninsula, the E.P. Burton Lumber Company, the A.C. Tuxbury Lumber Company and the North State Lumber Company began opening mills and buying and leasing timberland. By 1910 these companies held most of the timber acreage in Berkeley and Charleston counties.

The timber industry's growth on the Cainhoy peninsula came at a time when Berkeley County's population was declining in black and white residents, and South Carolina's population growth in general slowed compared to most other states. This population drain was due to black residents leaving rural counties for higher-paying jobs in the North, a higher death rate among African Americans, a decline in the production of rice in the coastal counties and a decline in naval stores and other industries throughout the state.

To support logging operations in Berkeley County, timber companies

A locomotive passes through the logging camp at Witherbee.
Source: Forest History Society.

built mills across the river in Charleston County. Tuxbury and E.P. Burton ran miles of railroad tracks across the Cainhoy peninsula to bring the felled trees from the forest to the mills. North State had lines in the area just west of Huger at the company's town at Witherbee. Logs were either placed on barges or lashed together and floated on the Cooper and Wando rivers to mills north of downtown Charleston.

In 1900 the North State Lumber Company moved its mill at the village of Parmele in North Carolina to Shipyard Creek on the Charleston Neck. The company floated barges loaded with logs from the company's property near the landings at Silk Hope Plantation on the Cainhoy peninsula to the mill. North State's logging operations were centered at Witherbee near Huger where it had a railroad shop. In 1910 the mill on the Cooper was cutting 50,000 board feet of lumber daily. Seven years later, North State's logging railroad was 15 miles long.

By 1936 the North State railroad operation was shut down. The last of North State's operations was over by 1956.

The A.C. Tuxbury Lumber Company in 1905 established one of the largest lumber mills in the Charleston area. Tuxbury's first logging operation was at Magnolia Plantation on the Ashley River. Logs were rafted to the Tuxbury mill on the Cooper River at Shipyard Creek near the North State Mill. Schooners at the company's dock were loaded with lumber for ports in South America, the West Indies and Europe. Later the company began logging at sites along the Cooper, above the Cainhoy peninsula.

In 1910 Tuxbury had 13 miles of railroad in Berkeley County. The Tuxbury line ran from Cainhoy to a large logging camp at Bethera. Logging spurs ran deep into the woods and surrounding swamp. By 1917 Tuxbury had laid 38 miles of rail line from Bonneau to Jamestown. In Berkeley County, Tuxbury built what is believed to be the first fire tower in South Carolina: a 100-foot tall wooden structure erected in 1927. Ironically, a woods fire destroyed the tower shortly after construction.

Because of its fast-paced cutting of trees, Tuxbury by 1924 needed more timber so the logging operation was extended to McClellanville and the Bethera logging camp was moved to the Awendaw area. A rail line hauled logs from Awendaw to Cainhoy where they had previously been dumped in the Wando and rafted to the Tuxbury mill on the Cooper. The Awendaw camp also had a turpentine distillery until August 1938, when the Tuxbury logging operations ended. The locomotives used to pull timber cars were later cut up for scrap steel to feed the demand for metal during World War II. Tuxbury closed its Cooper River mill in June 1939. The mill had cut 715 million feet of timber in little more than three decades. At the height of its operation, Tuxbury employed more than 400 hundred people.

When the mill closed, the company announced: "We have cut all our timber and there is not sufficient trees in this neighborhood to keep a plant of that size in operation and too much is tied up in the investment to operate on a smaller scale."

Henry Beer sold Limerick Plantation to the E.P. Burton Company in 1899. Also that year the company bought seven other tracts in Berkeley County. By 1906 Burton had purchased 48,000 acres of forestland on the East Branch of the Cooper River. The company also built a sawmill down river near what later became the Navy Yard.

The company laid a railroad to haul logs to a landing on the Cooper.

Workers load logs onto a rail car in Berkeley County.
Source: Forest History Society.

From there, the timber was rafted to the mill. To house its workers, the company built a village in 1902. The company called it Conifer, which means cone-bearing tree. Situated about five miles from the Cooper, Conifer was a clearing of several acres. The village's only street was lined with four-room houses for the white foremen and their families.

Near the center of the village was the company house, occupied by two foresters. At the far end of the street, the railroad crossed between the last three buildings, which included the superintendent's office, company store, blacksmith's shop and the company boarding house for unmarried men. Four other houses stood along the railroad. A distance away were the stable and cabins for black workers. The cost of a room ranged from $8 to $10 per month.

A cook's house prepared meals for the workers. The menu included rice, grits, ham, cabbage, beans, sweet and Irish potatoes, biscuits and coffee.

The well-stocked commissary supplied the needs of approximately 500

Darr Sullivan (far right) and his Berkeley Electric Cooperative crew extended electric service to the Cainhoy peninsula in the early 1960s. Sullivan,
who retired in 1981 as the utility's chief of operations and engineering,
supervised a crew that installed power lines along S.C. 41 and S.C. 98 past
Middleburg Plantation toward Cainhoy. Photo courtesy of Darr Sullivan.

people, including the workers' families. The goods were expensive. The
men were paid $1 a day for straight labor, the locomotive engineer got $2
a day, and the foremen were paid $50 a month.

By 1906 Burton was cutting 20 million board feet of lumber annually
with pine accounting for 18 million feet and cypress for two million feet.
The company also sold smaller amounts of oak, ash and yellow poplar.
Boston, New York and Philadelphia were its largest markets. The company's
rail lines covered 25 miles in 1912. The Burton mill on the Cooper closed
in 1923 after it caught fire. The company sold its uncut land to the North
State Lumber Company, which continued to cut timber at Silk Hope.

The lumber companies' private electric-generation stations powered
the logging camps on the Cainhoy peninsula before the Berkeley Electric
Cooperative ran its first line to Henry Lee Johnson's store in the Huger
area in the early 1940s. The Burton Lumber Company also installed a
telephone line from its Conifer camp to Charleston before Home Telephone

Company ran its first phone line from Cordesville to Johnson's store in 1963. Four miles of the company's 30-mile-long private telephone line ran under the Cooper River.

The cutting of timber in Berkeley County and elsewhere raised concerns of whether the coastal plains would see depleted forests on the same scale as what had happened in the Great Lakes and Northeast regions. Cutting the forest creates a series of land-management problems, including erosion, flooding and silting of streams and rivers. Conservationists argued that sustainable forest practices would enhance fishing, hunting and recreation, generate tax revenues and stable communities.

By 1926 there was a strong demand in the Carolinas and Georgia for the federal government to purchase coastal pineland to protect the trees. A decade later, the Francis Marion National Forest was established in Berkeley and Charleston counties. Tuxbury and North State land made up the core of the forest, which covers 260,000 acres in the two counties. North State sold 65,000 thousand acres to the federal government in 1936. Creating the forest not only began a process to protect the land but also provided jobs during the Depression.

President Franklin D. Roosevelt approved in 1933 the Civilian Conservation Corps, which had bases in national and state forests. The CCC put men to work on reforestation, firefighting, road-building and soil-conservation projects around the country, including the new Francis Marion Forest.

In the early 1930s the CCC enrollees built Charity Church Road in the Huger community at S.C. Highways 98 and 41. Fort Moultrie on Sullivan's Island near Mount Pleasant was headquarters for the South Carolina camps. On the CCC's third anniversary, Roosevelt told the workers in a national radio address that "through your spirit and industry it has been demonstrated that young men can be put to work in our forests, parks and fields on projects which benefit both the nation's youth and conservation generally."

In 1933, CCC camps were opened at Witherbee near Huger and Awendaw north of Mount Pleasant. Initially, the camps did not employ

Calhoun Umphlett, former president of Umphlett Lumber Co. in Moncks Corner, lived at Witherbee in the 1920s with his family when it was a logging camp for North State Lumber Co. Umphlett's father Mills "Bud" Umphlett supervised the cutting of logs. Pictured are the late Clifford Ackerman, (left) Calhoun Umphlett, the late Burton Ackerman, and the late Clyde Umphlett, Calhoun Umphlett's twin brother. Source: Forest History Society.

local people. Most workers came from New Jersey and many were sons of Italian immigrants.

A CCC camp inspector reported in 1934 that the arrangement was not working. "It is my impression that much of the trouble that exists between the foremen and the enrolled men lies in the fact that the foremen are unused to directing white labor of foreign extraction, but instead are more familiar with working Negro labor. A lack of understanding between foremen on the one hand and enrolled men on the other tends to promote friction."

CCC administrators responded to the problem in 1935 by transferring the New Jersey men out West and replacing them with black men from coastal South Carolina. The move also led to a national policy to open some of the military-style CCC camps around the country to black men.

In that year camps at Awendaw, Witherbee and a new one near Mc-Clellanville were filled with black enrollees supervised by white Army officers. White Forest Service employees directed the day-to-day work throughout the national forest.

Witherbee, designated as Company 5418, SC F-3, was one of 29 CCC camps in South Carolina. Six were for black recruits. Twenty-five men arrived on August 3, 1935, at Witherbee for early training as the camp leaders in advance of 200 enrollees who would join them two days later. Ben Gerideau was the first sergeant. Hercules Lucas supervised the supply room and Alexander Blake, said to be one of the best cooks in Dixie, ruled the kitchen.

Henry Smith (second from left) was a member of the Witherbee CCC camp quartette in 1935. Photo courtesy of the U.S. Forest Service.

Surprisingly, none of the workers came from the Cainhoy peninsula. The only local enrollee at Witherbee was Joe Thomas of Cordesville.

The day at Witherbee began with physical drills before the men went to work in the forest. A lunch truck carried their meals, but when it arrived at the work site, local people appeared seemingly from nowhere asking for food.

The camps had trade schools to teach cabinetmaking, gardening and chicken farming. The camp also had a basketball court and baseball team. When their assignment at the CCC camp was completed, many of the men joined the military or got jobs at the Charleston Navy Yard.

Henry "Dead Horse" Smith, a 23-year-old enrollee from Georgetown, was among the black workers at Witherbee. In its first year, the camp organized the Witherbee Quartette, a singing group composed of Smith, Winston Hemingway, Paris Graham and George Jackson. The group styled itself after the Mills Brothers.

In later years the group also included Bernie Long and "Bungy" Dewitt. They traveled often to Charleston to sing in the studio of radio station WCSC, located on the top floor of the Francis Marion Hotel at Calhoun and King streets. Smith became well known across South Carolina for his voice. In 1994 he was awarded the South Carolina Folk Heritage Award. Smith was the steward of the camp's canteen and a reporter for the camp's newspaper, Little Ethiopia.

During the Depression, Smith left his home in Georgetown to join the CCC camp so he could support his family. His father died and he quit school in the seventh grade to work. As the canteen steward, Smith was paid $45 a month of which $25 was sent home to his mother. Regular camp enrollees were paid $25, of which $20 was sent home to support their families. If managed properly, the $5 an enrollee kept could go a long way in a month's time.

But many lost money gambling. After the lights were ordered out at 10 p.m., the gamblers lit candles and found a place in the woods to play.

Smith sold more than just cigarettes and sodas from the canteen. He sold shots of moonshine for 50 cents and 25 cents. Working in the forest, the men often found moonshine stills. They'd dip a bucket into the still then hang it on the tractor to drink as they worked. One day the tractor driver got so drunk he ran the vehicle into the swamp and got stuck.

Smith worked at Witherbee for four years until it closed in 1939. Witherbee was re-opened in 1943 as a prisoner-of-war camp for German soldiers captured in North Africa during World War II. The site is used today as offices for the U.S. Forest Service.

Chapter 9: Moonshine

Army Colonel George C. Marshall Jr., commander of Fort Moultrie on Sullivan's Island, toured the South Carolina camps of the Civil Conservation Corps in August 1933. After the tour, Marshall said the chief problem wasn't the food or living quarters but the consumption of bootleg liquor.

* * *

In 1946 the baseball team for employees at the General Asbestos and Rubber Company (GARCO) was the champs of South Carolina's semi-pro league. They played at the Chicora playground in the North Area just above Charleston. While the team whipped their opponents on the field the fans sipped moonshine in the stands. Moonshine arrived at the games via milk trucks, bread trucks and a train called "the Boll Weevil." It also came by rowboat from Cainhoy.

* * *

In the late 1940s mortician apprentice Herbert U. Fielding was called to Cainhoy to pick up the body of a child the family wanted Fielding Home for Funerals in Charleston to prepare for burial. He placed a small casket in the rear of a hearse and drove over the Cooper River bridge to the family's home. When he arrived that night, a crowd had gathered outside.

As Fielding placed the body in the hearse, a man asked for a ride back to the city. The young mortician welcomed the company, but before he closed the rear door of the vehicle, the man slid a fancy suitcase next to the casket. When they arrived in the city, the passenger got out on Lee Street,

"Look here. It was hard times, you know. He had to make ends meet. If a man is a man he'd want to support his house. Most everybody was making moonshine."

– Florence Dickerson

Florence and Louis Dickerson of Huger. Courtesy of Florence Dickerson.

Berkeley County author William Dennis Shuler at the old Moncks Corner train depot where three men died during a May 1926 shootout between rival bootleggers. Photo by Herb Frazier.

retrieved his suitcase and opened it. Fielding saw that it was filled with small jars of moonshine. The man offered Fielding a pint.

Moonshine stills hidden in the Francis Marion Forest were once as plentiful as fiddler crabs in marsh grass at low tide. An estimated 9,000 people lived in or near the forest and most of them depended on subsistence farming, logging, moonshining or a combination of the three.

Pushed by a religious temperance movement, Congress passed the 18th Amendment to the U.S. Constitution in January 1919, outlawing the manufacturing and distribution of alcohol. Prohibition began and with it came a lucrative black-market liquor trade and associated violence, especially in Berkeley County. During the 1920s until the early 1930s, moonshine and the violence linked with it became the curse of Berkeley County. Black and white people from all walks of life were in its grips. Not even the church was off limits to bootleggers. Because the St. Thomas Church near Cainhoy was not used for regular services, bootleggers stashed liquor in the historic sanctuary.

"Berkeley was the nation's capital when it came to making and selling corn whisky — second to none — except perhaps to Harlan County, Kentucky," William Shuler wrote in *Short Stories about Life in Berkeley County, South Carolina.*

Federal agents and local police routinely raided moonshine operations throughout the county. One of the biggest busts was May 7, 1926, when five state lawmen and a federal agent smashed 10 moonshine stills operated by George D. McKnight in Hell Hole Swamp. They also confiscated 10,000 gallons of beer and 1,800 gallons of corn whisky. One of the stills had produced 1,000 gallons of moonshine per week for 14 months straight. McKnight was arrested but never brought to trial. Instead, he landed a job as a federal prohibition agent.

Bootlegging was a dangerous business. When the operators weren't tending their stills, they were dodging police, bullets and buckshot. But the cops weren't the only ones doing the shooting. Bootleggers often went after each other for control of the market. The shootouts became so common that the county was known as "Bloody Berkeley." The day after the Hell Hole bust, hot lead flew outside the train station in the center of Moncks Corner. The shooting started after two cars arrived at the railroad crossing. When it stopped, three men were dead in the street.

Moonshine from Hell Hole Swamp was shipped by rail to mobster Al Capone in Chicago, where operators of speakeasies sold what was known as Berkeley County Corn or BCC for short. Capone visited stills in Moncks Corner and Huger to inspect the liquor-making operations. In Huger, Capone's Lincoln was once spotted parked behind Henry Lee Johnson's ere the proprietor supplied local bootleggers with sugar and Mason car was covered with a tarp while the mobster mixed business with pleasure.

Good corn liquor is 60 percent alcohol. Bad 'shine was deadly. A dash of Red Devil Lye would hasten fermentation, but too much ruins the batch. The good stuff was produced in clean copper stills, but liquor made in an old automobile radiator came spiked with fatal levels of lead.

In neighboring Charleston County, Awendaw was the base for another large moonshine operation. The area also received and distributed liquor from Cuba smuggled in via the nearby Santee River.

Shortly after John G. Richards was sworn in as South Carolina's governor in 1926, State Sen. Edward Dennis of Moncks Corner sought his help in cleaning up the bootleg industry in Berkeley County. The bootleggers were furious and Dennis' political opponents claimed he was trying to corner the moonshine market.

Dennis was later indicted in federal court for conspiring to violate the Prohibition law. He stood trial and was acquitted. Following that, the governor removed Berkeley County Sheriff C.P. Ballentine from office after seized liquor, which was to be used as evidence, disappeared from the jail.

Violence erupted again in May 1930 when 19-year-old LeGrande Cumbee was killed and his father Sabb Cumbee was wounded during an ambush in Hell Hole Swamp. The Cumbees were politically aligned with Sen. Dennis.

Next, Dennis' political rival Glen D. McKnight was cut down by a shotgun blast outside his Moncks Corner home, but he survived. Two months later, Dennis told the Associated Press he had received death threats.

According to testimony, Glen McKnight was plotting to kill Dennis. W.L. "Sporty" Thornley, who stood five feet, four inches tall and weighed 105 pounds, was recruited to assassinate the senator. On July 19, 1930, McKnight promised to give Thornley "a little house" and provide for him if he killed Dennis. McKnight told Thornley, "If you kill Mr. Dennis and if they catch you and if they lock you up, don't worry about nothing. Tell them you don't know nothing about it, and I will prove in the Senate that you was crazy."

It was not the first time McKnight made such a request. Before McKnight was ambushed outside his home, he had offered Thornley $500 to carry out the plot, saying he wanted Dennis dead because the senator's friends were going to kill him.

Thornley refused the first time but later changed his mind. He told McKnight to get him a car, a shotgun and a half-pint of liquor.

On July 24, 1930, Dennis headed to his law office in Moncks Corner as he always did. He stopped at the post office first, then walked past the Rigby Hotel. Thornley was waiting behind the parked car that McKnight had provided. Thornley aimed the shotgun and fired. Dennis fell after being hit squarely by a round of buckshot.

Thornley ran. John Hill, a game warden, chased him. During the pursuit, he met Moncks Corner mechanic Clarence Rudloff, who told him he saw Thornley run by. He tried to speak with Thornley, but he didn't stop to talk. Then Thornley returned. He approached the men.

"Here I am. What do you want?" Thornley asked.

"If you're not guilty, then for your own protection, let's get out of here," Hill responded.

"Why sure," Thornley said. "I'll go anywhere; there's nothing wrong with me."

Dennis died the following day at Riverside Infirmary in Charleston. Thornley was charged with his murder. Thornley initially told police he couldn't remember shooting the senator but later confessed and implicated McKnight, who denied involvement. Thornley, 34, was convicted and sentenced to life in prison. But after serving only eight years and one month, Gov. Olin Johnston, who had only been in office a week, commuted the sentence to time served.

Years later the murdered senator's son, Rembert Dennis — who had been elected to the state Senate himself — told historian Dale Rosengarten that politics was behind Thornley's release, and bootleggers had arranged the assassination.

Thornley was a disabled veteran, Dennis said. "He had been gassed in the war and he wasn't mentally right. ... He was persuaded to do it by others. They furnished him the automobile, the gun and a half a pint of liquor to drink before he did it, and said they would take care of him and his family."

***

If a bootlegger had enough money to hire the right lawyer in Charleston, federal court cases moved slowly against some whites arrested for making moonshine. But the cases against black people who were arrested usually went to trial quickly in federal court. Like their white neighbors, black families on the Cainhoy peninsula made moonshine to get cash to survive. In both communities, people who made corn liquor weren't ostracized. Today, older residents readily admit they and their relatives made moonshine during Prohibition and after it ended in 1933.[8]

Huger resident Florence Dickerson, the oldest member of Zion United Methodist Church, speaks candidly about why it was necessary for her husband, Louis Dickerson, to make moonshine. Men turned to making moonshine when it was not possible to work in the forest cutting trees after a heavy rain soaked the soil. Some sold moonshine at retail prices, 25 cents a pint, or sold cases of quart jars at wholesale prices to the bootleggers. "Look here. It was hard times, you know. He (Dickerson's husband) had to make ends meet," Dickerson said sternly. "If a man is a man he'd want to support his house. Most everybody was making moonshine."

Louis Dickerson didn't get in trouble with the law. The Dickersons' daughter Vernelle remembers that when police patrolled the community she sometimes heard a loud explosion outside. When authorities found a still, they sometimes dynamited it so it could not be used again. If the police came too close to the family's house, her father would whisper, "Out the light."

---

8 After Prohibition, it was illegal to make, possess, transport or sell alcoholic beverages not taxed by the state.

Ernest Taylor made moonshine to support his family in Huger. Photo courtesy of Dorothy Scott.

Combined with fermented grapes, raisins or apples, moonshine could be made into a brandy used in home remedies. Mothers gave children a mixture of moonshine, lemon and an herb called Life Everlasting to break a fever.[9]

A felt hat came in handy too, according to Dorothy Scott, who grew up in the Huger area. She was in her early teens when her stepfather, Ernest Taylor, made moonshine. Dorothy and her siblings held Mason jars under a felt hat to filter the 'shine for consumption. "Everybody wanted to get Taylor's moonshine," she said. Helping her stepfather "proof" the moonshine was a way of supporting the family, she said. The family wasn't

---

9 Life Everlasting is illegal to grow and possess in South Carolina because it is considered to have an intoxicating effect when it is smoked.

overly concerned that making 'shine was illegal, she said.

When Buster Brown was a boy growing up on Rivers Reach Drive in Wando he was never tempted to drink moonshine, even though his family made it in the woods near a low spot where his father grew rice. "If you drink it and got drunk, you'd get a backside cuttin'," Brown said. He remembers the night his uncle David Venning loaded a rowboat with jars of 'shine and took it across the Cooper River to Charleston.

Black men often made moonshine for white bootleggers, who typically provided the still and the ingredients. The white man made the money, but it was the black man who went to jail, Brown said. "But later on, the black people get hip. They say, 'I can make 'em for myself.'"

Postal and Fredie Mae Grant Smalls. Courtesy of Norwood Smalls.

Postal Smalls

Before he died in December 2008, Postal Smalls said he made moonshine, and he didn't need help from a white man.

Smalls was born in the Brickyard community of Huger just off Steed Creek Road in a wood frame house he shared with his parents, Johnnie and Lousia Smalls; four brothers, Eddie, Enoch, Rudolph and Harold; and two sisters, Maybelle and Grace. He was the third child.

Smalls said he did not know his birth year was in doubt until he applied for retirement benefits. His parents told him he was born October 9, 1919. The Social Security office, however, said the Census showed he was born October 9, 1920. "I feel like I am 1919," he shrugged.

Smalls described his life as a boy in Huger, the first time he saw the lights and paved streets of Charleston and the economic hardship that got him into the moonshine business.

"They call it Hu-gee," he said about the name of his community. "But they should call it Hu-gerr."

When Smalls lived with his parents, there was not much to do other than eat and play. But it all changed before he became a teenager.

"I was 11 years old when my cousin come to my mother and asked her to let me come over here (to the Poyas community) with her to pick up corn stalks for two weeks. That was the second week in March 1932. And when I come over here, I had loved the place. I had all kind of activities over here.

"There were horses and wagons and plenty of cows and hogs, and I had loved it, and they learnt me how to plow. They grew corn, sweet potatoes, peas, beans and rice. They had a little patch of rice. They had a field and it had a trunk to turn the water on and turn the water off, and the old people taught me how to grow the rice."

His cousin Florence Grant, who was married twice and widowed twice, needed someone to help her with the chores. So Smalls packed his clothes and moved in with Grant, the daughter of Frederick Poyas, who owned 55 acres he had purchased for 50 cents an acre.

Smalls' first trip from the Poyas community near Huger to Charleston was on Labor Day 1935 when he hitched a ride with a clothing salesman. Smalls sat in the car's rumble seat as it bounced along dirt roads until they reached U.S. 17, a paved highway that led to the big steel bridge over the Cooper River. When they got to Charleston, Smalls got out at Lee and Meeting streets in an area locals called "the foot of the bridge."

In wide-eyed amazement he walked south along Meeting Street to Calhoun Street then to the home of his grandaunt, Elizabeth Stewart, at 34 Chapel Street.

"I was in a different world. I never thought I would ever see a place where ain't nothin' but pave; no dirt road. All I ever seen in my life was dirt road. I spent from Saturday till Thursday with her, caught the boat and come back to Cainhoy and caught the fruit truck back." While he was in the big city he didn't see the sites. His grandaunt didn't take him on a tour. But the trip made a big impression on him just the same.

Florence Grant's niece, Fredie Mae Grant, lived with her aunt when Smalls joined the household. They grew up together and later were married on Saturday, August 31, 1940, by the justice of the peace in Moncks Corner.

"I grew up with her, and I married her. She was a pretty youngster. I could go anywhere with her." They had eight children: Beatrice Smalls McGirth, Leon, Samuel, Jesse and Elijah Smalls, Carolyn Smalls Goodson and Norwood and Nathan Smalls.

The day after Postal and Fredie Mae Smalls exchanged vows he went to work with a crew that built S.C. Highway 41, a straight and wide two-lane road that runs from Wando through Huger.

Smalls had worked with North State Lumber Company and was paid 75 cents a day in 1936 to tote drinking water. "That was so much of money I didn't know what to do with it. The man who drive the log wagon got the top price, $1.35 a day!"

By 1939 Smalls was earning $5 a week. Later, he also farmed to feed his family. With the extra money from logging, he bought a 100-pound sack of sugar and went into the moonshine business. "I got out of it temporary. But when things got bad, I get back in it."

In 1949 Smalls sold a dozen half-gallon jars of moonshine for $30. It was liquid money and he was ready to pour a glass of it to get his truck's radiator patched. Two men agreed to help him fix it, but first they wanted a drink.

"No. No. Let's get this radiator fix, then I'll give you a drink," Smalls insisted.

"No. We need a spirit to work," one of the men said.

Smalls had a half a gallon of moonshine. He set it up and built a fire to heat the soldering gun. But before it got hot, a car rolled up in the yard. Two doors flung open and federal agents jumped out. Four of them approached Smalls. He wasn't scared even though the evidence was in plain view. One of the agents picked up the liquor and asked who lived in the house?

"I live here," Smalls answered. "Those boys don't know nothin' 'bout this stuff," he added as he pointed to his helpers.

The agent then asked Smalls where did he get the liquor?

"We picked it up on the road," Smalls replied.

"Boy, where did you get this liquor from?" the agent shouted.

"We picked it up on the road."

"Don't you think this stuff will kill you if you drink it?" the agent asked.

"Well, if I want to drink it I might as well die from the drinking or die from the wanting of it," Smalls quipped.

"Where you get all those jars?" the agent asked.

Smalls said he used the jars to can fruits and vegetables.

"If you can show me one case of fruit or vegetables, we will turn you loose."

"We eat them as fast as we jar them up," Smalls answered.

"OK, we'll buy that," the agent said.

Meanwhile, as Smalls was being questioned, two agents searched the woods near his house and found a 200-gallon still filled with moonshine. So, with an ax, they hacked it to pieces.

"Come here, Smalls," the agent said. "Sit in the car. We have to turn you in."

"Well, y'all is the law," Smalls said. "I will do what y'all say do."

Smalls spent the night in the Charleston County jail near the Cooper River bridge. Back then, the stout brick jail was known as the "Seabreeze Hotel."

Smalls woke up the next morning at breakfast time. A jailer shoved a tray through the crack in the door. Breakfast was green beans, meat skin and a cup of bitter coffee.

"Postal Smalls here?" someone asked.

"Yes, sir," Smalls answered.

"I come to get you."

"Who is you?"

"The United States marshal."

Smalls was handcuffed and taken to the federal courthouse at Broad and Meeting streets and faced a federal judge, who released him on bail.

Henry Lee Johnson, who sold sugar to Smalls, paid the $25 bond and gave him a ride back to Huger. The following day, Smalls went to Johnson's store to thank him for bailing him out of jail and to apologize for the inconvenience.

Smalls was later placed on probation for three years. The judge made it clear that he should avoid the moonshine business. But that was easier said than done because times were tough on the farm.

Smalls made more moonshine. He was arrested again. A federal agent carried him to the federal courthouse on February 4, 1955. He faced the same judge and probation officer from the first time he was arrested in 1949.

The probation officer told Smalls it had been six years and six days since the last time he was placed on probation.

"You couldn't be good?" he asked. "I could get you probation, but I have to see about it. Tell me a story now."

"Well, officer," Smalls said, "it was like this. In 1954 it was a hot and dry year. We didn't make nothin' on the farm. I couldn't buy a job if I had the money to buy it with. I got a wife and eight head of churrin' to feed, send to school and clothe. I just didn't know what to do.

"A man came by that Friday morning and asked me if I wanted to make some money. I asked him what would I be doing? He said make some liquor. I said I will try, and I got caught the same day I started. That is how I got in this position again this time."

The probation officer told Smalls, "Boy, you make yourself a damn good lawyer. You can lie. Yes, 1954 was a hot and dry year. You tell the truth there. I am sorry you had to violate the United States government law to make a living. For that, we could throw the book at you. But I am going to try to get you probation. If I can get you probation, could you get $100 in 30 days?"

"Yes, sir," Smalls answered.

It would be his last run-in with the law. He went to work on Charleston's waterfront and got his union card from George German, the first president of the International Longshoremen's Association. It was steady, good-paying work that gave him a way out of making moonshine.

"It was either go to the Longshoremen or go to jail," Smalls said. At that time, the union hall was on East Bay Street near the old WCSC television station. Smalls paid $35 for his union card. His first job was helping to unload a boatload of scrap iron. After Smalls retired from Charleston's waterfront in the mid-1960s, he held other jobs including working as the caretaker at Middleburg Plantation after its ownership was transferred from the Ball family to the Hill family.

Although Smalls had turned his back on moonshine, he still was grappling with unfinished work. He was on the path to find another spirit to fulfill his needs.

Smalls was not a churchgoer when he was making moonshine. But his children worshipped at New Hope United Methodist Church with their mother, Fredie Mae Smalls, and their maternal grandmother, Carrie Nesbit Ladson. Smalls' children also attended St. Philip AME Church, pastored by their maternal grandfather, Frank Ladson.

Beatrice Smalls McGirth asked her father why he didn't attend church like the other men in the community. Smalls said he wasn't told he had to do so. But in 1972, Postal Smalls changed his ways, although he only attended special services. At that time, McGirth and her husband were "added to" the Church of Christ. Her mother and two of her siblings also were added to the church. But Smalls resisted.

"He attacked me because I was the first one in the family to step out and went into a non-denominational church," McGirth said. Her mother also initially questioned her decision because without a church membership, she wondered, where would she be buried.

Having a plot in a church cemetery didn't matter to McGirth. "What was more important to me was my soul."

Smalls continued to search to find his faith. He studied the Bible with members of the Jacksonville Road Church of Christ in North Charleston for more than 14 weeks; then he began studying with the Jehovah Witnesses. After prolonged and intense Bible reading and study, he decided to join the body of Christ. He was baptized at the Jacksonville Road Church of Christ in 1979 and placed his membership at the Berkeley Church of Christ in Moncks Corner.

Smalls was not a Christian when he made moonshine. "If I was a Christian, I would have known better," he said. He also regrets he didn't attend church with his children and give each of them a Bible.

"I didn't know what it was all about until I went to church and I started hearing the gospel," he said. "They give me the Bible and everything that's done in the church come from the Bible. If you don't do it the Bible way, you just losing your time."

Gedney Howe's Bootlegger Story

The late Gedney M. Howe Jr., a prominent Charleston attorney and former solicitor for Berkeley and Charleston counties, was fond of telling stories. After his death, his family published a small book — "Re: Gedney Main Howe, Jr. 1914-1981" — filled with many of his tales that grew in size with each telling.

One of them is titled "Judge Grimball and the Bootlegger," a story he told at a South Carolina trial lawyers convention.

According to Howe, Berkeley County had a tremendous number of liquor cases when he was the circuit solicitor for a decade beginning in 1946. Because it was difficult to get a county grand jury to return an indictment, he attempted to persuade a federal prosecutor to take the case.

But the case didn't go to the federal court. Instead, it ended up before circuit Judge William H. Grimball. It involved a black man who had been arrested multiple times for bootlegging. The judge lectured the bootlegger, but by his tone Howe suspected the man would never get time.

"Boy, don't ever do this again," the judge finally said. "A hundred dollars or 30 days."

The defendant didn't move.

"Haven't you got the money?" the judge asked.

"No, Judge. I don't have that much."

"Well, 50 dollars or 30 days – you got that, haven't you?"

"No judge. I haven't."

"How much do you have?" Grimball asked.

The defendant reached in his pocket and pulled out some change.

"I got four dollars and thirty-seven cents."

Grimball reared back and roared: "The sentence of the court is 30 days or four dollars and thirty-seven cents."

Original Keith School building built in the mid-1920s. The school is named for Edward B. Keith Sr., who donated the land. Painting by John W. Jones.

Chapter 10: Education

Huger resident Florence Dickerson was 13 years old when she began school in 1926. At that time, education came second to feeding the family. Before her schooling started at Annie Kinlaw's house, Dickerson was already a seasoned farm worker. She picked cabbage and white potatoes on "Dan's Island" for the American Fruit Growers Co. Workers were allowed to keep some of the harvest. Dickerson's family stored burlap sacks filled with potatoes under the house.

When it was time for her to attend school, Dickerson walked about a mile and a half to Kinlaw's house on the Kinlaw Hill for instruction two days a week. "She would teach us what she knew, but she didn't know that much. I found out after I got older," Dickerson lamented. "I didn't learn that much."

Later, Dickerson and her siblings went to Elijah Collins' school in a house on the Lockwood Hill owned by Surry Lockwood. Collins, who Dickerson described as old and cross, taught there two or three months a year. At home she could recite her lesson, but in her teacher's intimidating presence, she forgot the answers.

"When we were coming up it was very tough because we didn't have school like they do now," she said.

Dickerson soon left Elijah Collins and enrolled in a school closer to home at Charity AME Church on Cainhoy Road. The teachers, she recalled, were Miss Lucille and Mr. Mark. The church soon built a school house on Charity Church Road.

"My father (Jake Howard) gave the acre of land for the school," she said. Florence Dickerson remembers Miss Lucille especially because the teacher slapped her left hand every time she tried to write with it. "From that, I can't do nothing else with the right hand but write. I do everything else with my left hand," she said with a laugh. Years later Dickerson worked as a cook at the Charity Church School.

Two decades before Dickerson began her schooling, groundwork was being laid to improve education for black children in Berkeley County and elsewhere. In 1907, Anna T. Jeanes, a Quaker from Philadelphia, contributed $1 million to establish a foundation to support schools for black students in the rural South. The Negro Rural School Fund lasted until 1936 when it merged with other funds to form the Southern Education Foundation to support the Jeanes schools.[10]

Jeanes collaborated with Booker T. Washington, founder of the Tuskegee Institute in Alabama. The Jeanes program ended in the 1960s following school desegregation. During the program's 60-year history about 180 black and white educators, mostly women, served as Jeanes supervisors of schools.

By the early 1950s Jeanes had opened 35 schools in Berkeley County. Four of them were on the Cainhoy peninsula: Brickyard School, in the Huger area; and the Greenbay, Keith and Shingler schools in the Cainhoy-Wando area. The school day at a Jeanes school began with prayer, scripture reading and the Pledge of Allegiance.

Postal Smalls was a student at the Brickyard School in the Huger area in the 1930s. "What I learned, I learned it off of mother wit. They taught the lessons in school, but I didn't learn it." Smalls handed off his schoolwork to a friend who completed it. "I would get an OK, and I thought I was

---

10 Julius Rosenwald, a Chicago philanthropist and president of the Sears & Roebuck Company, established a fund in 1917 to improve education for black children in the South. It built approximately 500 schools in South Carolina. Six Rosenwald schools were built in Berkeley County. They were the Berkeley Training High School, also known as the Dixie Training High School; Cordesville School; DuBoise School No. 2; Jamestown School; Pineville School and St. Stephen Schools.

learning something, but I was doing all the harm I could do to myself."

Lela Haynes Session, a graduate of Allen University in Columbia, taught at the Brickyard School from January 1944 until the following May. Her mother, Ida, had played with the Ball children at Middleburg Plantation in the latter part of the 19th century and benefited from the teacher who gave them private instruction.

Jeanes Schools helped students prepare for industrial jobs — making clothes and furniture, canning fruit and vegetables and farming — because college was not an option for many students. Jeanes teachers convinced the white community that the labor pool would have more qualified black workers if they were educated.

Helen Bess Brown also taught at the Brickyard School. Because Session lived in Moncks Corner, she would spend the workweek with Brown and her husband, Willie, a longshoreman in Charleston. Helen Brown was a graduate of Morris College in Sumter.

On school days, Session and Brown arrived early to prepare pots of vegetable soup on the wood-burning stove for about 60 students in first through ninth grades. Students' parents donated the vegetables. With money from the county, the teachers bought rice and bread from Henry Lee Johnson's store.

In addition to being the cooks and school nurses, Brown and Session gathered wood for the stove that warmed the classroom. At the end of the day, they cleaned the school.

White children attended a nearby one-room brick school, and by 1916 the county opened an elementary school for them. After completing the sixth grade, white students were provided with free room and board at a dormitory at Berkeley High School in Moncks Corner.

Berkeley High was established in 1912 with 11 students and one teacher. A decade later the school was accredited. By then it had grown to include dormitories for girls and boys who traveled to Moncks Corner over mostly dirt roads.

In contrast, black families bore the cost of sending their children to

Moncks Corner to attend Berkeley County Training School. Because there were no boarding houses for black children, they lived with friends or relatives.

After Session left the Brickyard School, she taught briefly at the Alston School in Summerville, one of the first institutions for black students in Dorchester County. She later moved to the upper part of South Carolina and took a job as a substitute teacher in Spartanburg at Carver High and Cross Anchor Elementary schools.

When her parents' health began to decline in 1946, she returned to the Lowcountry to teach science and math at Berkeley County Training High. Six years later, she was hired to supervise the Jeanes schools.

The condition of buildings and the availability of classroom materials varied widely at the Jeanes schools in Berkeley County when Session became supervisor. Some classes were held in barns with dirt floors. Others were in space provided by churches or in private homes. Most had no running water.

Few classrooms had blackboards. Students shared crayons, pencils and used textbooks. Meals consisted of government-supplied cheese, powdered milk, canned vegetables and flour, supplemented with the food grown by the students' families.

Despite these disparities, pupils and teachers found ways to cope while they hoped for change. Session often struggled to contain her anger and hatred toward the local and national governments for permitting such poor conditions in black schools. She also was upset that black people did not vote en masse to push for change.

Session's work went beyond the classroom. When timber cutting slowed because of excessive rain, Session co-signed loans for workers who needed money to feed their families and keep their children in school. William "Duley" Martin, president of the South Carolina National Bank in Moncks Corner, approved the loans, which ranged from $100 to $600. Many families in Huger owed money for food they bought from Johnson's store. When the men returned to work in the forests, they repaid the loans. No worker who received a loan with Session's help let her down.

Florence Jessie Dickerson of Huger (left lower row) is surrounded by three generations of her family. Her daughter, Vernelle Dickerson, Vernelle's daughter, Crystal Aisha, and Crystal's son, Zachery. Photo courtesy of Florence Dickerson.

The Jeanes Fund supported the Shingler School in the Yellow House community near Wando. The Rev. Benjamin Dennis and Albertha Jenkins attended the school that once stood along Clements Ferry Road near New Mary Ann Baptist Church that locals call "Anna Baptist Church."

Like most schools of its day, Shingler was in session three days a week. The teacher arrived at St. Thomas Island by boat on Monday evenings and left on Friday mornings, Dennis recalled. His father donated money he made from his boat service to and from the Charleston Neck to help establish the school, which most likely took its name from the nearby Shingler Plantation.

Benjamin Dennis left the island in 1938 to live with his aunt in Charleston to attend Buist School on Calhoun Street. His classes were held in a wooden building the children called the "chicken coop." During the five years at Buist, Dennis worked after school at Peter Pavalatos' grocery store at Calhoun and Alexander streets delivering groceries on his bicycle in the Ansonborough neighborhood. The store's unkempt condition earned it the nickname "Nasty Pete."

Lela Haynes Session speaks at the Keith School Museum dedication on November 9, 2007. Photo by Herb Frazier.

Benjamin worked alongside Pavalatos' son Jerry. They often did not get along. Being a little older and taller than Benjamin, Jerry tried to take advantage of him. One day Jerry threw a rotten tomato that smacked Benjamin in the face. "I snatched him off he bicycle, and I put a wearing out on him." That brought an abrupt end to Benjamin's time at Buist, Nasty Pete and Charleston.

"My aunt had to get a taxicab and bring me out of Charleston 'fore day clean (sunrise)," he said. The cab took him to the Etiwan fertilizer plant where his father worked in the Charleston Neck. He spent the night at the home of the plant's gatekeeper, Mr. Frost. Benjamin's father operated a boat that brought workers to the plant from St. Thomas Island. When his father's boat arrived that morning, he boarded and spent the day on it before returning to the island with his father. Benjamin later went to night school at Cainhoy High to complete the 11th grade.

Albertha Jenkins is one of 18 children born to Henry Jenkins and Florence Vanderhorst Jenkins. On the family's farm in the Yellow House community the children had to work, which accounts for Jenkins not having fond memories of the Shingler School. For her, school wasn't a place for learning. It was a place to work. She attended the school for several years, beginning in 1938 before she dropped out in the eighth grade, pregnant with her eldest daughter, Rosemary.

Jenkins lamented that instead of studying in the classroom she spent more time outside with the boys in the woods gathering firewood. She said her teacher insisted that she help gather the wood. The teacher taught only some of the children. "I wasn't learning nothing."

She told her mother that her time was divided between the classroom and the woods. But Jenkins' mother didn't believe her. By the time she was 18, she had a second child, Gloria.

After dropping out of school, Jenkins moved to Charleston and worked as a cook and house-cleaner. She later answered an ad for a sleep-in caretaker and was offered a position in New York

Edna Keith Goodman speaks at the Keith School Museum dedication. Photo by Herb Frazier.

City. She left her children briefly with relatives and promised to send for them once she got settled. She worked as a nursing assistant at the Jewish Nursing Home in the Bronx. She was reunited with her children. One of her nieces later joined them.

"When I went to New York I prayed to the Lord to bring me through. I didn't have the education, but I wanted my kids to get what I didn't get." And they did. Jenkins worked and saved for the next 25 years to put her daughters and niece through college.

Rosemary Jenkins-Varela earned a master's degree in business and is now a manager with the Port Authority of New York and New Jersey. Gloria Jenkins, who received an associate degree in business administration, is now the Huger postmaster. Jenkins' niece, Sadie Jenkins, used the bachelor's degree she earned in education to become an elementary school teacher at Chicora Elementary School in North Charleston.

The Wando area school for black children was named for Edward B. Keith Sr., who was born at Wando on September 16, 1881. The tall, soft-

Jacob Morgan stands in front of the original Keith School building in the early 1980s. By the late 1980s the building had become weakened by time. Hurricane Hugo in September 1989 destroyed it. Photo courtesy of Jacob Morgan.

spoken Keith was a carpenter. The tools of his trade were carried in a wooden toolbox that hung from his shoulder by a leather strap.

He worked primarily for Charlestonians who lived in the grand houses along the Battery. In addition he and his wife, Rebecca Brown Keith, managed their large farm on Rivers Reach Road. They sold their produce at the farmer's market in Charleston. The Keiths were never late for the market because Rebecca could tell time hourly by the sun's position.

The Keiths had nine children, eight of them boys: Edward Jr., Sam, George, Isaiah Ralph, Calvin Allen, Joseph Alonza, John, William Thomas and daughter Margaret.

In later years Keith's grandson Sam Keith traveled on the ferry to the city with his grandfather. Keith held his grandson's hand as they walked along King Street.

Leroy Keith (left) stands in front of the Keith School Museum with his sister, Mary Keith, their brother, Calvin Keith, and Calvin Keith's wife, Pastor Rose Keith. D.R. Horton, the builders of the Peninsula subdivision, in 2006 constructed the Keith School Museum a few yards behind the original school's brick foundation. Friends of the Keith School hope the museum will be used for community gatherings. Photo by Herb Frazier.

"Granddaddy walked head held high. He walked like he was proud. He would tip his hat to folks," Sam Keith recalled.

In the mid-1920s, Edward Keith Sr. donated the land for a school and every family in the Cainhoy-Wando vicinity took part in the building's construction. Marie Fordham, Isaiah Brown and Harold Lincoln were among those who helped. The new school was named after Keith.

Before the Keith School opened in 1926, children in Jack Primus walked 10 miles to a schoolhouse near the intersection of Cainhoy and Clements Ferry roads in an area called "The Hill," not far from Marie Fordham's house. She had been principal of the first school on that site and later headed up the Keith School.

Although the Keith School was closer to Jack Primus, the walk to school on cold winter mornings was tough. Fires were lit in steel drums stationed along Clements Ferry Road so children could warm their hands as they traveled.

After the students completed the sixth grade at the Keith School, they were taken in a county-provided bus to the Charity Church School in the Huger community.

Keith's granddaughter, Edna Keith Goodman, remembered her grandfather. "Papa was a man with a vision. He saw a need in this community for a school. The thought of children walking in the cold and rain was troubling to him. He was determined that a neighborhood school would afford them a better chance for a future. 'Education is the path. Go to school and get an education.' Those were his words."

Two rooms were added to the school in 1943. The following year, Goodman entered the school. She was a five-year-old first-grader. "I was so excited. Finally I would learn about those far-away places Papa had so often told me about and read the books we looked through that were in a big trunk that my daddy had in the house."

The Keiths provided room, board and transportation for the teachers, who came to Cainhoy in a rowboat from Charleston. Sam Keith, Goodman's brother, remembers the teachers. "I remember Mrs. Marie (Fordham), Mrs. Turner, Mrs. Logan and Mrs. Qualls. Mrs. Marie taught every one of us, including our daddy. They were old-school teachers, firm, and would smack us on the knuckles if we acted up. Mrs. Marie was a small woman with an impediment in her leg. Mrs. Turner was a large woman with a stiff leg, injured in a car accident."

Early in the morning a group of boys arrived at the school to light a fire in the wood-burning stove. The oil lamps were also lit and classes began. Part of the process was for younger students to observe what the older ones did.

"If they were using the blackboard to do math, we watched and learned," Goodman said. "We learned so much more by listening to other classes. The teachers let us know this was a place of learning, and they made sure we got the benefits of their educations."

When it was time for a restroom break, students followed a footpath through the grass behind the school to the outhouse. For Sam Keith, it seemed like a long way to get there, especially when nature was calling. "Sometimes, I wasn't able to make it."

Mary Keith, Sam Keith's sister, also remembers the older children "leaving you in their dust in the mad dash to the outhouse. I also remember the cooks who prepared the lunches. On our breaks, we would go next door and buy cookies from Mrs. Mabell."

Rebecca Keith was 62 when she died on Christmas Eve 1944. Five years later, Edward Keith Sr. died at age 67. They are buried in the Nelliefield Cemetery. The school remained open for about 30 years until the county built Cainhoy Elementary and High schools in 1956, two years after the U.S. Supreme Court ruled against public funding of segregated schools.

Mary Keith entered the Keith School as a first-grader in 1956 and transferred to the Cainhoy school when it opened later that year. It was one of many public schools built with money collected through a new three-cents sales tax in South Carolina. The tax was proposed years earlier. In his 1951 inaugural address, Gov. James F. Byrnes called for the tax to provide "substantial equality" of the state's segregated school system.

Willie Rembert was the first Cainhoy High School principal. Nathaniel Anderson was the first principal of the elementary school.[11]

Dora Bolden arrived at the new elementary school in 1956 as a fourth-grade transfer student from Shingler. Today, Dora Bolden Howard of Huger is a counselor at the Cainhoy campus. She remembers Anderson as quiet and self-assured. "I never heard him raise his voice," she said.

Principal Anderson moved along the halls with a smile, acknowledging not only the teachers but the students, too. "It didn't matter how many times you'd pass him during the day he'd always ask: 'What you're

11 In the fall of 1996 the students at Cainhoy High School were bused out of the community to Hanahan High School or the newly built Timberland High School north of Moncks Corner. That same year, the old Cainhoy elementary/high school building was converted into the Cainhoy Elementary/Middle School.

doing? Doing all right?' " Howard recalled. "That let you know you were important to him."

Anderson, who lived in Cainhoy, had an air that he was financially well off, but if he had money, he didn't flaunt it, Howard said. Students wondered: Was he married? Because he had a fair complexion, they also wondered about his race. Anderson's life remains a mystery even today for former students and Cainhoy residents alike.

The Big Leagues

At least two students who attended Cainhoy peninsula schools became professional athletes and one worked as an accountant for a major league baseball organization.

Robert Porcher III and Luther Rashard Broughton Jr., both graduates of Cainhoy High School, played in the National Football League. Emma Jule Gadsden Williams, who was a wiz with numbers, landed a job in the front office of the New York Yankees baseball team.

Porcher, a Wando native and a 1987 Cainhoy High School graduate, was a defensive lineman at South Carolina State University in Orangeburg before joining the Detroit Lions of the National Football League. He was a first-round draft pick in 1992 and played defensive end for the team for 12 seasons.

Porcher led the Lions in sacks for eight years and played in the Pro Bowl three times. He won numerous service awards in Detroit, including "Father of the Year" in 2000. Porcher now owns three businesses in downtown Detroit.

He also provided uniforms for the Cainhoy High School marching band in 1993 at the request of his mother, Marilyn Porcher. His father is Robert Porcher II.

Luther Rashard Broughton Jr. of Huger also played in the NFL. He was a 1992 honor graduate and class salutatorian at Cainhoy High, where he played basketball and football. Broughton received a full athletic scholarship to Furman University and played tight end. He graduated in May 1997 and in 2003 was inducted into the Furman Hall of Fame.

Broughton was drafted by the Philadelphia Eagles but didn't play much because of injuries. The Carolina Panthers hired him in December 1997. He was traded back to the Eagles for a year before returning to Carolina. He played for the Chicago Bears and Green Bay Packers before retiring in 2003. Broughton is the oldest son of Luther and Inez S. Broughton of Huger.

Emma Jule Gadsden Williams left her home in the Steed Creek Road area of Huger in the mid-1950s to be a nanny in Moncks Corner for Berkeley Training School principal Switson Wigfall. She also attended classes there and graduated in 1956. Lela Haynes Session made the move possible, placing Williams on the path of becoming an accountant.

Williams attended Allen University in Columbia and in 1957 moved to live with her aunt in New York City, where she attended Bronx Community College. She worked as an accountant with Lord & Taylor clothing store, Diners Club and CBS Television. She joined the Yankees front office after CBS chairman William Paley bought the franchise.

In the early 1970s, Williams returned to the Lowcountry and married Peter Williams. For a short time she worked at the CBS-affiliate WCSC-TV in Charleston before joining the College of Charleston's comptroller's office, where she worked for the next 26 years.

Williams is director of the East Cooper Interdenominational Mass Choir Scholarship Fund. Since its inception in 1984, the fund has given more than $150,000 in scholarships to students at Lincoln High School in McClellanville and Wando High School in Mount Pleasant. Scholarships also have been awarded to students in the Huger-Wando area who attended Bishop England High School on Daniel Island, Hanahan High School and Timberland High School in St. Stephen.

The old Wando post office in the new village of Cainhoy. Painting by John W. Jones.

Meeting Creek, which divides the village of Cainhoy, is flooded at high tide. Painting by John W. Jones.

Chapter 11: Remembering Old Cainhoy

Cainhoy is split by what was called Bridge Creek in the mid-1850s and is known as Meeting Creek today. When the tide is low the creek snakes through the marsh like a narrow muddy ditch. To the west is the old village; to the east is the new. Whites have their own stories to tell about Cainhoy.

Before Beverly Avinger Lahmeyer was born in 1943, families on either side of the marsh built, and later tore down, a narrow footbridge across the creek where it empties into the Wando River. Beverly's mother told her the bridge was demolished in reaction to an embarrassing incident that had festered for years.

"I can't tell you the story," Beverly said in a stubborn tone.

"Why not?"

"Because you'll put it in the book, and you can't do that," she said.

"That's what I need. A juicy story!"

"I can't tell you this juicy story," she laughed as we sat in the living room of her home that fronts the Wando in the old village.

If she's not going to tell that tale, she has plenty of others to share. She's one of a few who knows the history of Cainhoy's old houses, stores, boatyard and ferry landing, especially the nine buildings in Cainhoy that by 1982 were placed on the National Register of Historic Places. With that designation, the structures are considered worthy of preservation, but some have burned, deteriorated or been demolished. As a child, Beverly lived in one of Cainhoy's most historic houses.

But before she tells the story of Cainhoy, she has a tale to tell about her family, whose roots here date back to 1927. Beverly's grandfather Ernest Christopher Avinger Sr., a Charleston native, moved to the village from O'Hare Point on the Wando just east of Cainhoy. Before that, he lived on Daniel Island. After settling in the old village, Avinger operated a store and brokered the sale of Daniel Island vegetables. He was a classical pianist who studied at the Academy of Music in a massive building that once stood at King and Market streets across from today's Charleston Place Hotel. Prior to moving to Daniel Island, Avinger worked at a music house on King Street where he played sheet music for customers who wanted to hear a composition performed.

Beverly's grandmother, Eloise Goutevenier Avinger, was an 1897 graduate of the Memminger School in Charleston. She studied French and Italian and spoke both fluently. She also enjoyed reading Shakespeare for small groups that gathered in the living rooms of private homes. Beverly does not know how her grandparents met except that it wasn't in church. Eloise was a devout Catholic; Ernest was Lutheran.

Because Eloise was a Memminger grad, Cainhoy's leaders recruited her to teach at the community's one-room school house for white children. Eloise walked to school from the old village along a route that took her across the footbridge and Meeting Creek. Ernest was a school trustee. Eloise also briefly served as Wando's postmaster.

The Avingers had five children. Ernest C. Avinger Jr., born in Charleston in 1904, is the eldest. He is Beverly's father. He married Florence White, one of nine children from Awendaw. Florence's mother died when she was small. Her death split the family apart. As a result, Florence was passed from one relative to the next; from one community to the next; Awendaw to McClellanville to Cordesville. The instability frightened her; she longed for security, and she found it in Ernest, whom she wed when she was 16. When they were married in 1930, he was 10 years her senior. He had a gun, a horse and a dog. His father had a store, and his mother was a school teacher. With useful possessions and parents with influence, Ernest seemed likely to provide well for her.

When the Avingers were married, Cainhoy, like elsewhere, was in the grips of the Depression. "Black and white people around here were depressed for a long time," Beverly said. The isolation brought everyone closer. Still Cainhoy had its share of separation along the color line. Churches and schools were not integrated and the line boat to Charleston had segregated seating. Despite this, people in the country depended on one another. They even came together to make moonshine.

During the Depression the Cainhoy peninsula seemed more isolated than ever. Many residents had moved away. Older people with homes in Cainhoy also lived in Charleston, returning on weekends and holidays. It was difficult for Florence to have friends her age in isolated Cainhoy. She found her solace in Hattie Fishburne, a black woman who lived in Jack Primus with her husband, Richmond, and a dozen children. Florence hired Hattie to help clean the house and do the ironing. They'd both work a little then stop for lunch and talk. They talked more than they worked. They shared stories about their husbands and children. They became friends.

Beverly has always been curious about her mother's relationship with Hattie because Florence feared most black people. Florence's feelings on racial issues contrasted with her husband's acceptance of people regardless of their skin color. People in the community called Ernest "Happy." His wife sometimes called him "Ernst." Ernest's pragmatic attitude toward race surfaced at a potentially dangerous moment. One night he came upon a cross burning in the woods. Even though the Klansmen around the blazing cross were hooded, Ernest recognized some of them by their shoes. He called them out by name, telling them that what they were doing was wrong and they should go home. When he told Florence what happened, she feared for his safety. But there was no retaliation against him.

Beverly and her neighbor MaeRe Chandler Skinner belong to the Berkeley County Historical Society. Its members had suggested that Beverly and MaeRe give the group a tour of Cainhoy. Beverly said that it would be a good idea if there were something left to tour. Some of Cainhoy's most important architectural gems, including the historic house she once lived in with her parents and siblings, are gone.

Nevertheless, she graciously agreed to give a tour of the area. The first stop just beyond her driveway on Cainhoy Village Road was the spot where the Beresford Bounty House once stood at a bluff along the Wando. Beverly and her family lived in the house, an imposing three-story structure. Built in the mid-1800s with money from Richard Beresford's estate, it also served as a school for poor children and a rectory for the Episcopal Church.

Beverly said the dusty, unused sanctuary at one end of the house was once a special place. Its past elegance was reflected in the sanctuary's crushed-velvet seat cushions and stained-glass windows. An old mulberry tree that in 1939 was estimated to be 250 years old was just outside of the chapel.

The Avingers lived on the first two floors. Their landlord was millionaire Harry Frank Guggenheim. He hired Beverly's uncle George Avinger in the 1950s to demolish the massive house. Today, the lot is covered with trees.

When the Avingers moved from the Beresford House, they did not travel far. Avinger bought his mother's house near the river. He was a mathematician and inventor. The backyard was his workshop, where he built shrimp boats and repaired the family-owned *Viking*, a line boat that took people to Charleston. His boat-building apprentices were young men, black and white. Avinger designed and built a gasoline engine. He also invented and received a patent for a device to cut pine logs into shorter sections so they could be hoisted onto a truck.

The Avingers' two-story house, which sat on tall piers, had a front-side piazza. When the family sold the house, the new owners tore it down. Another family who bought the lot is building a larger, more modern frame house. "Look at what they are building," Beverly said with surprise. "Oh, my God! A house with two porches!"

When she was a child, the land across the road from the house was a storage yard for freshly cut pine. It was also Beverly's playground. She climbed on the sap-oozing logs stacked straight and high like rows of library books. The sticky sap dripped into her straight blond hair. It clung so tightly her mother had to cut out lengths of the matted mess.

An old dwelling just to the east of Beverley's home is the Miss Mary Lesesne House, one of the nine Cainhoy structures on the National Register. The two-story frame house is believed to have been built around 1790. During the Civil War, the house was used as a makeshift hospital. Some folks say the house is haunted. The current owner's daughter told Beverley that an upstairs window must be nailed shut. Otherwise, it won't stay closed.

The Mary Lesesne House in Cainhoy is on the list of historic properties. Photo by Herb Frazier.

Away from the river, Cainhoy Village Road ends at busy Clements Ferry Road. Just east is a lane probably named for Lewis Fogartie, the founder of the village. The spelling of this lane, however, is "Fogarty." Not far down Fogarty Lane is Fiddler Crab Lane, and just across from it is an open area that once was a pecan tree grove that extended to Meeting Creek. Beverly's great-aunt Carrie Murphy owned the grove. She'd recruit children to gather the nuts that she sold. She gave them pecans.

When Beverly was a child, Fogarty Lane was called Village Road. Back then it wasn't paved. The long tree branches that reach out over the lane have always kept it in dense shade. Saint Peters AME Church is on the high ground across from the old pecan grove, and it is the only church left in the village. Saint Peters is home to an African-American congregation organized on April 12, 1886. The original church was made of wood. The present white block building was completed in 1976. It took the small congregation at least a decade to raise the money for the new building.

In a May 1967 letter the church's pastor, the Rev. James Deveaux, asked Harry Frank Guggenheim for a contribution to the building fund. Gug-

Saint Peters AME Church is the only church remaining in the village of Cainhoy. Photo by Herb Frazier.

genheim had donated money to other local churches, including money for repairs and upkeep of St. Thomas Church on his Cain Hoy Plantation. In 1953 he also contributed $50 to the Greater St. John AME Church in Jack Primus, where his former employee Harold Lincoln still worships. In return for his generosity, the Greater St. John's pastor, the Rev. S.L. Boston, and the congregation prayed that Guggenheim would have a place in heaven after he passed away.

But the Saint Peter's request was denied. George J. Fountaine, Guggenheim's secretary, wrote on June 13, 1967: "Mr. Guggenheim has, for many years, given extensive support to St. Thomas Church; and he also feels that some of the colored people in the vicinity are so badly in need of church support that it is not possible for him to give support to all. He therefore regrets that he cannot be of assistance to you at this time."

About the same time, the white congregation at Wando Baptist Church also asked Guggenheim for money to build a new church. Their request also was denied.

The month after Saint Peter's was established, the founding members paid $18 to buy a quarter-acre from Ludwig Mayer, a mixed-race man who operated the village store and blacksmith shop near the church. Mayer also may have once served as the Wando postmaster. (A list of postmasters includes "Lutewick C. Mayer" as Wando's postmaster for nearly four years, beginning on October 18, 1910. See Appendix II)

Mayer's two-story store and blacksmith shop are listed on the National Register of Historic Places, although the building no longer stands. It is identified on the Register as the "Village Store-Blacksmith Shop," built around 1875. The commercial activity took place downstairs, and upstairs was a residence. When it was placed on the Register in the early 1980s, it was empty and in poor condition. Prior to the 1950s the village had another church in addition to Saint Peters. On the old village side of Meeting Creek, a few white families — the Coxes, Murphys, Villeponteauxs and Smoaks — worshipped at Wando Methodist Church. Services were held one Sunday a month and Sunday school weekly. Before the S.C. Highway 41 bridge was built, a church member with a rowboat brought the Rev. Mr. Betts to the village from the Mount Pleasant side of the Wando.

John Samuel Sanders III is standing in a driveway along Fogarty Lane. Sanders is the son of the late John Sanders, a longtime Cainhoy resident. The younger Sanders, nicknamed Sammy, owns four of the historic buildings on the National Register at the end of the lane: the Village Store, the Lewis Fogartie House, the Sanders House and the John R. Sanders House.

Next to the site of Mayer's store and blacksmith shop is the Village Store. The one-story building was built around 1905. It is not in use now but still stands adjacent to the Lewis Fogartie House. The village's founder built the two-story house around 1798, according to the registry. But Sammy said his father told him the house was built in 1792.

The ground floor of the Fogartie House was open to store carriages. Today the bottom floor is enclosed. It is a weatherboard building with a double-tiered porch on the south side facing the river. A separate kitchen building once stood next to the house, Sammy said. A covered walkway once connected the main house with the kitchen. The canopy was designed to be flimsy, so in case of fire it could be pulled down quickly to save the house.

Next to the Fogartie House, near the river, is the George R. Sanders House. The one-story weatherboard dwelling was built around 1866 and is typical of pineland village summer houses. It is set on high brick piers with a porch across the front. Sammy, a retired contractor, is renovating it.

The Village Store and Blacksmith Shop was a historic property in Cainhoy. Photo courtesy of the National Register of Historic Places.

Across the road from the George R. Sanders House was a small bakery that burned in the 1920s, Sammy estimates. As the story goes, the wind carried a spark from the bakery fire to the Fogartie House, igniting a sofa on the porch. That fire was put out, but the bakery was lost. In those days, Cainhoy didn't have a fire department.

Adjacent to the site of the bakery is the Sanders House, built in the late 19th century. Sammy said his ancestors built the Sanders House and the John R. Sanders House. The original Sanders House was a one-story frame dwelling on brick piers with a porch facing the river. Sammy, who now lives in the house, has modernized and expanded it.

The Humphrey House once stood just west of the Sanders House. It, too, was placed on the National Register, but the one-story frame house is gone.

The other buildings on the National Register that front Fogarty Lane are the Ward House and the old Wando Post Office. The Ward House was built around 1890. The original house had a shallow porch in the center with a five-bay facade that contained three doors with transoms.

The Lewis Fogartie House in Cainhoy has survived the centuries. Photo provided by the National Register of Historic Places.

Josie Worsham Smoak was born in the house on May 15, 1929, and lives there today with her husband, Thomas Smoak, a retired Cainhoy constable and magistrate. They met at Berkeley High School, where she lived in the boarding house for students. Soon after they were married on November 7, 1946, they moved to Cainhoy.

Worsham's mother, Daisy Legare Chandler Worsham, was Cainhoy's postmaster for 36 years before she retired in 1950. Josie Smoak followed her mother as postmaster and held the position for 34 years. Thomas Smoak, skilled in a variety of construction trades, built the post office in 1973. The tiny building that fronts Fogarty Lane is now a storage shed.[12]

Near the old post office, a road leads to the Charleston City Boatyard, the site of Murphy's Shipyard and How Tavern, a pre-Revolutionary War pub built around 1745. At the boatyard, a set of tracks extended to the water to launch boats into the Wando. Robert How established a ferry at Cainhoy around 1731.

The How Tavern and ferry formed the nucleus of the village. By the

---

12 See Appendix II: Wando-Huger post offices.

1760s the ferry was operated by Joseph Fogartie, who also brokered the shipment of various goods from Cainhoy. The Cainhoy ferry was at Fogartie's Landing. The ferry operation probably ended in the early part of the 20th century.

At the rear of the lot, Carrie Murphy lived in the one-and-a-half story tavern, which burned after it was placed on the register of historic properties. It once stood on short brick piers and the tavern was built on a frame made from heavy timber. The building had been altered substantially with the addition of two wings and large chimneys at each end.

Beverly said that as a child she'd rush upstairs there to see her great-aunt in her bedroom after she had become old and frail. Murphy told her how as a young woman she had wanted to study art in Paris, but her father wouldn't let her. Murphy was in her 90s when she died. The tavern and boatyard were on the east bank of Meeting Creek, upstream from the footbridge. Beverly again declined to say why the bridge was torn down, but she does tell another story about Murphy.

To earn extra money, Murphy grew fragrant lavender violets, bound them in bunches, placed them in buckets of water and loaded them on the *Viking*. The boat took the flowers to downtown Charleston where they were sold to black women who hawked flowers at the historic Four Corners of Law at Meeting and Broad streets. In that location today, black women still sit in the shade of the granite post office as they weave and sell sweetgrass baskets.

The end of Fogarty Lane was the central shopping district for a wide area around the village. Proprietors of five stores there near the water sold a variety of goods brought to Cainhoy on the ferry. As a boy, Sammy watched a man in one of the stores sit on a stool as he repaired cast nets that hung from the rafters. The lane was renamed in memory of Fogartie — albeit misspelled — after the 911 emergency telephone system was established. Just east of the Fogartie House was a cotton gin operated by Sammy's great-grandfather John Sanders.

A short distance west of the village is the intersection of where Cainhoy

174

Road ends at Clements Ferry Road. The intersection has a signal to control a stream of traffic that includes big trucks going and coming from the Nucor Steel and BP Amoco plants, which are located up Cainhoy Road. Near the crossroads where the Two Rivers Center now stands was Eugenia Broughton's clinic and George Avinger's store. Fronting the traffic signal at the crossroad is a towering oak that longtime residents call the Meeting Tree. Nearby is a short bridge on Clements Ferry that crosses the upper end of Meeting Creek.

A one-room school run by Beverly's grandmother once stood at the Clements Ferry and Cainhoy roads junction, which black people called "The Corner." Eloise Avinger taught first through sixth grades during the 1920s and 1930s in the school. It was for whites only.

But Eloise Avinger met monthly with Marie Fordham of the Keith School. They shared lesson plans and talked about their students. (Beverly's oldest brother, Ernest Avinger III, was one of them.) When students left Avinger's school, they usually went to the boarding high school in Moncks Corner. By the time Beverly reached school age, she was bused to Mount Pleasant Academy and Moultrie High School.

Eloise Avinger's husband, Ernest Avinger, was the superintendent of the school at The Corner. When he left the appointed position, he wanted his son Ernest Avinger Jr. to take his place. Young Ernest Avinger's wife, Florence, encouraged her husband to take that job and to oversee the all-black Keith School.

Ernest Avinger Jr. resisted, telling his wife he wasn't going to meddle in the affairs of the Keith School. Beverly remembers her father and mother arguing about it.

"Oh Ernst, you have to do this. This is your duty," Beverly's mother told Ernest.

"No. It has to be done by their own people," he said.

Several black families lived near The Corner: the Browns, the Bennetts, the Washingtons, the Smalls, the Fordhams and the Porchers.

Among them was Robert Porcher, whose house was near the Avinger school. Porcher was injured in the mid-1940s in an accident at the Charleston Navy Yard. Doctors amputated his left leg several months after a crane ran over his foot. Porcher didn't let his injury stop him from hunting squirrels in the woods around the McDowell Cemetery, named for the black man who was the caretaker in the early 1900s. Porcher lived at The Corner with his wife, Teresia Green Porcher, and their four children, Elizabeth, Gloria, Albertha and Robert Jr.

Porcher was admired for his ability to communicate with people of both races. He often sat in his brother Willie Porcher's store at The Corner and talked to customers throughout the day.

The Corner is still a place where people gather, particularly on Sundays after the service at Saint Peters AME Church. The Porcher family and their friends have been meeting at the home of the late Ella Carson Porcher for potluck dinners since the 1970s. Another Porcher family gathering began a decade before Ella Porcher died in December 2006. On her birth date in September, the family gathers for the "Big Cookout for Aunt Ella," a tradition that attracts relatives from other states.

It's an occasion where family members enjoy a meal, socialize and honor their ancestors. The children, especially, learn from the experience, said Robert Porcher Jr. The family discussions usually include the importance of getting a good education, marriage, raising children and devotion to Christ.

The McDowell Cemetery near The Corner is on the site of the Meeting House, or "Old Ruins," near Meeting Creek, about half a mile from the Wando River. Congregationalists built the Meeting House around 1700. Members were originally called Dissenters after they broke from the Church of England. The Dissenters were later assimilated into the Presbyterian Church.

The church, later called Bethel Presbyterian Church, was used during the Revolutionary War as a shelter for wounded American soldiers. By the late 1700s the church switched to the Methodist faith. The Meeting House was on a 10-acre tract that included an area for camp meetings. Only a few short brick pillars hidden in the tall grass are all that's left of the Meeting House.

The church has transferred the deed to a community group that has agreed to maintain the cemetery.

During the Revolutionary War, Gen. Francis Marion once traveled up the creek after stopping at How Tavern, Beverly said. The creek and the area surrounding it were dotted with artesian springs. No doubt Native Americans drank from them, she said, and Beverly ought to know. She received a degree in anthropology in 1996 from the College of

Willie James Porcher, the eldest son of the late Ella Carson Porcher, helps with preparing the food during the "Big Cookout for Aunt Ella" on September 25, 2010. Photo by Herb Frazier.

Charleston. When she and her brother played in the woods around the Meeting House, they found arrowheads, pottery shards and musket balls.

The Meeting House ruins and McDowell Cemetery can't be seen from the highway, but vandals have found it. A section of the property is used to dump trash. "Sad, isn't it?" Beverly noted.

Beverly's mother told her stories of Cainhoy as they walked along Black Snake Road, a footpath between the old and new villages. It was the route Beverly took as a child because the footbridge over Meeting Creek had long since been torn down. During one of those walks, Beverly's mother motioned for her children to look at some Mason jars on a carpet of pine needles nearby, explaining that a moonshine still was probably operated there at one time.

The tour ends where it began, on Beverly's front porch, where she decides she would tell the footbridge story as long as the central character's identity remains secret.

As the story goes, a flirtatious man had angered every woman in the community by making inappropriate comments when he met them on the footbridge. No woman in the village went unnoticed. Most were too timid to complain because of the man's status in the village.

But when the man spoke his "sweetness" to Carrie Murphy, her husband, Tom Murphy, was within earshot. The man had his say as he was coming over the bridge on horseback while Carrie Murphy was bent over and tending to her violets. A furious Tom Murphy later knocked the bridge down. It did not quiet the man's flirtatious tongue from wagging. In the years to come, women in the village either accepted it or they avoided him, Beverly explained.

Sometime after Tom Murphy demolished the bridge, the man flirted with Beverly's mother, Florence, who warned him that if he did it again she would tell her husband. Soon, people on both sides of Meeting Creek knew that Florence was steaming.

"My mom was like a Yankee the way she would tell people right out," Beverly said. "I never met anyone who was that direct."

S.C. 41 Bridge Dedication

On July 26, 1939, the S.C. Highway 41 bridge over the Wando River connected Cainhoy in Berkeley County with the Phillips Community, an African-American neighborhood on the Charleston County side of the river. The opening ceremony began when two motorcades, one from Charleston and the other from Moncks Corner, met at the center of the span. Police cars with blaring sirens escorted each parade.

The new bridge opened up a quicker route from Charleston to Wando, Cainhoy and the areas beyond the Francis Marion Forest.

Two young women, one from Charleston County and another from Berkeley County, served as "sponsors" among the long list of elected officials and business and community leaders at the ceremony.

Carolyn Avinger of Cainhoy, Beverly Avinger Lahmeyer's aunt, was the

Completed in 1939, the S.C. Highway 41 bridge opened up a quicker route from Charleston to Wando, Cainhoy and the areas beyond the Francis Marion Forest. Post and Courier photo.

Berkeley County sponsor. Carolyn, who cut the ribbon to open the bridge, was a college-educated social worker who later served as a Red Cross director in London at the end of World War II.

After she returned home from the war, she got a job distributing blankets and other aid to poor families in Berkeley County. A black man named Jackson was hired to drive her around the county so she could make the distributions.

It was an important job, but Florence Avinger, Beverly's mother, wasn't impressed. Always the cynic, Florence Avinger asked why Carolyn distributed blankets during the summer. Carolyn laughed, saying it didn't matter what Florence thought, adding she and Jackson had jobs and were paid good money to help poor people.

Carolyn Avinger later married Paul E. Shelton and they lived at Folly Beach, where in the 1970s she served on the Town Council. She also was the founder and supervisor of the Homemakers Service in South Carolina. She died May 16, 1999.

The Rev. Benjamin Dennis holds a picture of his father, Benjamin Dennis, who operated a boat service that took workers from St. Thomas Island to the industrial plants in the Neck Area of Charleston. Rev. Dennis is flanked by his son, Benjamin Dennis (right) and his grandson, Benjamin Dennis IV. The Dennis men are outside Intercession Reformed Episcopal Church where Rev. Dennis is an associate pastor. Photo by Herb Frazier.

Chapter 12: Boats, Buses, Civil Rights

The Rev. Benjamin Dennis was born November 15, 1925. From the time he was a boy growing up on St. Thomas Island, his father, Bennie Dennis, piloted a 70-foot wooden boat that took men from the Cainhoy peninsula to their jobs at fertilizer and lumber mills in the Neck area of the Charleston peninsula.

Before sunrise, two Model-A flatbed trucks owned by Dennis brought men to a pier on St. Thomas Island at the end of Clements Ferry Road. One truck, driven by a man named Moultrie, who lived in Huger, carried passengers from there to the dock. Ulysses "Dutchie" Vanderhorst drove the truck from the Jack Primus community.

At one point Dennis had as many as 85 passengers on the round-trip boat ride Monday through Friday. Dennis was the blacksmith at the Etiwan Fertilizer plant. Because of his skills, he earned a top wage of $50 a week; more than three times that of a typical mill worker. In their thick Gullah accents, the mill workers pronounced Etiwan as "Eighty-one."

By the 1950s Bennie Dennis became ill and could no longer operate the boat. Jake Vanderhorst took charge of it while young Benjamin worked at the Navy Shipyard. But in the early 1960s a lovers' quarrel placed Benjamin in charge of the boat. As he begins to tell his story, a smile curls the corner of his mouth.

Benjamin dated Vanderhorst's daughter, but "after me and Jake's daughter fall out, he put me down, so I had to quit the Navy Yard to come and take the boat over."

Benjamin Dennis and Sol Rivers then worked together on the boat. Rivers was the pilot and Dennis maintained the 24-horsepower gasoline engine. Passengers paid $2.50 a week for the 30-minute ride each way. One of Dennis' regular riders and part-time crewmember was his first cousin, Henry Rivers, a supervisor at the Etiwan plant.

Dennis worked in Eitwan's bag assembly room where burlap bags were sewn and printed with the company's name. Different-sized bags held 100 pounds and 200 pounds of fertilizer, which consisted of fishmeal, cottonseed meal, limestone and potash. He was paid 60 cents an hour to make the bags. Workers who made the fertilizer got 25 to 30 cents an hour. The plant was in full production from January through April. When work slowed, only a few employees remained on the payroll. "God blessed me. I was never laid off. But a black man never made much money until after (the Rev. Martin Luther) King came along. In the early '70s the wages started going up."

Not all workers in the dusty dangerous Etiwan plant were men. Women also pushed hand trucks loaded with fertilizer and assembled bags in the sewing room. The workday started at 7:30 a.m. and ended when all of the fertilizer orders were filled. "There was no such thing as a special hour to knock off. You worked until the work was done." If the shift ended at 9 o'clock, the boat returned to St. Thomas Island in the dark.

Dennis quit the plant in the mid-1960s after the new management told him to leave the sewing room for the dusty production area. He got a job at the Virginia Chemical Plant, a fertilizer mill on the Ashley River side of the Neck area. He was paid a dime more an hour to make bags.

By the 1940s workers on the Cainhoy peninsula opted to ride a bus to work. Jerry Fordham had switched his boat operation to a bus service after the state highway department built the S.C. 41 bridge over the Wando River.

Dennis couldn't compete with Fordham's bus service so he eventually closed the business. He continued to travel by water to his job at the V.C. plant. He bought a boat with an outboard motor, and his cousin Herbert

The *Viking* was one of the line boats that ferried passengers between Cain-hoy and Charleston. Photo courtesy of Beverly Avinger Lahmeyer.

Jenkins rode with him. The river was still the best way to travel because the workday at the mill ended at odd hours. Fordham's bus ran on a set schedule.

After tying up at the Etiwan plant, Dennis and Jenkins would pay 10 cents for a trolley-car ride up Meeting Street Road to the V.C. plant. If they were lucky, they'd hop on a northbound freight train. One morning a slow-moving train presented a chance for a free ride to work. Soon after they jumped aboard, however, the train sped up. It stopped in Moncks Corner, 45 miles away!

"It was one of those days I didn't have a dime in my pocket," Dennis recalled with a chuckle. "We had to walk the track all the way back."

The V.C. plant closed in January 1977, sending Dennis to the unemployment line. He went to the food stamp office in Moncks Corner to apply for benefits. A friend told him he wouldn't get aid because he wouldn't lie.

"Mr. Dennis, you own your own home?" the clerk asked.

"Yes."

"How many vehicles you have?"

"Two."

"Do you own a boat?"

"Yeah."

"How much you'd say your boat is worth?"

"About fifteen hundred."

The clerk paused, looked at him and said, "Mr. Dennis, there is no use for me to go any further with you. You got too much."

Dennis replied, "I need money because I don't have no payday coming and my money is gone."

"We are going to give you $60 worth of food stamps today but don't come back," the clerk said.

At 51 years old, it was tough for Dennis to find a job that paid as well as the $5 an hour he earned at the fertilizer mill.

"Let nobody fool you. They don't hire you when you are up in age," he said.

So Dennis decided to learn a new skill. He cleaned floors for a few months at the Charleston County Hospital during the day and at night he took a short course on janitorial work.

Soon afterward, Dennis and his son-in-law Joseph Grant launched the Grant Janitorial Service. Their first contract was with the Franklin C. Fetter Health Care Center on Meeting Street in Charleston. From there the client list grew to include the South Carolina Electric and Gas Co. and the Charleston Air Force Base. Their business also took them to North Carolina.

The money was good but Dennis' health was not. He had developed a heart problem as the stress of the business increased. He retired in 1985, which may have saved his life. His sister and a brother each died of heart attacks.

"My Daddy's Boat"

Starting in 1936 Rosena Virginia Fordham Moultrie lived with her maternal grandmother in Charleston to attend public schools. Her grandmother, Hester Kinlaw Williams, lived in a two-story beige-and-brown house next to the police station at St. Philip and Vanderhorst streets. Some weekends Virginia traveled on "my daddy's boat" to St. Thomas Island and spent the weekends with her parents and brothers at Yellow House, where her father, Jerry Fordham, was born and raised. Her mother, Lillie Jenkins Fordham, came from Daniel Island where Virginia was born on July 28, 1930, nine months after the stock market crash triggered the Great Depression.

Virginia was about five years old when she first saw her father piloting the *Viking*, which left Cainhoy with a stop at Daniel Island before passengers disembarked at Columbus Street in Charleston.

During the boat ride she read classic nursery rhymes between glances at her father. "It was exciting to see my dad running this boat, and I am on this boat and everything was cool!"

She didn't know then that everything wasn't cool with the boat's safety, or that the *Viking* wasn't her father's vessel. Decades later, she learned that he worked for the Avinger family, the boat belonged to them and it didn't have life vests on board. "It gives me goose bumps to think of it now," Virginia said.

In the late 1930s, Jerry Fordham started a boat service in competition with Benjamin Dennis. In 1939 after the S.C. 41 bridge was built over the Wando, Fordham closed his boat service and bought a bus to take workers from the Cainhoy peninsula to jobs at the fertilizer mills and the Navy Shipyard, where he worked as a rigger.

Fordham also helped other men from Jack Primus and Wando get work at the shipyard. By the mid-1950s, Fordham owned four passenger buses, and he hired his cousin Joe to drive one of them.

Churches chartered the buses for summertime excursions to Atlantic Beach near Myrtle Beach. Atlantic Beach was a popular gathering place for black people during the era of racial segregation. Fordham's buses also transported the Burke High School basketball team to away games, carried passengers south to Savannah, Georgia, for the Memorial Day weekend and took people to New York where local folk visited "home folk" in the big city.

In the Huger community, Willie Singleton also operated a bus service that took residents to Charleston.

Rosena Virginia Fordham – age 8. Photo courtesy of Rosena Virginia Fordham Moultrie.

After Fordham started the bus service in the early 1940s, the family moved from Yellow House to Wando. Next to the family's home on Cainhoy Road, about a half mile from "The Corner," Fordham ran a gas station and sweet shop. Inside, a jukebox or "piccolo" played 45-rpm records for a nickel.

"In the sweet shop we sold sodas, beer, cookies," Virginia said. The gas pump dispensed ten gallons of fuel at a time from a glass reservoir on top of the pump. "I

186

remember pumping gas into that big glass tube. Gas was 19 cents a gallon."

At night, Fordham and other men sneaked into the woods to do a business they couldn't carry on during the day. "Oh yeah, of course, he made moonshine," Virginia said.

Virginia never saw the still, but she knew her father's friends would station themselves along the road to watch for the highway patrol, also known as "wings." When a lookout yelled, "Wings over Jordan," everyone scattered like quail.

Virginia also recalled "private meetings" her father arranged at the family's home with two Civil Rights pioneers. Newspaper editor and publisher John McCray of Columbia and Johns Island activist Esau Jenkins came to Cainhoy to discuss local strategies to raise the number of registered black voters.

During the 1940s and 1950s, McCray was editor of The Lighthouse and Informer, South Carolina's largest black weekly.

Jenkins operated a bus service at the other end of Charleston County that brought schoolchildren and working adults from Johns Island to the city. During the daily commutes, Jenkins stressed to the adults the importance of voting and taught them to recite passages from the S.C. Constitution, which at that time was a requirement to vote in South Carolina. Jenkins ran other businesses too, including a record shop, fruit store and a motel/café in Charleston.

Virginia was most impressed with the tall, slender and well-educated McCray. For a young girl who had yet to travel far, she found him most impressive because he was a newspaper editor from the capital city.

From Virginia's teenage perspective in the late 1940s, black people knew their boundaries in a racially segregated Charleston, and black-owned businesses made life less stressful by providing everything their customers needed. "We were equally separated."

Henry Smith, an influential black businessman at the time, also visited the Fordham family at Cainhoy. Smith owned Safety Cab Company and an Esso gas station at Ashley Avenue and Fishburne Street. Smith helped other black people open businesses. They included Jerry Fordham, who bought Smith's station in the early 1950s. Smith then opened a Shell station at Coming and Cannon streets.

Virginia was the first-born and the only girl among the Fordhams' eight children. As such, she was pampered with clothes and shoes. Her father even bought her a $700 piano from Fox Music House on King Street and paid for her lessons. Fordham was well respected by whites and blacks, which meant Virginia could buy on credit at the stores on King Street.

Willie Singleton, Dorothy Scotts' uncle, operated a bus service from Huger that took workers to Charleston. Photo courtesy of Dorothy Scott.

Jerry Fordham dropped out of school in the fifth grade, but he wanted his children to get good educations. His sons Fred, Jerry Jr. and James attended Keith School. His younger sons John, Robert, Melvin and Jessie went to school in Charleston. Fordham encouraged his daughter to earn a college degree, become a teacher and work with his aunt-in-law Marie Fordham at the Keith School. Marie Fordham was married to Fordham's uncle Ben Fordham.

Virginia tried to follow her father wishes. She went to Allen University in Columbia but left after a year. Virginia wanted to be a secretary so she could help manage and build the family business along with her brothers.

So Fordham sent her to the Nashville School of Business in Tennessee. However, she took a secretarial position in the Charleston office of the North Carolina Mutual Life Insurance Company, the nation's oldest and largest black-owned insurance company.

Virginia met Jacob Moultrie in the early 1950s when the Moultrie family moved from Summerville to Charleston, where Jacob's father worked for the railroad. Jacob graduated from Burke High School in 1951. The next year he married Virginia, joined the Air Force and the couple left Charleston. They had three children. Jacob Moultrie retired after 26 years in the Air Force. Virginia Moultrie later ended a 30-year career with the Department of Defense. They currently live near Sacramento, California.

Cancer cut Jerry Fordham's life short. He was 48 when he died at a New York City hospital on Father's Day 1960, which also was Virginia's and Jacob's eighth wedding anniversary. Fordham is buried in the Greater St. John AME Church cemetery at Jack Primus.

Three of Fordham's sons also became entrepreneurs. Fred took over the bus business, Jerry operated a service station on Meeting Street in Charleston and James bought Henry Smith's cab company.

A line of Palmettos borders the high ground at the northern end of Daniel Island along Beresford Creek. Painting by John W. Jones.

Chapter 13: The Land

During the Depression years, many Blacks in this county continued to function well. As long as they had their land, they could farm and feed their families and survive.

— Dr. Lela Haynes Session, with Cynthia Hughes,
"Unconditional Love" (2004)

Rivers Reach Drive in Wando divides the six wooded acres Buster Brown inherited from his parents, Isaiah and Dora Venning Brown. The land is all that's left of the 13 acres Isaiah Brown farmed to feed a family of seven children squeezed into a two-room house. Buster Brown was born there on December 7, 1916.

"One (room) you cooked in and one you slept in," Brown explained. His mother cooked in the fireplace. Brown laughed when asked where the outhouse was located. "Didn't have an outhouse. Potties were dumped in the woods," he said. The family got an outhouse after two additional rooms, including a kitchen, were connected to the house. The outhouse was a fancy two-holer with wooden seats.

Brown's father worked at the Reed Phosphate Mill just north of the old Navy base. But when the seasonal job ended he returned to farming. Few jobs provided steady, year-round work. Buster Brown stood at the edge of his wooded property. He pointed to a depression in the earth where his father tended a small rice plot.

Isaiah Brown inherited the land from his mother, Martha Brown. Isaiah

Isaiah Brown's land was one of 13 tracts carved out of the Wilderness Plantation in May 1920. Plat courtesy of the Charleston County Register Mesne Conveyance.

Below: Buster Brown stands on the property he owns near Rivers Reach Road on the Cainhoy peninsula. Photo by Herb Frazier.

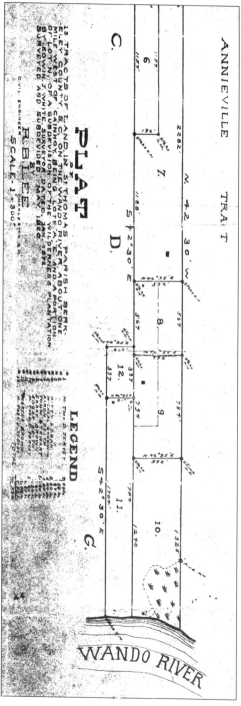

Brown's father was Comesee Brown. Before Isaiah Brown died in 1959 he sold about seven acres to relatives for a token amount. The remaining six acres, which Buster Brown now owns, is surrounded today by new subdivisions.

The pressure is on for him to sell it to developers. He has turned down all offers, fearful he won't get a fair price. "I've been doing all the holdin' for a long time, and I'm old. Now I can't go no more. The young members (of the family) have to pick up. I tell them I hold it for them so the white man won't get it."

Brown is a retired longshoreman who lives with his wife, Janie, on Alexander Street in Charleston. His nephew Jacob Morgan insisted that if the family sells part of the property, "I want the sale to be equitable. We don't want Uncle Buster and everybody who came before us to hold onto the land and then we turn around and give it away. My grandfather (Isaiah Brown) took land ownership for granted. It was understood the land would be passed to the children and always stay in the family."

The asking prices for lots in a subdivision near Brown's property start at $300,000 and increase to $800,000 closer to the Wando River, Morgan said. For Morgan, the land is more than a house spot. For him, it's the place of childhood memories.

In 1946 Morgan was a first-grader at the Keith School, named for his granduncle Edward Keith. The following year he went to schools in Charleston: Henry P. Archer, then A.B. Rhett, and later he graduated from Burke High. When summer recess arrived, he dashed back to Wando so his grandfather could show him "the old ways." Earl Johnson, Morgan's city pal since kindergarten, often tagged along. Both boys called Isaiah Brown "Grandpa.".

They helped Brown cut sugar cane, pick fruit from a grape arbor and collect pecans that fell from two trees. By the time Isaiah Brown was shadowed by his grandson he had stopped growing rice, but he told Morgan how he grew it. "They ate off the land," said a youthful-looking Morgan. "That's why I am so healthy today."

From his grandfather's porch, Morgan watched people head to the Wando for a religious ceremony seldom seen today. Some Sunday mornings, a black congregation from St. Paul Missionary Baptist Church filed along Rivers Reach Drive toward the Wando to baptize converts to Christianity. On the way they passed land owned by Cash Turner, John Stewart and Rebecca and Edward Keith. At the river, the baptismal candidates entered a small shack where they donned plain white ceremonial attire.

The baptismal site was at a place called "The Landing." It's where Morgan learned to swim and refine his skill of catching crabs with bait — usually a rancid chicken neck tied to the end of a string. In the river, men in rowboats hurled circular handmade nets in which they caught shrimp and fish. Horses and mules grazed on marsh grass and drank from an artesian spring.

Change isn't only marked by the modern houses at the edge of Brown's property. Change is as small as a brown beetle Morgan spotted trudging through the grass at the river's edge. It reminded him of an iridescent-green beetle commonly called a fingator. They were plentiful when he was young but now fingators are seldom seen since urban sprawl has gobbled up fields and pesticides have soaked the soil. Fingators aren't the only insects missing from Morgan's riverside playground. Lightning bugs and lady bugs are scarce, too. "There was once fruit here too along the river," he said. "Blackberries and raspberries. You don't see much of anything anymore."

Other elders in the community who want to pass inherited property to the next generation share Buster Brown's attitude about land ownership. They too have protected the land by paying the taxes and resisting offers to sell out.[13] Some of them, however, welcome change. They see it as an inevitable consequence of time.

Harold Lincoln predicted, "The whole place is going to be built up. Time brings changes, you know. I welcome the change because I sure don't want to go back to where I come from." He welcomes the change, however, as long as his family can retain its land.

One man's decision decades ago not to sell his land may have saved Jack

---

13 See Appendix III: How Land was Lost.

Primus, Lincoln recalled. "Guggenheim had wanted to buy this same section here, and he would have moved us out someplace else," Lincoln said with assurance. "But old Billy Vanderhorst said no, he is not going to sell his place. If he had done that there might have been no Jack Primus. I don't want that to happen. That's why I try to tell all the young people today to hold onto your property because once you sell

Jacob Morgan looks among the marsh grasses along the Wando River at the end of Rivers Reach Road. Photo by Herb Frazier

your property to the white man you can't get it back."

At the other end of Clements Ferry Road toward Daniel Island, the Rev. Benjamin Dennis, an associate pastor at Intercession Reformed Episcopal Church, preaches a similar lesson of land ownership to his wife, Mary

195

Porcher Dennis, and their six children. The family's one-and-a-half-acre home site is what remains of the 22 acres his grandfather James Dennis bought for 50 cents an acre after he came to St. Thomas Island from Daniel Island following World War I.

"I had a fella come here and offer me $1.9 million. I tell him when he see the sign 'side that road that say it is for sale, he can come back and talk to me. This is the only thing here that is in the Dennis name. I got six kids, 12 grand and seven great-grand. I got it fixed so good they can't even sell it. I want this to go down through history in the Dennis name. My father left something for me, so why not I leave something for my children?"

Living on Her Parents' Land

From her Victoria Road home on St. Thomas Island, Alice Washington has watched the changes on Daniel Island and at night she can see the lights at the nearby Blackbaud soccer stadium on the smaller St. Jogues Island. But another sporting venue, a professional tennis stadium on Daniel Island, stands near a special place for her family. The tennis stadium was built near the graves of her grandparents Cupeid and Hannah Shaw. "A lot of people are buried over there," she said. Washington didn't know her grandparents. They died before she was born on May 5, 1935. She was born on the island, as were her grandparents and great-grandparents just out of slavery.

Washington was a premature baby, so small that her parents, Gabriel and Victoria White, laid her in a shoebox. But she stands tall today. Her parents bought land on St. Thomas Island, farmed it and built a house. "Corn, watermelon and every vegetable you can name, they grew it. My daddy didn't have a tractor. A big ox — Billy Long was its name — pulled the plow."

Washington often rode on Billy Long's back. After the ox died, her father bought a horse and plowed with it.

Washington's education began at home with her mother. When she was six years old she was enrolled in classes at St. Luke Reformed Episcopal

Church on Daniel Island, where Philip Simmons first went to school. She attended the church on Sundays. By the time Washington reached the fourth grade, she had moved to Charleston and lived with a cousin on Brigade Street so she could attend Henry P. Archer School.

"My mother did most of the talking," Washington said. "Daddy was a quiet man who drank. (My mother) knew how to save money." Victoria White stuffed money in a moonshine jar and buried it in the chicken house. "If Dad found it he would drink it up. That's the way it was. She would bury coins and paper money."

Victoria White was industrious, too. "She had cows. She sold cows to make her money," her daughter explained.

Gabriel White was a fisherman. "My daddy would sell fish. The vegetables were to feed the family. The family from the city would come and get vegetables."

Washington was 17 years old when she married Peter Washington. They had seven children —two girls and five boys. "My husband worked for Guggenheim. He took care of the cows. He made sure they had water and feed. He had a big truck. That's how I learned to drive."

Washington, a former Roper Hospital cafeteria worker, lives on the six acres her parents left her. The old house was torn down more than 30 years ago. Her daughter built another house on the site and lives in it today. Now Washington is surrounded by her children. "I love here. I love the peace and quietness. You can go and leave your door like this and nobody bothers you," she said, glancing at the unlocked front door of her home. "Nobody steal anything." She's now concerned, however, that the expressway will bring too many outsiders and that security could be lost.

She said a developer once offered her family a million dollars for their land. After a family meeting, they declined to sell.

The pressure to sell still comes from another source. In recent years Alice Washington received her Berkeley County property tax bill. In one year, it increased from $318.43 to $3,508.

Pinefield Lost Forever

Johnnie Rivers could not save his piece of heaven at Pinefield before he died in January 2010.

The serenity of a country lifestyle there were the memories he shared during an interview before his death. He sat in a metal folding chair on the lawn outside his mobile home wedged onto a narrow lot just off Clements Ferry Road.

He was quick to note the house trailer did not compare to Pinefield, where he grew up and raised his family. He spent much of his life at that family settlement established by his great-grandfather Hector Rivers, who paid Susan B. Hay $250 on March 8, 1883, for 50 acres. The land was once part of the Shingler Plantation.

Rivers could only speculate as to why his great-grandfather named the land Pinefield. "I think why he called it Pinefield it was an open area, and it had a few pines," Rivers said in a serious tone. Within time Pinefield became an African-style family compound along Clouter Creek, a deep-water tributary to the Cooper River. Hector Rivers died before Johnnie Rivers was born on October 16, 1931, at Pinefield. Johnnie Rivers remembers his grandfather Hector Rivers Jr. farmed and raised cattle and hogs.

Rivers' parents, Alex and Eva Rivers, with their six boys and four girls, settled at Pinefield. When Rivers was young, his father's brothers joined the compound with their wives and children: Sam and Florence Rivers, Henry and Isabelle Rivers, Jack and Elizabeth Rivers and Peter Rivers. Each family had its own dwelling. They lived off the family land.

The houses had long porches, places to gather late at night when it was too hot to sleep. Then mosquitoes from the marsh were on patrol for warm bodies and fresh blood. The families were prepared. It was the custom, Rivers said, to use a hoe to scrap the yard to remove the grass. The grass was raked in a pile to dry.[14] When the mosquitoes became too pesky the grass was set on fire. Smoke repelled some of the intruders. "When it got cooler around midnight, then we'd all go to bed."

---

14 A grassless yard swept clean is a tradition brought from West Africa.

Johnnie Rivers no longer had convenient access to his favorite fishing spot after he lost Pinefield. Photo by Herb Frazier.

At Christmas, Pinefield's houses were gleaming white with fresh coats of whitewash. Porches were scrubbed clean with broken pieces of red bricks.

For New Year's, a hog was slaughtered. The meat was shared with people in Pinefield and beyond. Children delivered the meat to neighbors with a word of caution not to drop the package in the sand. "If you did," Rivers said, "you'd get your backside cut."

Decades later he lived in a mobile home situated a few hundred yards from the elevated portion of the Mark Clark Expressway where it crosses Clouter Creek. As his family grew, he allowed his five daughters and two sons to live at Pinefield with their children. He kept the grass cut, the bushes trimmed and the taxes paid. He only left Pinefield once for a nine-day stay in the hospital. He never left South Carolina. He wanted to stay close to his land.

For 23 years Rivers was employed on "Dan's Island" at Guggenheim's cattle ranch. "I worked there since I was a little boy," he said in a raspy tone. Rivers fed the cattle and tended them when they were sick. When his children were young Rivers didn't buy them toys at Christmas — Guggenheim did. "My children got more gifts than I got," he laughed. "He gave them cash. Everybody got a turkey, apples and oranges, and he'd bring them to the house. He'd sit down and talk to you. Guggenheim was a Yankee, but he was about the best man I ever worked for. When I left (Guggenheim), I worked at a fertilizer plant and when I leave from the fertilizer mill I went to Charleston County schools for 23 years doing maintenance work." After retirement, Rivers was enjoying life at Pinefield, surrounded by family and a creek to fish. He assumed he'd die there.

Eventually, Rivers and one of his sisters and their children were the only families left at Pinefield. Through the sale of some of the property, Pinefield had been reduced to 17 acres. Rivers then allowed other relatives to move to the compound. He had plans to pass the land to his children. But without a will, no one could lay legal claim to all of it.

Hector Rivers' descendants owned it jointly. Hector Rivers Jr., Johnnie Rivers' grandfather, didn't want to sell any portion of the property to his children because he didn't want them to sell the land to a stranger who might move into the family compound. But when land prices began to rise after the expressway opened, Johnnie Rivers had an argument with his sister Blondell Wigfall. This triggered a dispute among the heirs to property. The disagreement led to a lawsuit filed by Wigfall.[15]

In the lawsuit, Wigfall said her brother allowed his children to live on the land without permission from her and other relatives. Johnnie Rivers said Wigfall forced the sale to push the issue into the court.

Moncks Corner attorney William Peagler III filed a lawsuit in 1994 on Wigfall's behalf to clear up the title by selling the property. Money from the sale would be divided among the heirs. Peagler contacted nearly 30 relatives, including some who lived in New York, Florida and Georgia. After six years of legal wrangling, Berkeley County Master-in-Equity John B. Williams ordered in October 2000 that people living at Pinefield must move before the land was sold.

An investor offered $910,000 for the property. The judge warned Pinefield heirs living on the land that if they refused to move, sheriff's deputies could be called to force them out.

Rivers appealed but lost. In September 2001 the Rivers family was evicted, but Rivers and his wife, Ella Lue Rivers, were allowed to stay until the sale was closed.

On eviction day, 25 members of Rivers' family — children, grandchildren, great-grandchildren — were uprooted from Pinefield. Rivers told a Post and Courier reporter that several other heirs, including two brothers, jumped on the legal bandwagon. "A lot of them who want to sell don't live here," Rivers said. "They know what they're doing to me, but they don't care. They figure they can get some money."

Peagler, Wigfall's attorney, told the Boston Globe newspaper that typically in heirs' property disputes family members who still live on the property are not happy, but other relatives agree to sell all of the land instead of dividing it into smaller parcels. Dividing the Rivers land would have been complicated because it included marsh and deep water, he told the newspaper. "Everyone took their check and was happy," he said.

---

15 See Appendix IV: Heirs' Property.

ed about $27,000 and moved into a doublewide mobile
ot in the vicinity owned by his son. "We had a nice place
" River said. "I would not have sold one ounce, not as
.. Rivers leaned forward in his chair to pinch a blade of grass
..s feet, adding his grandfather had written on the deed that it should
not be sold. "So, I figured he wanted it to go from generation to generation, When I die it would have been just like my grandfather: you leave it
for the next generation. That's what I had planned."[16]

Pinefield was sold for $910,000. Eight months after the Rivers family
was evicted, the new owners, Clouter Creek Properties, placed the property
back on the market for $3 million.

Last Man on Daniel Island

Curiosity once lured Paul Alston to Daniel Island in a futile attempt to
find the plot of land where he was born on January 6, 1933. Alston lived
and worked on the island for 59 years. He left voluntarily in the early
summer of 1992 after he was told the island would be sold to a developer.
When he relocated to Yellow House, Alston departed as the last tenant
worker to leave Daniel Island.

Alston's parents Arthur and Julia McNeil Alston picked rows of vegetables on the island for American Fruit Growers and later for John F.
Maybank, a stockholder of American Fruit Growers.[17] Arthur Alston settled
on the island from the Snowden community near Mount Pleasant. Julia
Alston's kin came from Yemassee. In addition to Paul, their youngest child,
the Alstons had eight other children: Jack, Henry, Arthur, Freddie, Edward,
James, Etta and Leonora.

At different times the family lived in two company-owned wood-frame

---

16 See Appendix V: Dividing the Money.

17 American Fruit Growers purchased land on the island from A.F. Young and Company. A.F. Young established truck farming on the island. Truck farmers traditionally
didn't sell their goods for cash. Instead, they traded or bartered what they grew. The
word "truck" derives from the old English word "trukken," which means barter.

Paul Alston was one the cowboys on Harry Frank Guggenheim's cattle ranch on Daniel Island. Painting by John W. Jones.

houses close to a general store. Workers called the entire area "Big Store," which is near the site of today's Berkeley County Library. Well-manicured yards that front modern houses along paved roads and sidewalks have altered the landscape, obscuring Alston's search for his old homestead.

By the time Alston was seven his brothers had moved across the Cooper River to work in the fertilizer mills or enlist in the military. He started school at that time, walking five miles with his sisters to St. Luke's Episcopal Church, where Philip Simmons had been educated. Students gathered in the sanctuary during the week. Alston quit school in the 10th grade to join his parents picking vegetables.

During harvest time hundreds of people came to the island, many on foot from surrounding communities, to work in the fields. At the height of the farming operation during the mid-1900s, however, as many as eight families occupied company-built dwellings. They lived and worked on the island in exchange for free-rent accommodations. The simple wooden houses were surrounded by vegetable gardens. Every family had an acre or two of cabbage, greens, watermelon and other vegetables, Alston said. "You could take a piece (of land) as big as you want," he said as the aroma of lima beans and neck bones boiling on the stove filled his living room. "You had plenty of land to plant. People had cows and hogs for meat."

When he was a child, tasty dishes including cakes and pies covered the dinner table at Christmas. Toys under the tree made the season a happy time. Stockings, however, weren't stuffed with cash. Money was scarce during the Depression years. "But we had plenty to eat," he bragged. "We didn't want for nothing."

The ferry carried Alston and his family from the island to Charleston. As an adult, he drove his car to the city or the short distance to George Avinger's store near Nurse Broughton's clinic. Alston still calls the area "St. Thomas," harkening to the old parish name. A significant story from the parish's history is part of his childhood memories.

The elders boasted about the black victory at the Cainhoy gunfight in 1876. "They told me about the day the white people come on a boat and tried to surprise all the black people and started shooting. The black people shot them so much the white people ran and bogged in an old pond back in the woods," Alston said. "The colored people was used to the woods 'cause they lived back there." Life on Daniel Island in the 20th century was far more tranquil than those violent days of Reconstruction. Alston said families – black and white – lived on the island in peace.

By the early 1950s, Alston not only had a new boss he also was about to learn a new skill. Guggenheim began in the late-1940s acquiring property on the island for a cattle ranch. Within a decade, he had it all. He asked Alston to work for him. Alston was one of about six Guggenheim cowboys.

Their living arrangements did not change from the time they worked for the vegetable companies. Families stayed in the houses rent and utilities free. The wranglers rode on horseback among scattered groups of grazing cattle in a seemingly never-ending search for strays. They burned the Guggenheim brand "C H" – the initials for Cain Hoy – in the hide of red-and-white Hereford calves. By the mid-1960s the herd had swelled to well over 2,000 head on a ranch where cowboys often gazed at the distant lights of Charleston at night.

At six feet, four inches, Alston rode tall in the saddle. He wore a cowboy hat, chaps and spurs, and a cigarette usually hung from his lips. Alston was an African-American version of the Marlboro man. But Alston does not hold romantic memories of his days in the saddle.

"I didn't like to ride a horse. I didn't like nothin' about drivin' cattle. I was strong when I was a young man. It used to take two men to tackle a 600-pound steer. You had to throw 'em and hold 'em while somebody brand 'em. That was hard work." He preferred the lighter job atop a tractor or bulldozer on Guggenheim's property. Alston and Harold Lincoln worked together on the place. "I used to paint inside and outside the mansion. I'd cut wood for the winter time, but mostly I drove a tractor."

In addition to his lanky frame, Alston's other distinguishing physical feature is his voice. It sounds severely hoarse. Twice in the 1950s, Alston underwent operations to correct a twisted vocal chord. The procedures didn't correct the problem.

"I guess all the fellas I used to work with on the island done died: Julius Foy; Willie Brown; Peter Washington, that's Alice's husband," he said. He recalled when Nurse Broughton inspected the workers' homes and vaccinated the families. "Those shots made you sick, your arm started hurting, but I guess it was good for you," he conceded. Broughton wasn't the only nurse on the island. "Lula Shaw was a nurse midwife, and a Buncum lady who used to live on the Furman Tract was a midwife."

Alston's father died in the 1940s. When the health of his mother declined, she went to live in Mount Pleasant with her daughter Etta Alston

Paul Alston and his family once lived in this house on Daniel Island in an area called "Big Store." Photo courtesy of Brockington and Associates.

Buncum. Julia Alston died in May 1979 at age 79. Paul Alston said his mother changed her name in the 1970s back to her maiden name. Her headstone in the cemetery behind St. James AME Church on St. Thomas Island identifies her as Julia McNeil. She's buried there with her sons Arthur, Freddie and Edward. Alston attends the church today.

Alston missed his mother after she left the island. "I never had a wife. She was with me the whole time." His brothers Edward and Freddie lived with him for about six years following their mother's death, but after they moved away Alston was alone. He lived on the island during the week to be near the cattle and the Cain Hoy retreat. On the weekends he spent time in Charleston, where he met Patricia Norther of Yonges Island, a community south of the city. She moved to Daniel Island to live with him. They each have children from previous relationships. Alston has a daughter Julianne Wilson, who lives in Beaufort.

Alston and Norther were the only people on the island until they left in 1992. Alston covered his own moving expenses. His $900-a-month salary from the Guggenheim Foundation, he said, was more than enough to pay for the move. Besides, the foundation had allowed him to live on the island rent free, utilities included. "That was pretty good," he boasted. Even when Guggenheim was alive, Alston was pleased with the pay. "In the 1950s, we get paid off every other week, and I was making about $100 every two weeks."

When moving day came, Alston and Norther were eager and ready to leave. "It was lonesome 'cross there." Loneliness haunts Alston. His immediate relatives are gone now and Patricia died in June 2008.

View of the southern edge of Cainhoy peninsula from Beresford Creek.
Painting by John W. Jones

Chapter 14: Protecting Gullah Culture

3:31 p.m., Friday, Sept. 29, 2006

Michael Allen is in the Atlanta airport waiting for a flight to Charleston after attending the funeral of a close friend when his cell phone rings.

"Are you sitting down?" asks Danny Cromer, an aide to U.S. Congressman James Clyburn. "The bill has passed."

"What bill?" Allen asks softly, not making the connection between "the bill" and the nine years of work it has taken to get a federal law passed to interpret and preserve the Gullah/Geechee culture. Once he realizes the unexpected has happened, he cries.

For Gullah/Geechee people, the passage of the law is monumental.

Generations of Gullah/Geechee people had been ridiculed because of their speech and customs. Clyburn's bill was a long overdue recognition of the significance of them and their culture.

Allen hails from a Gullah community near the town of Kingstree in Williamsburg County, further inland than the Cainhoy peninsula. Gullah is Allen's profession and passion.

He is a community partnership specialist for the Fort Sumter National Monument and Charles Pinckney National Historic Site, managed by the National Park Service. The 28 acres of the Pinckney site in Mount Pleasant are all that remains of Charles Pinckney's 715-acre Snee Farm, a former rice and indigo plantation. Pinckney was a signer of the U.S. Constitution.

Allen also is known widely as the Park Service's coordinator of the

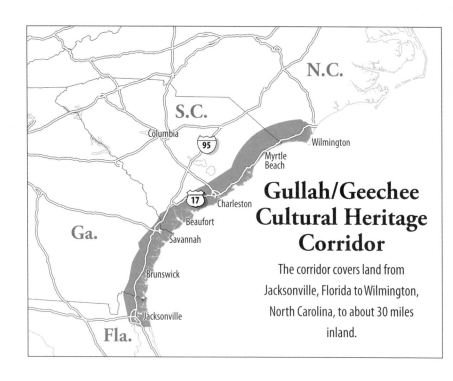

Gullah/Geechee Cultural Heritage Corridor

The corridor covers land from Jacksonville, Florida to Wilmington, North Carolina, to about 30 miles inland.

Gullah/Geechee Cultural Heritage Corridor. The corridor, created by the Gullah/Geechee bill, is one of 49 National Heritage Areas set aside by Congress to tell the nation's history. The law defined the boundaries of the corridor as a coastal region 30 miles inland from Wilmington, North Carolina, to Jacksonville, Florida. The legislation also established a commission made up of residents from the four states within the corridor.

Years before the Gullah/Geechee bill was conceived, the Park Service developed a plan to tell the Gullah story through its mission at the Pinckney site. The legislation that created the site specified that the department must highlight Pinckney's contributions to the Constitution, tell America's transition from a colony to a young nation and describe the inhabitants of the site, Allen explained. That gave the Park Service the license, he said, to include the Gullah story.

The work to tell the Gullah story at the Pinckney site and elsewhere led to a Gullah Consortium in the late 1990s. It consisted of historic and cultural sites and community groups. Meetings were held in coastal cities from Georgetown to Beaufort and in Columbia. The information gathered confirmed the assumption that there had been no communications among Gullah people, authorities on historic sites and the state Department of Archives. Around that time, Allen, Pinckney site superintendent John Tucker, historian Joseph Opala and Gullah community leader Emory Campbell in Beaufort County attended a Park Service conference in New Orleans and offered a proposal to expand the telling of the Gullah story.

Following that conference, Jannie Harriot, a member of the S.C. African American Heritage Commission; Marquetta Goodwine, of the Sea Island Gullah/Geechee Coalition; and the others met with Clyburn aide Cromer. The following year, Clyburn secured Congressional funding for a Lowcountry Gullah Study.

Allen and historian Cynthia Porcher, the Park Service's southeastern regional office in Atlanta, the Penn Center in Beaufort and the Sea Island Gullah/Geechee Coalition collaborated on how to develop the study with input from the community. It took nearly five years to complete it in 2005 because it went deeper than anticipated, Allen said. "After we finished the study we reported it back to the Park Service and Congressman Clyburn, who used its findings in writing the bill. The central recommendation was to establish another National Heritage Area for Gullah culture."

A problem, however, arose that needed immediate attention. African Americans in Georgia and Florida said they call themselves Geechee, not Gullah. Hence, the title of the legislation Clyburn filed encompassed both Gullah and Geechee cultures.

Longtime Jack Primus resident Harold Lincoln uses the Gullah word "kuta" for turtle. He roasts sweet potatoes in his fireplace. He recalled that his father grew rice. Gullah ways have been a part of his life since he was a boy. But he does not call himself a Gullah. People of African descent were called "Geechee," he said. "Gullah" was not considered a flattering term.

However, Rosa Lee Gibbs of Huger said she didn't like the word "Geechee."

"It didn't sound right to me. It seem like it was something that they would call you if you were a bad person," she said.

But the Rev. Benjamin Dennis was not offended when his classmates in 1938 at Buist Elementary School in Charleston called him a "country Geechee" or "Benjamin the Geechee," Dennis said. "I accepted it because I was from out the country."

Moncks Corner resident Bertha Roper Davis doubts "Gullah" was a word her maternal great-granduncle Hope Lloyd and paternal great-grandfather Frank Roper used when linguist Lorenzo Dow Turner came to Cordesville in the early 1930s to record their speech.

"When I heard (Lorenzo Turner's recording of) Hope Lloyd, how could you miss it? That was Gullah he was speaking," she said. When she was growing up in Moncks Corner before she moved to California, Davis didn't know Gullah was the name of the language. But it wasn't until after the 1970s that it became a widely used descriptor of the culture, the people and the language.

Historian Joseph Opala, who taught a Gullah language course at James Madison University in Harrisonburg, Virginia, said the term Gullah first came into use after 1750. Whites used it to describe Africans from Senegal through Nigeria to Angola. "In some parts of South Carolina, people were called Geechee and in other parts they were Gullah," he said. There are instances, he said, where people were referred to as Geechee but they spoke Gullah.

The term Gullah is thought to have been used to refer to people from Angola. Geechee may have become more popular in Georgia because fewer Angolans were taken to Georgia, Opala said, adding that the term Geechee may have been used to describe people who lived along the Ogeechee River near Savannah, Georgia.

Lela Haynes Session recalled that in the 1930s when she was a student at Avery, Gullah was used to identify the language and culture. "At Avery we took Latin and French, and our teacher, Alphonso Halsey, exposed students to other languages," she said. During a field trip to the Penn Center on

St. Helena Island, the Avery students received an explanation of Gullah language. They took the trip down to Beaufort because English teacher Margaret Rutledge wanted to expose students to Gullah.

In 1943 when Session arrived at the Brickyard School near Huger, the students and their parents spoke Gullah and followed Gullah customs, she said. Consequently, the students were caught between two worlds.

"In the classroom, we wanted kids to speak proper English. The teachers were trying to implant in them the use of correct English," she said. Some teachers accepted Gullah while others did not because they were anxious for students to speak only English. Session said Gullah culture and the language is diminishing, but it will survive.

Many traditional Gullah/Geechee communities have been reduced in size by real estate development, encroachment by outsiders and the migration of people from the community. Eddie Carson said he hoped the commissioners who oversee the Gullah/Geechee corridor will encourage developers to discuss their plans with a community and consider the heritage of the people.

In many ways the Cainhoy peninsula is similar to Hilton Head Island in southern Beaufort County. Commission chairman Emory Campbell grew up on Hilton Head and later became executive director of the Penn Center, where he managed social and educational programs, including workshops to teach local people how to protect heirs' property. He is the author of "Gullah Cultural Legacies."

In November 1989, Campbell led a group of 13 African Americans to Sierra Leone. A documentary film crew from South Carolina Educational Television recorded the event and later produced "Family Across the Sea," the story of Gullah people who went on a homecoming to that West African nation.

Before Hilton Head was transformed into an oceanside resort with condos, golf courses, malls and single-family homes, it was farms, woodlands and a community of Gullah families who lived in compounds like Johnnie Rivers' Pinefield. The loss of Pinefield has been used as an example throughout the corridor of what not to do to preserve land, Campbell said. Within the Gullah/Geechee corridor, people live on land they typically wouldn't have been able to afford if it hadn't been in their families since the 1800s. The rise in taxes is making it a struggle to keep the land.

"We have to avoid those situations. We have to look at public policy to prevent families from being disrupted," he said. "We have a number of instances where the culture is being disrupted by resort development through the sale of land, highways and planning laws that don't recognize traditions and customs of the culture.

"You have memories on that very land that you grew up on, memories of working the fields, stories told in the field or under a familiar oak tree and memories of walking through your grandmother's yard. It is because of those memories that the Gullah/Geechee culture and its people have bonded to the land.

"Historically, we have been insulated geographically as well as insulated from land speculators. But that has changed because the coast is no longer an inconvenient place for people to live," Campbell said. "Bridges connect islands. The coast used to be an uncomfortable place to live in the summer, but the pests are being controlled, waterways are no longer a hindrance and now we are threatened by other cultures."

The commission is young but we "are organizing our communities to get them involved in the preservation of the culture," he said. "We want to find out what it is they'd like to see preserved in Gullah culture."

Historic places and family property and the issue of escalating taxes head the list, he said. The commission has no policing power. However, it can go before policy makers to encourage them to recognize the value of Gullah/Geechee culture as they consider development or plan for growth.

In the late 1990s, St. Helena Island residents were successful in having a cultural conservation district created with a higher zoning density that allows for up to four single-family homes on an acre. It permits families to live together in a traditional family compound. The zoning also prevents gated communities. With no provision for a gated community, the land becomes less attractive for developers, he said.

"Land provides Gullah people with their historic ability to survive independently. As long as Gullah people have land, they can grow food and practice family traditions. That is the reason why we have been able to sustain the culture so those traditions can be passed on. Gullah people are the only people who know their neighbor as kinfolk. They know their cousins because they've lived on the same land where the knowledge and skills are passed down from generation to generation."

The corridor has limited congressional funding. It doesn't have a headquarters or staff beyond Allen, who has other responsibilities. One of the commission's first functions was a series of community meetings in 2009 to hear what Gullah/Geechee people in the corridor think should be done to preserve the culture. At a meeting on Johns Island that summer, Benjamin Dennis IV stood up to announce that he had come to represent his grandfather, the Rev. Benjamin Dennis of St. Thomas Island.

At that time Dennis was a 31-year-old old aspiring chef at restaurants in Charleston. He sat patiently during the meeting until it was his time to speak. Then he told the audience and the commissioners what he had learned about Gullah culture from his grandfather.

"He sits down with me all the time. Because for me to know who I am as a man, I got to know where I came from." Benjamin told the story of his great-grandfather Bennie Dennis' boat service that took Cainhoy peninsula people to work at the fertilizer mills in the Neck Area above Charleston.

"My grandfather still plants an acre of okra. We got sugar cane," he said. "I help him get in that yard and cultivate the land and pick okra. Because I'm his grandson, I feel that's the right thing to do."

His grandmother Mary Porcher Dennis also shares stories with him. "My grandmother would tell me that, when she was young, the ladies used to carry the baskets on their heads, walking around with the laundry. So we're not too far gone from past generations of true culture."

Benjamin also talked about his great-great-grandfather's land on St. Thomas Island:

"Twenty-two acres that he bought. And he passed that down to his son, his sisters … his daughters, and that went to my granddaddy. And all we have now is an acre and a half. … Every other week (we) have somebody come to my granddaddy's house and (ask), 'When you going to sell the land? We give you $900,000 for the land.'

"Money don't mean nothing," Benjamin said. "It's about heritage and about where you're from. My great-great-grandfather was the one who left that (land) for his grandchildren. And my granddaddy is leaving that for his grandchildren. And I told my granddaddy I would never, never sell."

Benjamin once lived on another island called St. Thomas. In the Virgin Islands, Caribbean people on St. Thomas were intrigued to meet a Gullah man from South Carolina.

"People would hear me talk and they would say, 'Well, where are you from? You from St. Lucia? You from Barbados?' … They wanted to hear the accent. They would just be so intrigued."

The future of Gullah/Geechee culture indeed depends on the public programs that will come from the commission to expose people here and elsewhere to the important contributions of Gullah/Geechee people. As the commission matures, its members will no doubt seek to acquire the clout to guide public policy that affects the use of land in Gullah/Geechee communities.

Across the Cainhoy peninsula and elsewhere in the corridor, however, the most effective guardians of the culture and the land will be people of Benjamin's generation who still listen to their elders, the voices of the past, who understand the importance of family, extended family, money and land. Either they will determine the future of the Cainhoy peninsula or the developers will do it without them.

216

The James B. Edwards Bridge connects Mount Pleasant (left) with Daniel island. Painting by John W. Jones.

Chapter 15: Voices of a New Generation

Sit There

You sit right there
Do nothing but pray
Justice will come
To you one of these days

Sit right there
And think money will come
If you do nothing
You'll have no fun

You have got to work
To get your pay
Why waste your time
With TV all day

You sit right there
And hope friends will help
Sit right there
Sit right there

– Carrie Bennett, Huger

Huger resident Carrie Bennett's poem expresses the self-determination of a new generation on the Cainhoy peninsula. People born in the 1940s and 1950s were learning the old ways and lessons of survival as the outside world was calling. They attended public schools and completed their homework but still were expected to pitch in on the family farm.

Life in the country wasn't always hard work for them. By their teen years, paved roads on the peninsula were lined with juke joints where they danced on Friday and Saturday nights to the music of Motown. If a car and money were available, they'd drive to County Hall in Charleston to see such headliners as James Brown or head to Riverside Beach, a segregated amusement park on the Cooper River at Remley's Point, where a century before Tena White had been enslaved on Venning Plantation.

During the daytime some of the juke joints also served a Gullah cuisine of shrimp gumbo, okra soup, black-eyed peas, cow peas and collard greens with ham hocks, fried chicken and, of course, every variety of rice — red, brown, yellow and white.

Children listened to their elders, who knew the importance of family, extended family, money and land. "When you have a dollar, you have a friend," Carrie Bennett remembered being told.

The elders were proud people who sacrificed so their children could get the college degrees they never had. With this new knowledge, their children traveled farther, were more mobile and worldly and better prepared to win the civil-rights struggle.

Family after family share similar stories of children who left the Cainhoy peninsula for opportunities in Philadelphia, Washington, New York City and elsewhere. In many cases the girls left and the boys stayed behind to work. Those who left are retiring now and returning to build homes on family land. Among them have emerged new community leaders.

Today they are members of volunteer groups who keep a watchful eye on land developers and press for more services from local government. Eddie Carson and Fred Lincoln are among them.

The day after Carson graduated in 1962 from Cainhoy High School,

Eddie Carson of Huger with his grandniece Joely Morgan Carson. Photo by Jeanine Carson.

he left Huger and joined the Marine Corps. "I wasn't going to work on anybody's pulpwood job cutting logs," Carson said before he died in August 2007 at age 64.

After nearly five years in the Marines and a long career as an investigator with the U.S. Postal Service in West Virginia, Pennsylvania and Columbia, S.C., Carson retired and returned to Huger in 1998. He became president of the board of the United Methodist Relief Center. He was a no-nonsense leader in protecting the community from adverse changes brought on by development as well as securing a fair share of services from Berkeley County government.

When Carson returned he moved into a house on Charity Church Road in the Huger area. He reconnected with the people of his childhood who went to church, appreciated their ancestors and sought to protect their land. Carson said he had noted that in politics the term "conservative" isn't used to describe African Americans. "But our people are conservative," he said.

"They have kept it (the land); they've paid taxes on it."

He also was pleasantly surprised that the people from the scattered communities on the Cainhoy peninsula were no longer segregating themselves from the outside world. From Yellow House to Huger and Jack Primus to Greenbay, residents seemed to think of themselves as one big community now. Their shared history of slavery is what binds them, Carson said.

Fred Lincoln (left) is chairman of the 12-member Cainhoy Volunteer Fire Department. Shaun Gadsden is a paid part-time member of the department's Station No. 3 on Clements Ferry Road in the Yellow House community. The station opened in 1996. Gadsden is also a captain with the Isle of Palms Fire Department. Photo by Herb Frazier.

Fred Lincoln spent the first four years of his formal education at the Keith School. After he graduated from Cainhoy High School in 1964, he worked as a dishwasher for a year at a Charleston restaurant, but it soon became clear that he couldn't tolerate a segregated South, so he had to go elsewhere. Like many children in his family before him, he set out for New York City to live with his father's oldest sister, Alma Binyard. He soon realized he had as many relatives in New York as he did in Jack Primus. Three aunts, four uncles and lots of cousins were scattered from Manhattan and the Bronx to Long Island. When he arrived in New York at age 18, Lincoln got an education he never would have received in the South. He learned about economic and political concepts such as capitalism, socialism, communism and black nationalism. He also was exposed to people who called themselves atheists.

"It was a wealth of knowledge that I had never heard down here. I was fortunate enough to meet Malcolm X on 125th Street in Harlem. People were proud to be black, and you didn't call yourself a Negro."

During the day Lincoln worked in a factory that made cardboard boxes. He attended night classes at the City College of New York, but he first had to take remedial courses because his high school education was incomplete. "I never had American history. All they taught me was South Carolina history and Civil War history."

Just as he was settling into his school work, the U.S. Army offered him a job overseas. U.S. troops were fighting in Vietnam. "I was angry. I was getting situated in school and doing pretty good," he said. "I was already against the war and aware of my blackness and how I fit into society."

Lincoln was certain he was going to Vietnam. Instead, he spent two years as a military policeman in Seoul, South Korea. After the military, he returned to New York to enroll in the RCA Institute, an electronics school. He took additional courses at City College. He married Peggy Butler, a Philadelphia native. They met in New York before she graduated from a nursing school in the city. For many years, Kwanza Lincoln was their only child.[18]

---

18 After a prolonged adoption process, Fred and Peggy Lincoln in September 2010 became the "proud parents" of three children from the West African nation of Ghana. Kwesi Lincoln, 16, (boy); Ama Lincoln, 10, (girl); and Afua Lincoln, 8, (girl) live with the Lincolns in Jack Primus and attend local schools.

Fred Lincoln went to work at the New York Stock Exchange in the stock-transfer department. He left Wall Street three years later and launched his own business, a concession stand in an office building on 43rd Street where he sold newspapers, magazines and candy. By the end of 1980 Jack Primus was calling him home. He returned to work as a volunteer doing whatever the community needed.

He soon joined the Mount Pleasant Fire Department, which gave him a flexible schedule that allowed him to do community work and help organize the Cainhoy Volunteer Fire Department, which today has three stations along Clements Ferry and Cainhoy roads.

Lincoln built a two-story brick home on an acre lot at the end of Sarah Lincoln Road, which was named for his grandmother, a small but strong woman who could walk a long way with a 100-pound sack of rice on her shoulder, he said.

Against one wall in his large den is his workplace, a black lacquered desk with papers, books and a computer. On the far wall, a fireplace is surrounded by mementos. Above the fireplace hangs a wooden horse collar used on the animal that plowed the field that fed the family. Near it is a two-man saw that cut the wood to burn in the stove that warmed the family. The saw belonged to his grandmother. When he was a boy, Lincoln was on one end of the saw pulling as his uncle Louis Lincoln pushed. A shotgun on the wall was used to hunt 'possum and 'coon. Oil lamps on the mantle once were used to light the family home, along with a black iron, used to press the clothes.

Families in Jack Primus have retained a sense of independence, reflected in the community's decision not to be annexed in 1991 into Charleston. "We don't need master. We can do it on our own."

But sometimes, he said, it is good to have friends when going up against a wealthy developer or a powerful state agency. For that reason, Lincoln has formed an alliance with MaeRe Chandler Skinner of Cainhoy.

As children in the Wando area, MaeRe and Fred were about the same age and lived less than three miles from one another, but they were worlds

Fred Lincoln and Peggy Butler Lincoln cut their wedding cake after they exchanged vows on June 12, 1970, at St. James AME Church in Harlem. Photo courtesy of Fred and Peggy Lincoln.

apart culturally. They first met after Charleston annexed Daniel Island and nearby residents were worried. Today they work hard together to protect their communities from unwise development.

Decades ago such an alliance between a white woman from Cainhoy and a black man from Jack Primus probably would not have been possible, Lincoln said. "Before, we weren't an asset but now we can be an ally" as a result of the multi-racial makeup in local government, he explained. "All of that is a reflection of how things have changed."

Like Lincoln, Skinner's passion to protect the community seems to consume much of her time. But the origin of Skinner's first name and its unusual spelling are the first questions most people ask before she can talk about Cainhoy.

Butch and MaeRe Skinner stand at the end of Cainhoy Village Road. Photo by Herb Frazier.

Skinner's first name is a fusion of the names of grandmother Mae Louis Habersham Laurence, aunt Mae Habersham Millar and mother Mary Elliott Millar Chandler. Initially, Skinner's mother had planned to take Mae and add to it the last two letters of her first name to get MaeRy. Instead, she changed the "y" to "e" to make it MaeRe, Skinner explained.

When she was a teenager she grew tired of being asked about her name. Once in awhile somebody would say, "Well, that is a pretty name. Is that French?"

Skinner would simply respond, "Oh, yes," with a confident toss of her head.

"I am proud of it. Most of the time, I just say it's homemade Southern." And she is as Southern as you can get, right down to soft-Gullah touches in her Lowcountry brogue.

Skinner was born in 1948 at Roper Hospital. The first five years of her life were spent with her parents and two older sisters, Kathye and Jean, near the hospital in a two-apartment house on Rutledge Avenue near Calhoun Street. They lived across from the old Charleston Museum, where Skinner played among the spooky exhibits of stuffed big game and mummies.

Her father, Thomas Burgess Chandler, owned the house in Cainhoy on the Wando at the end of Cainhoy Village Road that he inherited from his parents. The family went to the house during the summers. It was wired for electricity in 1948 but had no running water.

Nevertheless, her mother, who went by "Elliott," wanted to leave Charleston and live full time at Cainhoy. She was tired of the small Charleston apartment. But before they moved, Thomas Chandler had to install a bathroom in the Cainhoy house. When that was done, Isaiah Brown helped the Chandlers move in 1954.

MaeRe started school in 1955 and her mother, an accomplished singer, volunteered to teach music appreciation at Mount Pleasant Academy and Whitesides Elementary in Mount Pleasant. "She did that for eight years, and she never received a penny for it," Skinner said.

Skinner decided to go off to Gulf Park College, an art school, located on the Mississippi coast, after reading an advertisement for the school on the back page of Seventeen magazine. "I want to go there!" she told her parents. Two years later, she had an associate of arts degree and art certificate. Then she got married and "that was the end of that!"

Jean Chandler Patten (left), MaeRe Chandler Skinner, and Kathye Chandler McGregor surround Lavenia Broughton Porcher. Photo courtesy of MaeRe Chandler Skinner.

In a Washington, D.C., library she found a way to pursue other passions — history and genealogy. From 1977 until 1979, Skinner was a genealogist at the Daughters of the American Revolution headquarters near the White House. When a woman applied for DAR membership, Skinner checked the library's volumes to verify if she was the descendant of a soldier who fought for American independence. The interest, one might say, is genetic. As a 30-year DAR member of the Rebecca Motte Chapter in Charleston, Skinner's connection with patriots goes back six generations in South Carolina.

Skinner has another "family" connection that is just as important to her even if it does not follow her blood line. From the time Skinner was five years old until she was 17, she had "two mothers" — one white, the other black.

Lavenia Broughton Porcher "was my nanny, my best friend, and she was like a second mother to me." (Porcher's brother Joseph was executed for the murder of Yellow House storekeeper James Elias DuTart, as noted in Chapter Six.)

By 1965 Porcher was seriously ill and no longer worked. But that didn't end the relationship. Skinner visited Porcher many times afterward, including those critical days following Hurricane Hugo's devastation in September 1989. Skinner took a vanload of water and food for Porcher and the community.

After the storm, Porcher's health worsened and she was moved to a nursing home. She died the last day of June 2003.

"It broke my heart. I loved her. She was so special in my life," Skinner said.

MaeRe and husband Butch attended Lavenia Porcher's funeral, "a three-hour homegoing" at St. Paul Pentecostal Temple in Huger. "I was so proud to be there."

French Quarter Creek residents Mary Anne Lane (left), and Kuniyo Grainger, and Jennet Williams of Steed Creek Road, are founding members of the Sew Sew Quilters. Lane is chairperson of the group that meets the first three Mondays of each month at the Huger Community Center. Formed in 2000, the quilters gather to promote the craft and socialize. Many of their colorful quilts are given away as gifts. Photo by Herb Frazier.

The Rev. David Riley (far left) watches as his wife Mary Riley and June Oglesby, the Riley's cousin, unveil a headstone on November 7, 2009, at the grave of his great-great-grandfather David Sparkman in the Grove Cemetery on Daniel Island. Sparkman fought for the Union Army during the Civil War. The 54th Massachusetts, Co. I, Civil War Reenactment Regiment, color guard fired a salute to Sparkman. Photo by Herb Frazier.

Postscript: Saving Cemeteries

A fight Fred Lincoln, MaeRe Chandler Skinner and their allies routinely face is the threat to old and sometimes forgotten burial grounds. There are at least three cemeteries that concern the activists. The Rev. David Riley, an Episcopal minister in Charleston, also has his eyes on two burial grounds on Daniel Island.

Somewhere behind St. Paul Missionary Baptist Church on Clements Ferry Road is the Nelliefield Cemetery, an abandoned graveyard that holds the remains of enslaved people, Skinner said. Rebecca and Edward Keith, founder of the Keith School, were buried there in the 1940s. "We better find that cemetery before those developers get in there," she warned. It was a slave cemetery with graves marked with wooden crosses that have long since turned to dust.

Skinner is also worried about two other cemeteries. She and others have revived the old Cainhoy Methodist Church and Cemetery Corporation that was chartered in 1988 to protect the Meeting House ruins and cemetery. Skinner's father was its chairman. One section of the graveyard is for whites. The other was used by blacks. The white graves are marked with stone markers, but the black graves are unmarked. "Fred and I are in the process of locating the African-American section of this graveyard."

The Methodist Church has transferred the deed to the cemetery group so it can receive a nonprofit status to raise money to repair the existing fence and install a gate. In addition to Skinner, the chairman, the other board members are her husband, Henry "Butch" Skinner, vice chairman;

W.G. Dudley III, secretary-treasurer; and at-large members Elizabeth O. Anderson, Skinner's daughter; Thomas Chandler Skipper Owens, Skinner's son; Thomas Smoak and Joseph and Paula Wells.

Josie and Thomas Smoak remember when burials were held in the black section of the McDowell cemetery as recently as the late 1940s. Thomas Smoak said black families used an area between the white section of the burial grounds and Meeting Creek. "The lady (Essie Brown) who used to help me with my children, her daddy is buried there," Josie Smoak said. The wooden markers are gone.

A long dirt road on the Cain Hoy Plantation cuts through a forest of tall pine. Before Guggenheim bought the land, the dirt road was called Clements Ferry Road and at one time was lined at one-mile intervals with stone markers dating back to the 1700s. The road ends at the Cain Hoy mansion. It also is the route to the old Venning Cemetery, where granite tombstones mark 20th century graves alongside an unknown number of unmarked plots that hold the remains of enslaved people. Some of them are Fred Lincoln's relatives and other Jack Primus ancestors. Fred's grandparents, Peter and Sarah Lincoln, are there.

The cemetery is near where the workers lived. The quarters for enslaved workers was torn down when the people left, but they'd return to bury their dead. The dry grass under Lincoln's feet crumpled as he walked to the far side of the cemetery. He stopped at a marker that indicates the boundary. He knelt at the grave of William Leroy Brown Jr., who died in 1948. Lincoln pointed to another granite headstone beyond the boundary line.

At that spot the owners of the Cain Hoy Plantation designated the outer limit of the graveyard, "but you can see a tombstone there beyond the boundary," Lincoln said. "This is all that they want to give, but it is not a question of giving. Once they allowed the slaves to be buried there it becomes a graveyard. You can't come now and say we are going to put limitations and exclude all the graves back there."

Lincoln estimated the graveyard's boundary extends at least another 300 feet toward a nearby marsh. He spoke of the people buried beyond

Thomas and Josie Worsham Smoak pause at the graves of Josie Smoak's parents, Richard Joseph Worsham and Daisy Legare Worsham, who are buried at the site of the old Wando Methodist Church in the old village of Cainhoy. Photo by Herb Frazier.

the boundary as if they are still in bondage. "These folks have suffered too long to still be owned by someone, even in death."

Several months after Lincoln's visit to the cemetery, Peter Lawson-Johnston II, Guggenheim's cousin, said in a prepared statement, "the Trustees of this trust have been working closely with Fred Lincoln to ensure the continued protection of this cemetery. At Mr. Lincoln's request, the Trustees engaged a professional team to use sophisticated technology to identify all bodies within the cemetery. We did this because many of the graves did not have headstones. We have also had the cemetery surveyed with input from Mr. Lincoln. The Trustees have worked with Mr. Lincoln to enlarge the cemetery to be able to accommodate a modest number of additional gravesites. The Trustees have indicated a willingness to enter into a formal

Operating Agreement with an entity that represents the local community. Finally, the Trustees are placing a fence around the cemetery to improve its overall aesthetic and as further protection."

After residential construction began on Daniel Island, Riley, Fred Lincoln and others prepared an inventory of the cemeteries. They asked the Daniel Island Company for help to protect the burial grounds. Riley also addressed City Council. "We saw that some of the graves were damaged," he said. "Once you open up a place for development and people take shortcuts through the woods, then headstones are disturbed."

In a prepared statement, Matt Sloan, president of the Daniel Island Company, responded: "From the start, the plan for Daniel Island's development has involved honoring the history of the area, including the African Americans who were in some way connected to this land. This is why we forged a close relationship with Philip Simmons and the Philip Simmons Foundation early on, hiring him to create an identifying mark for the island (the Daniel Island logo), dedicating a prominent park in his honor and assisting his foundation over the years. It's also why we invested in the restoration and ongoing maintenance of three African-American cemeteries on the island. Like the island's parks, these cemeteries will be carefully maintained by the property owners association on an ongoing basis."

Three African-American cemeteries on Daniel Island are fenced off and tucked away in wooded lots along marshy creek banks. Finding them is easy. Settling on what to call them is not.

A cemetery at the edge of Ralston Creek on the north end of the island is referred to as the Daniel Island Park Cemetery in the book *Daniel Island*, written by Michael K. Dahlman and his son Michael K. Dahlman Jr. The Rev. Benjamin Dennis said that when he was a boy, black people on the island called the burial grounds the Alston graveyard. His father Bennie Dennis and grandfather James Dennis are buried there.

"Alston" is most likely a modification of "Ralston," according to Charleston writer Jack McCray. "Minority groups often permutated pronunciations of people, places and things from the culture of the majority. That might

Ernie Nelson, site manager at the BP Amoco Chemicals Company Cooper River Plant, reads the names of people buried in the Grove Cemetery that was part of the Grove Plantation. Boy Scout Troop 502 at East Cooper Baptist Church in 1997 repaired a fence around the burial grounds. The plant is on the former Flagg and Grove plantations. Photo by Herb Frazier.

be the case here."

At the south end of the island, the Rev. David Riley watches over two African-American cemeteries. One of them is hidden behind the towering grandstands of the Family Circle tennis complex. The other is in a serene setting near the island's sales office. Both of them are referred to as the Grove Cemetery, depending on who you ask.

The burial ground near the tennis stadium has been referred to by at least two names – the Simmons Cemetery and the Lesesne African-American Cemetery. Blacksmith Philip Simmons' grandfather William Simmons and his granduncle William Simmons are buried there. Philip Simmons remembered when his granduncle William left home for World War I. The cemetery is referred to as the Lesesne African-American Cemetery by the Dahlmans due to its proximity and historical connection with the Lesesne Family Cemetery, which holds the remains of the Lesesnes and other prominent planters on the island during the 18th and early 19th centuries.

As the Rev. Riley explained who is buried in the Simmons/Lesesne African-American cemetery, he looked across the grounds and realized the flags were missing. Two years previous, he stuck small American flags in the soil at each grave. Only two remained at the burial grounds near the tennis complex.

"I had them (American flags) on every grave and someone took them off," he said. "I wanted people to see that we as African Americans have a history of serving this country. I put the flags there to honor them, and to say thank you."

Further south is a burial ground that Riley calls the Grove Cemetery, near the island's sales office. When the Dahlmans were researching their book, Riley said, he mistakenly identified the cemetery as the Simmons Cemetery. The Grove Cemetery holds the remains of Riley's relatives in addition to those of the Pickens, Fordhams, Jenkins and veterans of conflicts here and overseas. The cemetery is well maintained today, but there was a time when large tree limbs and high brush covered the grounds. The city of Charleston and the Daniel Island Company removed the debris and exposed scattered tombstones. The cleanup makes it easier to do routine maintenance of the grounds, he said.

In the mid-1970s, Riley began regular visits to Grove Cemetery along with his great-grandaunt Ethel Bellinger Bennett, who lived on Daniel Island when it was farmland. Riley considers her to be his mother. "She raised me from the time I was three months old until I became a man."

They and other family members tended to the graves but couldn't do much of a general cleanup until the city and the developer offered to help. Riley, Ethel Bennett and others planted flowers, trimmed the grass and straightened toppled headstones. She taught him the importance of family. She told him of her mother, Jane Bellinger, who died in her 70th year. She was buried at Grove in April 1942, seven years before Riley was born.

During visits to the burial grounds, he often wonders about the location of the unmarked grave of his great-great-grandfather David Sparkman. Born in 1838, Sparkman fought in the Civil War with the 33rd U.S. Col-

ored Troops. Riley read records in the National Archives th
Sparkman's three years in the military before he was discharge
1866, and settled on the island. The military records show th
was buried in the Grove Cemetery. Riley said he also remem... ....
who are buried there referring to it as the Grove Cemetery.

When Riley visits the burial grounds, he has regrets that his aunt is not
there. She died in 1983. Her funeral procession couldn't reach the cemetery
because the hearse and pallbearers on foot could not traverse the long stretch
of deep furrows in the vegetable fields that blocked access to the cemetery.
Instead, Bennett was laid to rest in the cemetery at Intersection Reformed
Episcopal Church on St. Thomas Island.

"She wanted to come back here to her family graveyard," the minister
said. "She was born here in a place called Mitchell, but we couldn't get
through. Somebody ought to be responsible for the relocation of her body."

When Paul Alston, the lanky ex-cowboy who wrestled Guggenheim's
steers, strolled through the cemetery, he called it by a different name. Under
a thick carpet of pine needles are the remains of Alston's grandmother Julia
McNeil in an unmarked grave.[19]

"No, this is the Village Cemetery," Alston insisted after a few paces
beyond the gate. In his Gullah accent, he pronounces the v sound as a w.
"That's what everybody called it."

Alston lived on Daniel Island near the Mitchell area on the south side
of the cemetery and across the marsh. "My grandmother is buried right
in here," he said, waving his long arm over a clearing just beyond the gate.
She died around 1940 when Alston was about seven years old.

The last time Alston stood in the cemetery was for the burial of his cousin
Ernestine Venning, whose grave is near his grandmother's. She died Sept.
13, 1973. Reading the names on granite headstones reminded Alston of
people he knew as a boy.

Thomas Glover died March 13, 1940. He was a World War I veteran.
Two small American flags are stuck in the ground near his headstone,

---

19 Paul Alston's mother and grandmother were both named Julia.

sumably placed there by Riley. "I was a little boy when (Glover) died," Alston said. "He lived on Daniel Island. He lived in Mitchell. I remember him good. He was a fella who liked to drink and have a good time like 'dem old fellas I used to know. Those fellas used to get together at a little hall they had at Mitchell."

If this is not the Grove Cemetery then where is it? Could it be near the tennis stadium?

As Alston walked past the tennis stadium, he paused to observe the area. It all was once covered with trees, he said. As he walked closer to the cemetery's fence, he paused again. "This is the Grove graveyard. That's what everybody call 'em." When he worked for Guggenheim, he rode to the island's cemeteries on horseback, where he often found stray steers. "This is the Grove."[20]

A Road, A Bridge, Then Change

Edward Keith, who helped establish the Keith School, predicted in the 1940s that one day the area would get a bridge from North Charleston. That came to pass in 1992 when the Don N. Holt Bridge was completed over the Cooper River. His family calls him a visionary, but even Keith might have been surprised by the degree of change brought by the Mark Clark Expressway. Along the highway flows a stream of traffic from both directions — North Charleston and Mount Pleasant —and with it came development on Daniel Island that has spilled over onto St. Thomas Island and the tip of the Cainhoy peninsula.

Before the expressway's construction, Daniel Island was in view of mo-

---

20 The confusion over the names of the cemeteries near the tennis stadium and the sales office presents an opportunity for additional research to clarify their identities. Michael Dahlman said he and his son were "very careful not to attach names to the sites that they could not authenticate. I know there is deep history to these sites, and it is out of the deepest respect for the men, women and children that are buried here that we worked to catalogue all of the known names and markers. It is my continued hope that additional research enables us to even more deeply understand the lives of those who lived and worked and now rest on Daniel Island."

torists from the two steel bridges that once spanned the Cooper River. Yet the island was out of the way by road. By the mid-1980s, fewer than a dozen people lived on the island. As the expressway's completion drew closer, it heightened the anxiety of what would happen to the island. Harry Frank Guggenheim, who owned most of the island, never was interested in selling. He noted in his will that he wanted the island to remain pristine. After his death in 1971, trustees of the Harry F. Guggenheim Foundation honored his wish.

An editor at The Evening Post newspaper in 1985 wrote: "Those who would like to see Daniel Island's special charm preserved as much as possible can take some encouragement from the fact that the directors of the trust have engaged land planners to recommend the best usage of the island. Such considerations would seem to leave open the possibility that the island might be utilized for scientific research or for educational purposes — either of which tend to ensure protection of the natural beauty — rather than for industrial or commercial development, with the adverse impacts that have come to be associated with either."

Charleston annexed Daniel Island in 1991 in a highly publicized tug-of-war between Mount Pleasant and North Charleston. The island was still farmland. Since then, Daniel Island has grown into an upscale residential and commercial community. Now that some 3,000 homes have been built on the island, its population is estimated at 6,500 people. As many as 5,000 commuters arrive daily to work at offices, schools, restaurants and retail shops. A decade after development began to change the island's character, Mount Pleasant historian Suzannah Smith Miles asked why Guggenheim's wish wasn't honored.

"The island has become a developer's dream and a property owner's nightmare," she said.

That depends on where you live, however. For the 200 residents of Jack Primus who live in about 50 homes, the Daniel Island annexation was a problem initially but now it's a benefit, Fred Lincoln said. "It is nice to have the tennis court with its concerts, the shopping, the banks and supermarket nearby," he said. "That's not a bad thing."

Matt Sloan, president of the Daniel Island Company, said:

"It's natural for folks to be concerned about development and its impact. There are far too many instances where inappropriate development practices have done more harm than good. Negative consequences of development — such as increased traffic, the impact on property values (and taxes), and environmental concerns — have unfortunately occurred in many places because those in charge were not sensitive to these issues when planning. In many instances, these impacts have been caused by developers who move into a community, make their money and leave. Fortunately, the development team at Daniel Island has been sensitive to these issues since the inception of the master plan, and has taken a long term approach to community building. That's why we've tried to build a community lined with sidewalks so people can walk to school, the grocery store and the library. It's why we painstakingly design buildings and homes around existing trees to minimize disturbance to the environment. It's why we have developed a world-class parks system that is accessible to the public. And it's why we have been determined to make sure that Daniel Island becomes a friendly neighbor within Cainhoy and not a separate community up the road."

Development also began to take over a portion of Clements Ferry Road from the expressway to Jack Primus. The subdivisions, office parks, retail businesses and trucking terminals have drawn in outsiders and rush-hour traffic. The most unexpected change came in the form of a stream of commuter traffic along Clements Ferry from the S.C. 41 bridge. The increased traffic along Clements Ferry also has triggered a spate of traffic accidents, some fatal.

Traffic does not bother St. Thomas Island homeowner Alice Washington. "I'm glad that the expressway is there. I don't have to drive all the way around through Wando to get anywhere."

Huger resident Florence Dickerson lives about six miles from the residential and business expansion along Clements Ferry Road. She's aware

The Mark Clark Expressway bridges over the Wando River are part of the modern highway that links the once remote Cainhoy peninsula to metropolitan Charleston. Photo by Herb Frazier.

of it. But what troubles her most are urban trends that have spread to the country. She's noticed escalating drug sales on Charity Church Road where some young people don't respect their elders and black teen-age boys wear their pants so low they reveal their underwear. There is a declining devotion to God. These are the kinds of changes, Dickerson said, that have made country life less tranquil.

After Guggenheim died, ownership of Cain Hoy Plantation was transferred from his foundation to three separate groups. The land is now owned by the Cain Hoy Land & Timber LLC, 5,700 acres; Trust I owns three separate parcels that total about 1,860 acres; and Tract 7 LLC owns about 1,573 acres.

The largest portion of the property, owned by the Cain Hoy Land & Timber LLC, extends north from Beresford Creek to just north of the St. Thomas Church.

One of the Trust I parcels borders Sarah Lincoln Road near Jack Primus and includes the old Venning Cemetery. A smaller Trust I tract is on the Wando south of Cainhoy. The third Trust I tract is on the Wando River and Beresford Creek.

Tract 7 is to the east and north of Jack Primus and just south of the BP Amoco chemical plant off Cainhoy Road.

Lincoln and others wonder what's going to happen to the property. When the city annexed the property, there was concern that a potential development would harm the community. Building on the property, he said, could spur additional growth, bringing more traffic and the loss of land to widen the roads. It could also further boost property taxes and raise the potential of families losing their land to a developer through heirs' property disputes. Cainhoy residents have similar concerns. Part of the tract owned by the Cain Hoy Land & Timber borders the village.

Peter Lawson-Johnston II, Guggenheim's cousin and the managing member of Cain Hoy Land & Timber, said in a prepared statement that the three current owners of the Cain Hoy property "do not have any development plans at this point in time. Our family continues to use the property exclusively for recreational purposes and as a timber growing business."

The owners signed a development agreement with the city that commits Charleston to provide services to the area, such as water, sewer and fire and police protection and sets zoning regulations for various portions of the land. When Daniel Island was annexed into the city, the Guggenheim Foundation saw another opportunity on the horizon. They believed at that time that the chance to build a "city within a city" also created the best conditions for the eventual development of the Cain Hoy Plantation property.

Although there are no specific plans to develop the property, a skeptical Lincoln countered: "They have plans. People don't buy land for the beauty of it." If the property is sold and developed, the neighbor who's in the best position to do it is the Daniel Island Co.

The annexation of Guggenheim's property brought an unexpected problem that angered some Jack Primus residents. Following the annexation, Charleston police patrolled Clements Ferry Road. The police presence didn't stop there. For about six weeks after the annexation, police placed a checkpoint at the entrance to Jack Primus, Lincoln recalled. Upset residents demanded an explanation as to why they were being stopped on their way home to a community with little crime. They also asked why roadblocks weren't placed at Cainhoy, Lincoln said. The roadblocks stopped after community members met with Police Chief Reuben Greenberg. "He just went crazy with the roadblocks in the black community," Lincoln recalled.

As development crept toward the Cainhoy peninsula, circumstances brought Skinner and Lincoln together over their common interest of saving the rural character of the Cainhoy-Wando community. They had no idea then, however, that they and others would go up against a powerful state agency.

In 1985, after Cainhoy's historic houses and stores were added to the National Register of Historic Places, residents were called into action in their first effort to contain development. The community was protesting a planned marina in the village. Then the Daniel Island annexation got their attention. "Everyone had concerns," Lincoln said. "That's when we started meeting to discuss what our area would look like in the future." Skinner and Lincoln met at that meeting. "She knew of my activity in the community, and that led to a conversation to what we could do as far as zoning to protect our area," Lincoln said.

The community is organized so people work like firemen, ready to answer an alarm. When they get a hint a developer has plans for a project, Skinner and Lincoln make the phone calls and the community springs into action. They attended planning commission and county council meetings in Charleston and Berkeley counties and appear before Charleston City Council.

"I am actively involved in protecting this community because of my roots here, my love for its beauty, history and all of its people who come together in a time of need, and I know Fred feels the same," Skinner said. "That is one reason I have such a deep respect for (Fred) and have enjoyed working with him."

In 1999 the South Carolina State Ports Authority, a state agency that manages the container-ship terminals on the Cooper and Wando rivers, proposed to build a Global Gateway facility at the southern tip of Daniel Island. That sounded a loud alarm because the SPA wanted to bring a rail line directly through a black neighborhood on St. Thomas Island to Daniel Island. The residents responded to the Global Gateway by forming a group called the Wando Concerned Citizens Committee. "At that time, we had about 16 active members," Lincoln recalled. The group is remembered for its rallying cry "Contain the Port."

"We started a train and others started jumping on," Lincoln said. "It got press coverage. Save the Wando (an environmental group) joined with us. The Coastal Conservation League was one of our biggest allies. Arthur Ravenel (a former member of the U.S. House of Representatives) is a big environmentalist, and we got his attention," Lincoln said. "We got students from Tulane University (in New Orleans) and Morehouse College (in Atlanta) to write letters for us to whoever would listen around the country."

The community's protest was turning public sentiment to their side. Lincoln knew the protest was working when the SPA offered the community $5 million to accept the Global Gateway plan. "We rejected the port's offer to give us $5 million," he said. "Now where can you go to find any black community that well organized?" Eventually, the port retreated.

Before the community's victory, he said, "very few people had it in their minds that we could beat the port. But we did, and we knew that we had to fight them and stand up and say, 'No, not through our backyard.' People said we were wasting our time. The port usually gets what they want, and the port was telling us they would get what they want."

As the port fight was ending, the community organized the Wando-Huger Community Development Corporation. The multi-racial group was chartered to seek funding for community projects and promote specific causes. Key members included Skinner and her husband, Henry "Butch" Skinner, Louise Smalls, James Meyers, Jerry Burns, Laverne Skipper, the Rev. David Riley and Vernelle Dickerson, Lincoln said. "They were the ones there day and night," said Lincoln, who was the group's first chairman. Today, he holds the position of vice chairman. Frank Wright is the chairman.

Since its inception, Lincoln said, "The biggest projects the CDC has done was the Keith School Museum and the rehabilitation of the Venning graveyard. We are much stronger because the community had gained confidence after the victory over the port. The organization gained a sense of legitimacy that as volunteers they can make change."

The CDC's efforts haven't always paid off, however. "We have lost zoning battles," he said humbly. "The biggest one we fought and lost was in 2004 before Berkeley County Council to have every area of our community zoned that single-wide mobile homes would be allowed," he said. "We were defeated by the property owners near the Mark Clark Expressway. I fought the hardest for that because our community does not need any limitations," he said. "If you can afford a single-wide mobile home, you should be able to live in our community."

Membership in the Wando-Huger CDC includes people across the Cainhoy peninsula. "We are just one community," he said. "We have people on the CDC from Huger, Greenbay, Jack Primus, and all over the place." Members attend county council and planning board meetings when it is necessary to monitor and speak out again rezoning requests. But the CDC can be stronger, Lincoln admitted. "Just a few of us are making the decisions," he said. "In certain areas, people will come out when there is a zoning issue adjacent to their property. We need to come out in full force no matter what segment of the community is being attacked." The existence of the CDC is a lasting asset from the anti-port battle that could again be called upon if the community faces another major development or is confronted with a health issue with widespread implications on the Cainhoy peninsula.

As developers come looking for land, there is a concern that community needs might get overlooked. With funding from the Daniel Island Community Fund, the Coastal Community Foundation hired consultant Karimah Moore to prepare a community-needs report. In the summer of 2004, Moore met with 48 people during meetings, focus groups and one forum. She concluded that the community lacks strong community groups, affordable housing, after-school programs, recreation facilities, infrastructure improvements and a holistic community center. To satisfy these and other needs, the report recommended a coalition among existing neighborhood organizations. "A coalition can be formed to bring community leaders together on a regular basis to share information, define common links, develop joint projects, and create a unified, accountable leadership collective," Moore wrote.

In a prepared statement, Matt Sloan, president of the Daniel Island Company, said: "The Daniel Island Community Fund, which has invested heavily in organizations that are working to make Cainhoy a better place, was established by our company to make sure that this historically underserved community is not neglected as development of the region continues. We decided in the early stages of the fund that its giving would be based on geography, meaning that grants would be distributed only to organizations planning to use them in our geographic service area (the Cainhoy peninsula). The Fund has partnered with the Coastal Community Foundation and provided funding for a needs assessment study of the Cainhoy, Huger, Wando, and (St.) Thomas Island communities. It has provided funding to the Center for Heirs' Property Preservation so that they can advance their mission of helping today's generation of Cainhoy residents hold on to land that has passed from generation to generation. It's taken a lead on efforts to improve the facilities at Cainhoy Elementary and Middle School, funded Boys and Girls Club programs, funded scholarships for Cainhoy children to attend Daniel Island camps, and assisted numerous residents with critical housing repairs. A large portion of the funds for the restoration of Keith School came from this community.

"There are many other examples — too many to mention — where this community, with the aid of the Daniel Island Community Fund, has embraced its neighbors on the peninsula. Perhaps our greatest achievement has been to engage other service providers and get them focused on the Cainhoy community. Were it not for the Fund's matching grant program, many service providers may not have ever entered the community."

The changes on the Cainhoy peninsula following the opening of the expressway also offer a forecast of the impact development could have if the other end of the Mark Clark Expressway is extended to Johns Islands.

Dana Beach, executive director of the Coastal Conservation League, said, "What puzzles me about the debate on Johns Island is that no one has acknowledged that what happened to Cainhoy could happen on Johns Island." The Clements Ferry area is an example of how arbitrary investment in a new highway has inconvenienced and destabilized an entire community, he said. "And unlike the Cainhoy experience, there is no evidence that extending 526 to Johns Island will do anything but worsen traffic congestion in the region." In retrospect, the planning for the expressway across the Cainhoy peninsula and Daniel Island could have taken a different approach, he said. "Assuming that the expressway was a desirable thing to connect Mount

Pleasant and North Charleston, I would have worked with the families who live there to clear titles (to avoid heirs' property disputes), identified areas for development, and imposed high standards. I would have established a limit on the amount of commercial and industrial development to reduce the truck traffic on Clements Ferry. Cainhoy should have had a master plan under which local residents would have benefited." Instead, "all of the decisions were made to the advantage of the Guggenheim property owners and to the detriment of the community." The city, Beach said, sacrificed "the Cainhoy community to lure the Guggenheims into annexing Daniel Island. It was a huge mistake not to impose any restrictions on the use of the land on the Cainhoy peninsula."

The Future

Two urban planners with jurisdiction over land at opposite ends of Berkeley County offer predictions of what might happen to property on either end of the Cainhoy peninsula within the next half century. Mark E. Davis, a planner with the Berkeley County Planning and Zoning Department, and Christopher Morgan, Charleston's director of Planning and Neighborhoods Division, based their forecasts on projects that are underway and prior patterns of development.

Two projects – The Keystone Tract and Brightwood Plantation – will set the pace for growth around Huger in the Francis Marion National Forest, one of the last large stretches of undeveloped land in the Lowcountry.

The Keystone Tract is considered a low-density development on 4,500 acres that will cater to people who want an equestrian lifestyle and a home in a rural setting within an easy drive of Mount Pleasant and Charleston, Davis said. "Keystone is getting developed slowly but surely," he said. "It is a very low-density development that varies from tract to tract. Overall, the project will have 890 homes. Inside this substantial amount of acreage, parcels (set aside for developers) will range from 15 to 100 acres and each will have a varying number of homes." The Keystone developers have a 50-year development agreement with the county.

Brightwood, however, is a different kind of community. Although it is smaller than Keystone, when Brightwood is finished it will have 114 single-family houses packed on 40 acres. It is a higher-density development that does not fit into the rural makeup of the area at this time, Davis said. "I don't think more of that will show itself in that area. However, in the future the area near Brightwood on Cainhoy Road where sewer lines currently exist, more of this type housing option could be developed in the future."

Overall growth in the Huger area is expected to be slow because a majority of Huger lacks sewer and a network of major roads to handle the capacity of traffic, he said. It is a simple formula for growth. "Once you bring sewer and roads, density will follow," he explained. New home construction also is expected to spread slowly because much of the land is heirs' property, which often takes time to acquire, and conservation easements have placed Middleburg Plantation and other large tracts off limits to development.

Berkeley County has received public input as it updates its comprehensive plan for growth. The comprehensive plan, titled "Planning the Future While Preserving the Past," is intended to be a guiding document to help steer the county's growth. However, the plan does not specifically consider the historic nature of African-American communities on the Cainhoy peninsula. "No one community gets that much depth in the comprehensive plan," Davis revealed. "However, the plan does have an historic and cultural category which touches upon and recognizes that areas of the county are different and addresses needs based on the uniqueness of an individual area."

In the middle of the Cainhoy peninsula, the sprawling timber land of Cain Hoy Plantation has the potential to ignite a building boom that will change the rural landscape near Cainhoy and Jack Primus. But so far, the owners of the property have announced no specific plans.

Morgan said Cain Hoy Plantation, the majority of which is in the city of Charleston, "is a massive amount of area that is very important to the future of Charleston. It is one of the bigger areas of undeveloped land within the urban context of Charleston. It is an area of land that is equal to, if not greater than, the Daniel Island development."

As such, Morgan predicts that what might occur there is a combination of light industrial sites, office buildings, mixed-use projects with high- and low-density residential areas, dotted with gathering places at major crossroads. A golf course, affordable housing and schools are possible. The area also could have high-density development with lower density projects near Cainhoy, Jack Primus and Yellow House. To lessen the impact of traffic, cars and trucks will be routed off Clements Ferry to a new network of streets.

The city wants to prepare a development plan from the southern tip of Daniel Island north to the fringe of the Francis Marion Forest, Morgan said. "But it depends on funds and staff."

As growth in the Huger area slowly creeps through the forest, Dorothy Scott predicts that Huger could become a town. The construction of houses, she said, will draw people of both races to the community. "Huger is going to change, and it is going to change for the better in terms of the quality of life," but it also could mean that African Americans may no longer be in the majority, she said. "The people who are moving to the area could very well be better educated and forward thinking and as a result be more vigilant to monitor issues that affect the community," she said.

If signs of major development begin to show around Jack Primus, it will most certainly heighten the anxiety there. To protect the land, Fred Lincoln said, Jack Primus should be placed on the National Register of Historic Places. Lincoln admitted, however, that's unlikely to happen. Jack Primus doesn't meet the criteria to gain a historic designation because none of the present-day houses are historic. "The type of houses that slaves built, they tore them down to build more modern houses. They need to change the criteria. When plantations are placed in protected easements, the old rice fields are protected from development, but the black communities aren't. How can you value the rice fields more than you value the people who created the rice fields?"

Lincoln said the people who settled Jack Primus made a monumental shift when they went from slavery to freedom and then landowners. "The old-timers say that this is the first property we owned, and that was the factor that made you free," he said. "Land separated a free man from a slave. Because these are the first properties former slaves owned there is an emotional attachment to the land," Lincoln explained.

Most property owners want their land value to rise, but he said "if you don't plan to sell your ancestral property you want your value to decrease because of the tax concerns." Developers don't easily grasp that concept. "They say (development) is going to appreciate your property value so they are ready to put a commercial development next to these communities because, in their eyes, this will help you, but it doesn't help us, it helps force us off our property.

"If a person is working at McDonald's, all they can buy is a mobile home, but they will own that mobile home on their own property and that gives them a sense of pride of accomplishment," Lincoln said. "They could hold onto that mobile home so one day they could build a nice home, but if we allow property values to increase they can't hold onto the property, if the taxes go up."

Lincoln is adamant that local government should help communities like Jack Primus exist. "We don't need a lot of services," he said. "We get little police protection. I have an uncle who lives on Hanover Street in the city. I asked him, 'Where are you safer? You have all of the cops, but we are safer in Jack Primus. What makes my area safe is all of my family live here.' That's my argument for maintaining these self-sufficient areas. We aren't a burden on taxpayers. We don't have any homeless people. Yes, we have mobile homes, but we own them. We didn't beg anyone for them. The old-timers say once you come free, everyone should own an inch of dirt and be self-sufficient. That's what was instilled in us."

If it weren't for progress in the South, Lincoln said, he would not have returned to Jack Primus from New York. "We benefit from the change; we benefit from development," he said. "But we've come to a point now that those changes and those developments, if you are not careful, could be detrimental to us."

Acknowledgments

I am grateful to many individuals and organizations. Suzannah Smith Miles recommended me for this project. Madeleine McGee gave me early support when she led the Coastal Community Foundation of South Carolina. I appreciate their confidence.

I thank Richard Hendry at the foundation for his endless patience while I pursued yet another story. Steve Hoffius elevated this work with his editing skills and knowledge. He continuously motivated me to "finish the book!" Chuma Nwokike traveled with me around the Cainhoy peninsula to take the pictures that inspired artist John W. Jones, whose work adorns this book.

These stories come from people. They also come from paper filed in libraries and archives. The people who welcomed me into their homes to share their stories and those who granted interviews are listed in the bibliography. To each of them I extend many thanks.

Special thanks also goes to Fred Lincoln for his entrée to the community and his insights. Benjamin Bess, Gail Carson, Vernelle Dickerson, Beverly Avinger Lahmeyer, Peggy Lincoln, Vonnie Porcher Lincoln and Butch and MaeRe Skinner also were my guides through the community. I also owe a special thanks to Macky Hill for access to Middleburg Plantation and for sharing his passion of history.

I appreciate the support and kind words from the relatives of the people I interviewed. They read portions of the book or assisted in other ways. They included: Inez Broughton, Beatrice Dennis-White, Fred Fordham, Jerry Fordham Jr., Gloria Jenkins, Rosemary Jenkins-Varela, William Jenkins,

Calvin Keith, Leroy Keith, Tom Lucas, Al McCormack, Carey Lucas Nikonchuk, Georgette Rivers, Rufus "Thornley" Rivers, Norwood Smalls and Maxine Smith.

To the elders who have passed on: Eddie Carson, Gladys Lincoln, Elizabeth Rivers, Johnnie Rivers, Philip Simmons, Postal Smalls and Margaret Wade-Lewis.

Jane Aldrich, Michael Coker and Mary Jo Fairchild made my time at the S.C. Historical Society enjoyable and fruitful. Nic Butler, Marianne Cawley, Alicia Thompson, Liz Newcombe, Molly French, Christina Shedlock and Dorothy Glover in the South Carolina Room at the Charleston County Library. All were tireless in their pursuit of details. The Charleston Library Society staff and Leila Potts-Campbell, Harlan Greene, Curtis Franks and Deborah Wright at Avery Research Center for African American History and Culture helped to dig out the facts. My research friends "from off," Leslie Anderson, Alexandria, Va. Library, and Toni Carrier, Africana Heritage Project at the University of South Florida, kept the e-mails coming.

Eric Poplin at Brockington and Associates, Bernard Powers, Gene Waddell, Robert Stockton and Elijah Siegler at the College of Charleston, Kerry Taylor at The Citadel, Rossie M. Colter at the Philip Simmons Foundation and Robert T. Morgan with the Francis Marion Forest provided valuable assistance at the start of this project. Along the way, I received help from other scholars: Damon L. Fordham, Spring College and Virginia College, Charleston; Daniel Littlefield, University of South Carolina; Jim Piecuch, Kennesaw State University, Georgia; Richard Dwight Porcher Jr., The Citadel; Dale Rosengarten, College of Charleston; and author Roy Williams, Sullivan's Island.

I also received advice and research assistance from: Alcione Amos, Smithsonian's Anacostia Community Museum, Washington, D.C.; Marilyn Graf, Archives of Traditional Music, Indiana University; Richard W. Hatcher III, Fort Sumter National Monument; Brian Cuthrell, South Caroliniana Library; Tommy Townsend, Charleston County School District; and Libby Wilder and Pam Liles, The Post and Courier library. Thanks also goes to Pierre Manigault for the opportunity to write something that will be remembered longer than a newspaper story.

Others who were invaluable in the hunt for nuggets of information were: Josh Gelinas, Department of Corrections; Linda McClelland and Jeff Joeckel, National Register of Historic Places; and Harry Spratlin, U.S. Postal Service, Columbia. Elaine Bozman and Bob McEntyre, Charleston County Register Mesne Conveyance office helped me flip through maps and deeds. Additional guidance came from real estate title abstracter Mike Rourk, who should write a book of his own.

Thanks also goes to Jan Malloy, Daniel Island Co.; Steve Tuttle, S.C. Department of Archives and History; the Rev. Canon Jim Lewis, Episcopal Diocese of South Carolina; Dr. Julius Barnes, Diocese of the Southeast of the Reformed Episcopal Church; Gena Austin, Home Telephone Co.; Pam Bailey, Berkeley County School District; Marlene Estridge, City of Folly Beach; Carolyn Pilgrim, Berkeley County Museum; Dan Moon, Berkeley County Sheriff's Department; Thom Berry, S.C. Department of Health and Environmental Control; Crystal Smith, National Library of Medicine, Bethesda, Md.; Cynthia Nieves, Guggenheim Partners, New York; and Peter Poore and Jane Mayberry, S.C. Department of Transportation.

I'd like to thank those who read portions of this book: Edie Blakeslee, Peter David Brown, P.J. Dickerscheid, Dennis Fassuliotis, Thomas Fetters, Liz Marshall, Dick and Joanie Reed, Charles Rudloff, Richard Stoney, Ida Spruill, Joseph and Felicity Thompson and Valencia Williams. Tony Bartleme and Chuma Nwokike helped me to settle on the book's title.

James B. Edwards opened the gates to Limerick Plantation. Peter Lawson-Johnston Jr. granted access to the Cain Hoy Plantation, and Jake Wilson guided me through the mansion. Ernie Nelson at BP Amoco and Ray Sims at Nucor Steel Berkeley provided insightful history lessons during tours of the plant sites.

I also gained support from others who are passionate about history and Gullah culture. Among them are Michael Allen, Charlie Black, Barbara Fordham Collier, Ruth Cupp, Martha Dangerfield, Dena Davis, Jerri Eddings, Charlie Gates, Eleanor Kinlaw-Ross, Kaye Koonce, Ron Menchaca, Karimah Moore, Gia McKenzie, Walter Rhett, John Slayton and Edmund Varner.

I also owe a debt of gratitude to Jack McCray and Joe Opala. They support me when I need reassurance. Adrienne Troy-Hamilton knows a lot about this book. She's my best friend and confidante.

A special thanks to Emily James at G.W. Heyward Mortuary for providing a copy of the program from Eugenia Broughton's funeral and sending me to Nurse Broughton's cousin Geneva Broughton Dansby, who was an art teacher at Buist when I was a student there.

I'd like to thank E. "Jackie" Williamson at the Berkeley County Clerk of Court. Coincidentally, she is the godmother of my granddaughter Lauryn Michelle Thomas for whom this book is dedicated.

Henry W. Brevard II, a retired Berkeley County educator, referred me to Lela Haynes Session, who shared more than her knowledge of the county's education history. She helped me find the descendants of Hope Lloyd and Frank Roper. She later surprised me with details about my past. She knew my aunt Blossom Mack, who left Berkeley County for Baltimore.

My family's history is in Cordesville. My maternal great-grandparents, Joseph and Elizabeth McNeil, and my maternal grandmother, Mable McNeil Frazier, were reared there, as the family story goes. Now that the book is finished, I will look for my family's Berkeley County story.

Finally, God sustained me over the five and half years it took to collect these stories. My parents, Benjamin and Albertha Frazier of Wadmalaw Island are blessings beyond description. I appreciate all of my siblings and my son-in-law Prentiss Thomas. The love from my daughters, Angela Frazier Thomas, Amanda Frazier and Adrienne Frazier, makes me feel so young. And I thank their mother, Brenda Young Frazier, for her gift of three beautiful ladies.

Appendix I: Berkeley County Licensed Midwives in 1951

The following women were identified as licensed nurse-midwives in the "Berkeley County Midwife Year Book 1951," compiled by the Berkeley County Health Department.

Charlotte Bennett, Emma Bradley, Rebecca Broughton, Mariah D. Brown, Alphin Brown, Lurlene Brown, Lizzie Brown, Pearl Bryant, Victoria Canty, Virginia Cooper, Ivalina Davis, Annie Fladger, Daisy Gaillard, Geneva Gillins, Lucile Gourdine, Ellen Gourdine, Lila Graham, Phyllis Green, Lucy Green, Senie Johnson, Nancy Joy, Irene Ladson, Sara Jane Limehouse, Lucile McCray, Lula Miller, Sara Owens, Nellie Pasley, Cora Lee Preacher, Lucy President, Mattie President, Janie President, Wilhelmina Prioleau, Lillie Ramsey, Isabella Reid, Janie Richardson, Jane Richardson, Rosabelle Robinson, Catherine Scott, Mary Jane Shine, Emma Stevens, Mary Stretch, Rebecca Taylor, Sara Vanderhorst, Martha Walker and Isabella Washington.

Broughton and Callen, certified nurse-midwives and registered nurses, and Edith Baylor, a licensed practical nurse and midwife, served on a six-member advisory committee that supervised the county's corps of nurse midwives.

Appendix II: Huger-Wando Post Offices

A Cainhoy post office was in operation briefly from April 12, 1880, until December 1, 1880. Samuel H. Poyas was its only postmaster.

The Wando Post Office in the village of Cainhoy was established on May 5, 1886. It was discontinued on September 14, 1887. Mail was then routed through Charleston.

The Wando Post Office was re-established on March 7, 1888. Josie W. Smoak was the last person to serve as Wando's postmaster. When she retired on November 30, 1984, the post office was housed in a tiny white building on Fogarty Lane. It had fifteen general delivery customers. Letter carriers delivered mail to about ninety mail boxes on Daniel Island, up S.C. 41 toward the Greenbay community and a few homes on Cainhoy Road near Clements Ferry Road. Service was suspended on January 17, 1992, and discontinued on July 31, 1993, according to information provided by the U.S. Postal Service. The postal service also compiled a list of postmasters who served the Huger and Wando communities.

Wando Post Office

Name	Title	Date appointed
Mary L. Lucas	Postmaster	May 5, 1886
Kate L. Clute	Postmaster	February 16, 1887
Emma E. Venning	Postmaster	March 7, 1888
Eloise G. Avinger	Postmaster	June 2, 1908
Rosa E. Worsham	Postmaster	October 13, 1909
Lutewick C. Mayer	Postmaster	October 18, 1910
Daisy W. Chandler Worsham	Postmaster	May 22, 1914
Josie W. Smoak	Acting Postmaster	May 31, 1950
Josie W. Smoak	Postmaster	August 14, 1950
Carolyn Murphy	Officer-in-Charge	November 30, 1984

Huger Post Office

The post office in Huger was originally established as the "Hugers" Post Office. John C. Inabnett was appointed the first postmaster on November 27, 1890. On May 8, 1894, the name was changed to the Huger Post Office. Following are the men and women who served as postmaster.

Name	Title	Date appointed
John C. Inabnett	Postmaster	November 27, 1890
William E. Cook	Postmaster	July 16, 1894
Lester A. Coward	Postmaster	December 4, 1896
Annie J. Elliott	Postmaster	May 20, 1904
George W. Murray	Postmaster	October 6, 1904
William D. Austin	Postmaster	August 30, 1905
Amanda Cumbee	Postmaster	August 12, 1906
Benjamin P. Gibbs	Postmaster	October 30, 1914
Adeline C. Williams	Acting Postmaster	August 1, 1942
Myrtle V. Thomas	Acting Postmaster	January 16, 1943
Adeline C. Williams	Acting Postmaster	November 27, 1943
Myrtle L. Murphy	Acting Postmaster	January 24, 1945
Myrtle L. Murphy	Postmaster	October 14, 1946
Margaret Ann Johnson	Acting Postmaster	July 5, 1960
Margaret Ann Johnson	Postmaster	April 26, 1961
Annie G. Morris	Officer-In-Charge	March 17, 1972
Annie G. Morris	Postmaster	August 19, 1972
Robert Bogart	Officer-In-Charge	January 15, 1985
Rosie Brown	Officer-In-Charge	(No date listed)
Edna M. Wrenn	Postmaster	April 13, 1985
Gale Hughes	Officer-In-Charge	June 30, 1995
Harley D. Crosby	Postmaster	August 5, 1995
Ervin E. Lambert	Officer-In-Charge	May 7, 1996
Mary L. Levine	Officer-In-Charge	September 19, 1996
Gloria Jenkins	Officer-In-Charge	November 8, 1996
Gloria Jenkins	Postmaster	December 7, 1996

Appendix III: How Land was Lost

Land was often seized by the government for unpaid taxes and sold off to the highest bidder. Folks on the Cainhoy peninsula also lost it to shrewd storeowners who allowed them to buy food and other necessities on credit.

University of Michigan graduate student Terry Yasuko Ogawa, who grew up in Charleston, wrote about one such example in her master's thesis titled "Wando-Huger: A Study of the Impacts of Development on the Cultural Role of Land in Black Communities of the South Carolina Lowcountry." A local resident, who Ogawa identified only as Victoria, said her father helped a family recover land that had been signed away to pay a bill at George Avinger's store.

"When people couldn't afford groceries, he'd credit them food, and when they weren't able to pay the bill, he would have them to sign away property because a lot of the older people didn't know how to read and write," Ogawa quoted Victoria as saying.

Appendix IV: Heirs' Property

A report prepared by the Coastal Community Foundation in 2001 identified about 1,300 tracts covering 17,000 acres in Berkeley County that were jointly owned by relatives. With heirs' property, each relative has the right to sell his or her share of the property to a non-relative, who can force the sale of all of the land, if no agreement is reached.

"There are no winners when family members cannot agree on how their land should be used," according to Jennie L. Stephens, executive director of the Center for Heirs' Property Preservation in Charleston. "Without agreement, the odds are increased that the family will be forced to sell their land and divide the proceeds from the sale among the heirs. When this happens, it's not just the loss of land, but the loss of a legacy, the loss of history and the loss of a promise; a promise made by the ancestor that all family members would have a place to live, to come back to and enjoy indefinitely."

Access to the correct information and readily available resources are the most powerful tools heirs' property owners have to keep their land, she said.

"A lack of knowledge and no family agreement and limited access to affordable legal services have been some of the main reasons heirs' property owners have lost the precious gifts of land that have been left to them by their ancestors. Heirs' property owners need to have a working understanding of heirs' property ownership and the various strategies to achieve clear title to their land. Once this is achieved, they can make informed decisions and come into agreement with their families and take affirmative steps to jointly protect their properties."

A new S.C. law was enacted in 2006 to solve the problem of land acquisition through heirs' property disputes. The law requires that family members be given the first right of refusal to buy the property. The law still can be used against black land owners, said Dorothy Scott, a Huger native and president of the Charleston Branch of the NAACP. Land in heirs' property disputes is typically under-appraised in anticipation that a member of the family will not have the money to buy the property, she said. Historically, as is still the case today, she said, many properties that were owned by black heirs have literally been stolen by creative manipulation of the law.

Appendix V: Dividing the Money

Money from the sale of Pinefield was divided between sixteen heirs and four lawyers.

The money the heirs received ranged from a low of $11,700 to a high of $93,900. Rivers' share included a reimbursement for three years of property taxes he paid. The money the heirs received was calculated on what remained after the lawyers' fees and costs were deducted.

The lawyer fees were calculated on the gross sales price. William Peagler III, Wigfall's attorney, received about $104,000. Three attorneys for the heirs — John M. Bleecker Jr., Mark Lund and S. Tom Worley Jr. — each received $45,500.

Bibliography

Introduction

Suzannah Smith Miles, *East Cooper Gazetteer* (Charleston: The History Press, 2004)

Suzannah Smith Miles, *Writings of the Lowcountry* (Charleston: The History Press, 2005)

Karimah Moore, "Study of the Huger and Wando Communities," Prepared for the Daniel Island Company, July 2, 2004

Research Assistance: Suzannah Smith Miles shared unpublished research and correspondence on Daniel Island history and early inhabitants; Irving B. Fordham of Stone Mountain, Georgia, a descendant of Cain Walker, shared unpublished research about his ancestor

Voices: Harold Lincoln

An 1877 deed recorded in the Charleston County Office of the Register of Mesne Conveyance shows William L. Venning Jr. selling an acre for $1.00 to the trustees of St. Johns Chapel, which later became Greater St. Johns AME Church. The land was once part of the Hartford Plantation

Interview: Harold Lincoln of Jack Primus

Voices: Philip Simmons

John Beaty and Ralph Bailey, "A Historic Architectural Resources Survey of the Upper Peninsula, Charleston, South Carolina" (Charleston, S.C.: Brockington and Associates, 2004)

Harry Frank Guggenheim Papers (receipt for payment to "P. Simmons, blacksmith," July 17, 1962), Manuscript Division, Library of Congress, Washington, D.C.

Mary E. Lyons, *Catching the Fire: Philip Simmons, Blacksmith* (Boston: Houghton Mifflin Co., 1997)

John Michael Vlach, *Charleston Blacksmith: The Work of Philip Simmons* (Columbia: University of South Carolina Press, 1992)

Interview: Philip Simmons

Chapter 1: Native Americans

Chapman J. Milling, *Red Carolinians* (Columbia: University of South Carolina Press, 1969)

Eric D. Sipes and Eric C. Poplin, "Archaeological Testing of 38BK1799/1802, Charleston Regional Business Center, Berkeley County, South Carolina," Prepared by Brockington & Associates, 2001, for Charleston Regional Business Center, LLC

Gene Waddell, *Indians of the South Carolina Lowcountry, 1562-1751* (Spartanburg, S.C.: Reprint Company, 1980)

Gene Waddell, "Ignorance and Deceit in Renaming Charleston's Rivers; Some Observations about the Reliability of Historical Sources," South Carolina Historical Magazine 89 (January 1988): 40-50

Interview: Heidi Varner, former member of the Wassamasaw Council of the Wassamasaw Tribe of Varner Town Indians

Chapter 2: Africans and Europeans

"An Abundance of Game," Charleston News and Courier, December 15, 1889

An Account of the Late Intended Insurrection Among a Portion of the Blacks of this City (Charleston: the Corporation of Charleston, 1822)

"Records of the Assistant Commissioner for the State of South Carolina Bureau of Refugees, Freedmen and Abandoned Lands, 1865-1870," National Archives Microfilm Publication M869, Roll 34, Reports of conditions and operations July 1865-Dec. 1866

"Registers of Signatures of Depositors in Branches of the Freedmen's Savings and Trust Company," Records of Office of the Comptroller of the Currency, www.africanaheritage. com (Accessed June 2, 2010)

The Charleston Morning Post and Daily Advertiser, February 17, 1782 (Advertisement: An enslaved man named Primus who ran away is suspected of hiding in the Cainhoy area. The advertisements for enslaved people who ran away were found at www.GenealogyBank.com)

The Charleston Morning Post and Daily Advertiser, March 6, 1786 (Advertisement: Molly Dean ran away and is well known in the Cainhoy area.)

City Gazette and Daily Advertiser, October 9, 1795 (Advertisement: An enslaved man named Moses, who ran away from Johns Island, had lived at Cainhoy); June 11, 1798 (Advertisement: An enslaved man named Moses who ran away was seen at Cainhoy); February 27, 1809 (Advertisement: $10.00 reward: An enslaved woman named Manema, who was raised in St. Thomas on the Cooper River, was sold to Necca Decoster in Charleston before she ran away. She has numerous friends at Cainhoy); February 7, 1821 (Advertisement: $50.00 reward offered for Massa, an enslaved woman, who ran away from Columbia, South Carolina. She was born and raised on Daniel's Island.)

Nicolas Butler, Records of the Commissioners of the House of Corrections, 1868-1885 (Charleston: Charleston County Public Library, 2008)

Leland Ferguson, *Uncommon Ground: Archaeology and Early African America, 1650-1800* (Washington, D.C.: Smithsonian Institution Press, 1992)

Emma S. Gilchrist, "Middleburg Plantation, Its History and Its Romance," Charleston News and Courier, April 4, 1926

William Dollard Lucas, *A Lucas Memorandum* (Self-published, 1985)

Miles, East Cooper Gazetteer

Miles, Writings of the Lowcountry

Julie Saville, *The Work of Reconstruction: From Slave to Wage Laborer in South Carolina, 1680-1870* (Cambridge, U.K.: Cambridge University Press, 1994)

Dr. Lela Haynes Session, with Cynthia Hughes, *Unconditional Love* (Goose Creek, S.C.: Williams & Williams Printing and Coastal Publishing Inc., 2004)

State Gazette of South-Carolina, May 24, 1787 (Advertisement: An enslaved woman named Sarah ran away from Cainhoy, brought to New Work-House.)

Lois A. Walker and Susan R. Silverman, *A Documented History of Gullah Jack Pritchard and the Denmark Vesey Slave Insurrection of 1822* (Lewiston, N.Y.: The Edwin Mellen Press, 2001)

Nathaniel Williams' will, November 16, 1729, Charleston County Probate Court, Charleston, S.C.

Carter G. Woodson, ed., *Free Negro Owners of Slaves in the United States in 1830* (Westport, Conn.: Negro Universities Press, 1924)

Research Assistance: Toni Carrier, founding director, Lowcountry Africana, Africana Heritage Project, University of South Florida, Tampa, Florida, shared records from the Freedmen's Bank; Harriott Cheves Leland, researcher and archivist, The Huguenot Society of South Carolina, shared research on the French Protestants; Suzannah Smith Miles shared unpublished research and correspondence on Daniel Island history and its early inhabitants and Richard Beresford

Interviews: Bertha Roper Davis of Moncks Corner; Leland Ferguson, distinguished professor emeritus, Department of Anthropology, University of South Carolina; Max "Macky" Hill, a Charleston Realtor, whose parents own Middleburg Plantation; Simon Lewis, co-director of the Carolina Lowcountry and Atlantic World Program at the College of Charleston; Richard Roper of Moncks Corner; Cleola Reid Roper of Moncks Corner

Chapter 3: The Cainhoy Riot

Charleston News and Courier, "The Crime at Cainhoy," October 18, 1876; "The James Island Meeting," October 18, 1876; "The Cainhoy Slaughter," October 24, 1876; "The Fight at Cainhoy-Marshal Wallace's Report," October 25, 1876; "A Roland for an Oliver," August 29, 1888; "Race Clash Feared at Cainhoy," September 27, 1911; "Many Arrests at Cainhoy," September 28, 1911; "Cainhoy Trouble Over," September 29, 1911

Alexia Jones Helsley, *South Carolina's African American Confederate Pensioners 1923-1925* (Columbia: South Carolina Department of Archives and History, 1998)

Melinda Meek Hennessey, "Racial Violence During Reconstruction: The 1876 Riots in Charleston and Cainhoy," South Carolina Historical Magazine 86 (April 1985): 100-112

The Indianapolis Sentinel, "The Mount Pleasant Rage," October 25, 1876

The New York Daily Tribune, "The Fight at Cainhoy," October 21, 1876

Elise Pinckney, "The Cainhoy Riot as Remembered by Jim Alston," South Carolina Historical Magazine 86 (April 1985): 158-160

John S. Reynolds, *Reconstruction of South Carolina 1865-1877* (Columbia, South Carolina: The State Co., 1905)

The State (Columbia, S.C.), "Fined for Rioting," October 2, 1911

Research Assistance: Suzannah Smith Miles shared unpublished research on the Cainhoy riot

Interviews: Florence Dickerson of Huger; Tammy Wilson Giannelli, caretaker at St. Thomas Church; Fred Lincoln of Jack Primus

Chapter 4: Turn of the Century

"Born in Slavery: Slave Narratives from the Federal Writers' Project, 1936-1938," Tena White, enslaved on the Venning Plantation at Remley's Point in Christ Church Parish

Lydia C. Ball, "Limerick, Part of Cypress Barony," Charleston News and Courier, August 8, 1929

Damon L. Fordham, *True Stories of Black South Carolina* (The History Press: Charleston, South Carolina, 2008)

Lorenzo D. Turner, *Africanism in the Gullah Dialect* (Chicago: University of Chicago Press, 1949)

Lorenzo D. Turner Collection, Georgia and South Carolina, Sea Islands, 1931-33, Recorded interviews of Hope Lloyd and Frank Roper of Cordesville, S.C., Indiana University Archives of Traditional Music

Margaret Wade-Lewis, *Lorenzo Dow Turner: Father of Gullah Studies* (Columbia: University of South Carolina Press, 2007)

Interviews: Lela Haynes Session of Moncks Corner; Margaret Wade-Lewis, associate professor, Department of Black Studies, State University of New York, New Paltz, N.Y.

Chapter 5: Domestic Workforce

Herb Frazier, "Holding on to the Memories, Generations of Care Created Close Bond," Charleston Post and Courier, November 24, 2005

John G. Richards, "The official roster of South Carolina soldiers, sailors and marines in the World War, 1917-18 / compiled under the direction of John G. Richards, Governor, Jas. C. Dozier, the Adjutant General" (Columbia: Printed under supervision of The Joint Committee of Printing, General Assembly of S.C., 1932)

United States Federal Census 1920

Research Assistance: Robert B. Cuthbert, a Charleston scholar, shared research on Langdon Cheves III from the Cheves Papers at the South Carolina Historical Society

Interview: Dorothy Scott of North Charleston

Chapter 6: A Family Tragedy

Augusta Chronicle (Georgia), "J.B. Hyer Acquitted for Killing Duthards," November 12, 1908

Joseph Broughton's prison records, South Carolina Department of Archives and History, Columbia, South Carolina

James Cochrane, *Dewees: The Island and its People* (Charleston: The History Press, 2007)

Charleston News and Courier, "L.A. DuTart Killed at Cainhoy," August 11, 1908; "Witnesses Tell of the Tragedy," August 13, 1908; "Second Inquest Held," August 15, 1908; "Merchant Slain in Cainhoy Store," August 1, 1938; "Negro Confesses DuTart Slaying," August 3, 1938; "Negro Sentenced to Death Chair," May 12, 1939; "Berkeley Negro Dies in Chair Today for Cainhoy Shooting," June 23, 1939; "Berkeley Negro Pays State for Murder of Cainhoy Man," June 24, 1939

South Carolina Department of Corrections, "Exccutions in South Carolina – August, 1912 to Present."

The State (Columbia, S.C.), "Negro Dies for Murder of Merchant," June 24, 1939

Interviews: Rev. Benjamin Dennis of St. Thomas Island, Beverly Avinger Lahmeyer of Cainhoy, Johnnie Rivers of Yellow House and Mary Ann DuTart Silver of Charleston.

Chapter 7: Birthing a Community

Avery Research Center for African American History and Culture, College of Charleston, Charleston, S.C.: Programs for "Paying the Fiddler," a three-act comedic drama, written by Lillian Mortier, performed at Avery Institute, March 10, 1933; the Avery Dramatic Club's presentation of "The Call of Youth" written by Katherine Kavanaugh, April 21, 1933; the Annual Girls' Speaking Contest, Avery Institute, May 30, 1933; and the Avery Institute Sixty-Seventh Graduating Exercises, June 7, 1933

Eugenia Broughton files, the American College of Nurse-Midwives Archives, History of Medicine Division, National Library of Medicine, Bethesda, Maryland

Charleston Evening Post, "H.F. Guggenheim, Cainhoy Plantation Owner, Dies at 80," Jan. 22, 1971

Harry Frank Guggenheim Papers (Correspondence between Anita Eugenia Broughton and Harry Frank Guggenheim), Library of Congress, Manuscript Division, Washington, D.C.

Lavinia Baskin, RN., supervisor of public health nursing in Berkeley County, compiled a history of health and welfare services in Berkeley County in January 1958, Berkeley County Museum

Thomas R. Waring, "Wall Street Competence Backs Up Ranch For Raising Cattle in the Lowcountry," Charleston News and Courier, April 27, 1950

Interview: Carolyn Britt, Geneva Broughton Dansby of Charleston, Beverly Avinger Lahmeyer of Cainhoy, Beatrice Smalls McGirth of Huger and Johnnie Rivers of Yellow House.

Chapter 8: Timber

Charleston News and Courier, "Tuxbury Lumber Mill Shuts Down," June 23, 1939

Civilian Conservation Corps, "Official Annual of District I, Fourth Corps Area," 1936, provided by Robert T. Morgan, heritage program manager, Francis Marion & Sumter National Forests

Thomas Fetters, *Logging Railroads of South Carolina* (Forest Park, Il.: Heimburg House Publishing Co., 1990)

Al Hester, "From Sustained Yield to Sustaining Communities: The Establishment of Francis Marion National Forest in South Carolina, 1901-1936," Applied History Internship paper, U.S. Department of Agriculture Forest Service, 1997

William B. Lees, "Limerick Old and in the Way: Archeological Investigation at Limerick Plantation," Anthropological Studies 5, South Carolina Institute of Archeology and Anthropology, University of South Carolina

Little Ethiopia, CCC Camp newspaper, District I, Civilian Conservation Corps, Fourth Corps Area; May 1, 1936; June 19, 1937; October 30, 1937; March 9, 1938; July 1, 1938; July 15, 1938

Barbara Moore, "City's Good Will Ambassador Uses Talent to Educate Others about Life on the Waterfront," Georgetown Times, April 29, 1995

Robert T. Morgan and Al Hester, interview with Henry Smith, "Memories of the Witherbee Civilian Conservation Camp at Francis Marion National Forest, 1935-1939," 1998

Interviews: Calhoun "Clyde" Umphlett of Moncks Corner; Darr Sullivan of Moncks Corner

Chapter 9: Moonshine

Rembert C. Dennis, "Rembert Coney Dennis (1915-1992)," interviewer Dale Rosengarten, transcribed and edited by Colleen Bradley, Modern Political Collections, South Caroliniana Library, Columbia, S.C., 1995

Charleston News and Courier, "Bootleg Trouble in Forest Camps," August 13, 1933; "Two Killed, One Wounded in Gun Fight," May 9, 1926; "Five Berkeley Prisoners Here," May 10, 1926; "Senator Dennis, Shot Down In Berkeley, Lingers Near Death; Nab Man at Scene," July 25, 1930; "Doesn't Remember Shooting, Thornley Tells Governor," July 26, 1930; "Woodward, Thornley, Artis Wanted in Dennis Killing, Arrested and Imprisoned," July 30, 1930; "He Killed Senator Dennis At Bidding Of McKnight, W.L. Thornley Tells Jury," July 31, 1930; "W.L. Thornley, McKnight Held by Inquest Jury as Dennis Slaying Principals," August 1, 1930

Ruth W. Cupp, *North Area Scrapbook* (Charleston: Cupp Publishers, 1988)

Harry Frank Guggenheim Papers (letter from John G. (Jack) Leland, April 4, 1967), Library of Congress, Manuscript Division, Washington, D.C.

Marybelle Higgins Howe, Gedney Main Howe III, Robert Gasque Howe, Donald Higgins Howe and Belle Howe Stoddard, Re: Gedney Main Howe, Jr.: 1914-1981 (Adamsville, Ala.: Action Printing Co., 1985)

"Influencing Appointments to Postmasterships and other Federal Offices, Washington, D.C.," Report of the Subcommittee of the Committee on Post Offices and Post Roads, United States Government Printing Office, 1930

William Shuler, *The Ole Days in Berkeley County, South Carolina* (Bloomington, Ind.:

1st Books Library, 2002)

William Shuler, *Short Stories About Life in Berkeley County, South Carolina* (Bloomington, Ind.: AuthorHouse, 2007)

W.L. Thornley, court and prison records and pardon, South Carolina Department of Archives and History

Interviews: Buster Brown of Charleston; Florence Dickerson of Huger; Vernelle Dickerson of Huger; Herbert U. Fielding of Charleston; Beatrice Smalls McGirth of Huger; William Shuler of Moncks Corner; Postal Smalls of Huger

Chapter 10: Education

"Early Education in Berkeley County," a historical sketch provided by Pam Bailey, Berkeley County School District

"The Jeanes Supervisors, University of South Carolina-Aiken:" http://www.usca.edu/aasc/jeanes.htm (Accessed June 2, 2010)

Kimberly B. Lewis, "Cainhoy band gets uniforms," Charleston News and Courier, February 4, 1993

Rosenwald-Day Programs, March 30, 1928, and March 15, 1929, South Carolina Department of Archives and History, Columbia, South Carolina

Dr. Lela Haynes Session, with Cynthia Hughes, *Unconditional Love*

"South Carolina's Rosenwald School Buildings" Database: http://www.state.sc.us/scdah/afamer/rosenintro.htm (Accessed June 2, 2010)

Interviews: Rev. Benjamin Dennis of St. Thomas Island; Edna Keith Goodman of Charleston; Dora Bolden Howard of Huger; Albertha Jenkins of Wando; Mary Keith of Charleston; Robert Porcher Jr. of Wando; Lela Haynes Session of Moncks Corner; Postal Smalls of Huger; Emma Jule Gadsden Williams of Mount Pleasant

Chapter 11: Remembering Old Cainhoy

Capt. Ernest Christopher Avinger III's obituary, Charleston Post and Courier, January 27, 1999

Elias Ball Bull Papers, "The Cemetery at Cainhoy," South Carolina Historical Society, Charleston

W. David Chamberlain, Berkeley-Charleston-Dorchester Council of Governments, and Suzanne Pickens and John Wells, National Register of Historic Places Inventory-Nomination Form for the Cainhoy Historic District, November 28, 1980, South Carolina

Department of Archives and History, Columbia, South Carolina

Charleston News and Courier, "Work on Cainhoy Bridge is Begun," July 22, 1938; "Historic Trail Will Be Renewed," July 26, 1939; "Cainhoy Bridge is 'Safety Valve'," May 20, 1963

Harry Frank Guggenheim Papers (correspondence with members of Greater St. John AME Church, Saint Peters AME Church and Wando Baptist Church), Library of Congress, Manuscript Division, Washington, D.C.

Carolyn Avinger Shelton's obituary, Charleston Post and Courier, May 19, 1999

Robert P. Stockton, "Carolina Landmark," Charleston News and Courier, December 24, 1978

Interviews: Beverly Avinger Lahmeyer of Cainhoy; Fred Lincoln of Jack Primus; Robert Porcher Jr. of Wando; John Samuel "Sammy" Sanders III of Cainhoy; MaeRe Chandler Skinner of Cainhoy; Josie Worsham Smoak of Cainhoy; Thomas Smoak of Cainhoy

Chapter 12: Boats, Buses and Civil Rights

Herb Frazier, "Esau Jenkins (1910-1972)," Walter Edgar, ed., The South Carolina Encyclopedia (Columbia: University of South Carolina Press, 2006)

Herb Frazier, "John Henry McCray (1910-1987)," Walter Edgar, ed., The South Carolina Encyclopedia (Columbia: University of South Carolina Press, 2006)

Interviews: Rev. Benjamin Dennis of St. Thomas Island; Rosena Virginia Fordham Moultrie of Foresthill, California

Chapter 13: The Land

Tony Bartelme, "Heirs Property tangle leads to loss of land," Charleston Post and Courier, December 24, 2000; Bartelme, "Father dreads family's eviction in heirs' property dispute," September 27, 2001; Bartelme, "Heirs Land at Risk," June 23, 2002

Susan B. Hay, sale of fifty acres for $250 to Hector Rivers, 1833 deed, Berkeley County Office of the Register of Mesne Conveyance. The land was once part of the Shingler Plantation

Terry Yasuko Ogawa, "Wando-Huger: A Study of the Impacts of Development on the Cultural Role of Land in Black Communities of the South Carolina Lowcountry," University of Michigan School of Natural Resources and Environment, Ann Arbor, 2008 http://hdl.handle.net/2027.42/61366 (Accessed June 2, 2010)

Tatsha Robertson, "Developer Land Rush Divides Black Families," The Boston Globe, November 23, 2002

Dr. Lela Haynes Session, with Cynthia Hughes, *Unconditional Love*

Blondell Rivers Wigfall, plaintiff, Sandra Kappers Mobley, et al, defendants, Berkeley County Court of Common Pleas, Case No. 94-CP-08-1497

Interviews: Paul Alston of Yellow House; Buster Brown of Charleston; Rev. Benjamin Dennis of St. Thomas Island; Peter Lawson-Johnston Jr. of Greenwich, Conn.; Fred Lincoln of Jack Primus; Harold Lincoln of Jack Primus; Jacob Morgan of Charleston; Johnnie Rivers of Yellow House; Dorothy Scott, president of the Charleston Branch of the NAACP; Matt Sloan, president of the Daniel Island Company; Jennie L. Stephens, executive director of the Center for Heirs' Property Preservation in Charleston

Chapter 14: Protecting Gullah Culture

Interviews: Michael Allen, a community partnership specialist for the Fort Sumter National Monument and Charles Pinckney National Historic Site and the National Park Service's coordinator of the Gullah/Geechee Cultural Heritage Corridor; Emory Campbell, chairman of the Gullah/Geechee Cultural Heritage Corridor Commission; Eddie Carson of Huger; Rosa Lee Gibbs of Huger; Bertha Roper Davis of Moncks Corner; Rev. Benjamin Dennis of St. Thomas Island; Benjamin Dennis IV of Charleston; Harold Lincoln of Jack Primus; Joseph Opala, lecturer, James Madison University, Harrisonburg, Virginia; Lela Haynes Session of Moncks Corner

Chapter 15: Voices of a New Generation

Interviews: Carrie Bennett of Huger; Eddie Carson of Huger; Fred Lincoln of Jack Primus; Harold Lincoln of Jack Primus; MaeRe Chandler Skinner of Cainhoy

Postscript: Saving Cemeteries

Karimah Moore, "Study of the Huger and Wando Communities," Prepared for the Daniel Island Company, July 2, 2004

Interviews: Dana Beach, executive director of the Coastal Conservation League; Michael K. Dahlman, who along with his son Michael K. Dahlman Jr., wrote Daniel Island; Mark E. Davis, a planner with the Berkeley County Planning and Zoning Department; Florence Dickerson of Huger; Peter Lawson-Johnston Jr. of Greenwich, Conn.; Fred Lincoln of Jack Primus; Jack McCray of Charleston; Christopher Morgan, Charleston's director of Planning and Neighborhoods Division; Rev. David Riley of Charleston; Dorothy Scott, president of the Charleston Branch of the NAACP; MaeRe Chandler Skinner of Cainhoy; Matt Sloan, president of the Daniel Island Company; Alice Washington of St. Thomas Island; Josie Worsham Smoak of Cainhoy; Thomas Smoak of Cainhoy

Index

Hill
- Jane, 49
- John, 139
- Max "Macky" III, 49

Hilton Head Island, S.C., 213
Home Telephone Company, 129-130
Holt, Don N. Bridge, 238
Homemakers Service, 179
Honey Hill, 18
Hoover, Herbert, 27
Horlbeck
- Ann, 54
- Ben, 54
- Dinah, 54
- Ellen, 54
- Hector, 54
- Jacob, 54
- Jacob, Jr., 54
- Lemiel, 54
- Lewis, 54
- Michael, 54
- Miley, 97
- Sergeant, 97
- Stepny, 54
- Syke, 54

Horton, D.R., builders, 159
House of Corrections, inmates: July Pinckney, 52; Rose Alston, Godfrey Bryant, Scipio Green, Anna C. Hardgraves, Joseph Pinckney, 53
Howard
- Dora Bolden, 161-62
- Jake, 76, 152

Howe, Gedney M., Jr., 148-49
Huger
- Daniel II, 17
- Daniel, 17

Huger, S.C.: location, 15, 18; communities near, 18; moonshine stills in, 137; postmaster of, 157; Community Center in, 229; community representation of, 246; growth of, 248-50
Huger-Wando: community, 118; black nurse for all white clinic, 118
Huguenots (French Protestants): 17, 37; French Quarter, 45; Orange Quarter, 45, 63; Huguenot Cross, 63-64; Huguenot Society of South Carolina, 63
Hurricane Hugo, 158, 229
Hyer, Julius B., 105

– I –

International Longshoremen's Assn., 147

– J –

Jack Primus community: location of, 14, 18, 21, 67; Lincoln family compound in, 22-23; family life in, 24-27; Thom's Creek pottery found in, 35; convicted murderer from, 104, 106-109; Keith School near, 159-60; Greater St. John AME Church located in, 170; keeping the land in, 194-195; annexation rejected by, 224; impact of nearby development on, 239-40, 243; community representation by, 246; future development affects on, 250-51
Jackson
- George 133
- Mr. 179

Jeanes Fund, 155
Jeanes schools: Brickyard School, in the Huger area, 152; and the Greenbay, Keith and Shingler schools in the Cainhoy-Wando area, 152
Jeanes, Anna T., 152
Jehovah Witnesses, 148
Jenkins family, 115, 236
Jenkins
- Albertha, 155-57
- Esau, 187
- Florence Vanderhorst, 156
- Gloria, 157
- Henry, 156
- Herbert, 182-183
- Sadie, 157

Jenkins-Varela, Rosemary, 156-57
Jews, 45
Jim Crow, 76
John, alleged Denmark Vesey co-conspirator, 49
Johns Island, S.C., 51, 187, 215, 247,
Johnson
- Earl, 193
- Henry Lee, 114, 129-30, 137, 146, 153-54
- Jane, 76-78

Johnston, Olin, 139
Jordan, W.W., 76-78

– K –

Keeper of the Wild, (wildlife shelter), 42
Keith School Museum, 156-57, 159, 245
Keith School, 116, 150, 152, 158, 160, 175, 188, 193, 222, 231, 238, 247
Keith
- Calvin Allen, 158
- Calvin, 159
- Edward B., Jr., 158

George C, 134
John, 58
Martin, William "Duley," 154
Matthews, Josephine, 119
Mauzé, Caesar, 63
Maybank
  John F., 202
  John F., Jr., 123
Mayer, Ludwig, 79, 127, 131, 171, 163, 166,
McCray
  Jack, 234
  John, 187
McGinnis, Mack, 78
McGirth, Beatrice Smalls, 114, 144, 147-48
McGregor, Kathye Chandler, 227-28
McKinlay, W.J., 71-73
McKnight
  Ethel, 22
  George D., 137
  Glen D., 138-39
McNeal family, 23
McNeil family, 115
McNeil
  Alexander, 74
  Julia, 237
Medical University of South Carolina, 119
Medill, Joseph, 121
Meeting Creek: 164; original name of, 165;
  location, 165; footbridge story, 166, 174,
  177-178; evidence of a still near, 177;
  burials near, 232
Meeting House, 176-77, 231
Meeting Tree, 175
Mellish, Dorothy, 61
Memminger School, 166
Memorial Day, 186
Methodist Church Native American Minis-
  try, 42
Methodist Church, 231
Meyers, James, 245
Miles, Suzannah Smith, 239
Millar, Mae Habersham, 226
Mitchell
  Kit, 78
  Reuben, 31
mobile clinic, 110, 115, 117-18
Moncks Corner, S.C.: 131, 136; cotton gin
  in, 24; jail in, 78; Hyer trial held in, 106;
  Broughton trial held in, 108; midwife
  training in, 114; WIC program in, 119;
  violence in 137-39; education for blacks
  and whites in, 153-54, 175; South Caroli-

na National Bank in, 154; S.C. 41 bridge
  dedication starting point in, 178; food
  stamp office in, 183
Montell, F.M, 55
moonshine: 136; stills in forest, 19, 133-134,
  136, 186; sold at baseball games, 134;
  named Berkeley County Corn or BCC,
  137; was reason for nickname "Bloody
  Berkeley," 137; Hell Hole Swamp , 137;
  Henry Lee Johnson's store sold supplies to
  make, 137-138; shipping of, 137; violence
  because of, 137-39; economic survival
  reason for making and selling, 140-48;
  bootlegger story about, 148-149; race,
  money and, 167; jars found along Black
  Snake Road, 177
Moore, Karimah, 246
Moore's Corner, 18
Moreno, Henry, 122
Morgan
  Christopher, 248-50
  Jacob, 158, 193-94
Moultrie High School, 175
Moultrie
  Jacob, 189
  Mr. (driver), 181
  Rosena Virginia Fordham, 185-89
Mount Pleasant Academy, 175, 227
Mount Pleasant: 218; blacksmith shop in, 32;
  John P. Grace Bridge to, 33; Indian an-
  cestor tree in, 42; after Cainhoy riot, 74;
  Charles Pinckney National Historic Site
  in, 209; Mark Clark Expressway connec-
  tion to, 238-39, 247
Murphy family, 171
Murphy
  Carrie, 169, 174, 178
  Tom, 178
Murphy's Shipyard, 173
Murray, John, 80
Myers, P.E., 108

– N –

Nashville School of Business, 188
National Heritage Area, 210-11
National Park Service, 209-11
National Register of Historic Places, 76, 165,
  169, 171-72, 174, 243, 250
Native Americans: first people, 15; Cherokee,
  30, 32; Wando, 16, 36, 40; Etiwan, 17,
  36-41; Kiawah, 36, 40; Sampa, 36, 39,
  40-41; Sewee , 36, 38, 41; Ashepoo, 40;
  Coosa, 40; Cumbahee, 40; Cusabo, 40;